EUROPEAN POLITICAL FACTS
1848–1918

EUROPEAN POLITICAL FACTS 1848–1918

Chris Cook and John Paxton

Facts On File

119 West 57th Street, New York, N.Y. 10019

First published 1978 by

FACTS ON FILE INC.

New York

Library of Congress Cataloging in Publication Data

Cook, Chris, 1945–
    European political facts, 1848–1918.

    Bibliography: p.
    Includes index.
    1. Europe—Politics and government—1848–1871.
2. Europe—Politics and government—1871–1918.
I. Paxton, John, joint author.   II. Title.
JN10.C66 1978   320.9′4′028   77–21138
ISBN 0–87196–376–0

Christine Steinberg
with affection

CONTENTS

PREFACE

In compiling this volume the editors have aimed to gather together, in one volume, as many of the important political facts as possible for a critical period of European history. In addition this book has also been designed as a companion volume to the existing *European Political Facts 1918–1973* and to the forthcoming *European Political Facts 1789–1848*. Once again the editors have taken all the countries of Europe, from Portugal and Spain to Tsarist Russia and the Ottoman Empire.

Throughout the aim has been to provide comparable material, even though this has not always been easy to achieve, most particularly in the earlier part of this period, when reliable sources were extremely limited. For simplicity, the editors have adopted the use of the Gregorian calendar in this work.

The editors have been helped by an enormous number of people. In particular they would like to thank Anthony Bax, Eve Beadle (who also compiled the index), Stephen Brooks and Sheila Fairfield for very substantial help. Penny White did her usual typing marathon with good humour and eagle eye.

The editors would like to be informed of any errors or inconsistencies so that these can be taken into consideration when revision takes place for the next edition. Suggestions for additional chapters will also be warmly welcomed.

Chris Cook
John Paxton

London and Bruton
July 1976

1 THE MAKING OF MODERN EUROPE

Between 1848 and the outbreak of the First World War, the map of Europe underwent a dramatic transformation. Two major powers (Germany and Italy) achieved their unification. Elsewhere, nationalist aspirations against Ottoman rule in the Balkans led to a series of revolts and insurrections; the disasters encountered by the Turks after 1877 led to the independence of Romania and Bulgaria. The Balkan Wars further changed the map of South-East Europe.

There were other changes also: thus in Scandinavia, Norway achieved her independence from Sweden in 1905.

Elsewhere, however, nationalist aspirations were less successful. Despite successive insurrections, Poland only received a shortlived independence in 1918. Elsewhere in the Habsburg Monarchy, Pan-Slav aspirations were held down by the joint interests of Vienna and Budapest. Meanwhile, the cause of Irish nationalism achieved only partial success with the establishment of the Irish Free State in 1922.

The chronology of these nationalist movements impinges at almost every level on the history of modern Europe. This chapter sets out to arrange these events by area in chronological format. In addition, there are biographical notes on the key figures of the respective nationalist movements together with a section on the major frontier changes affecting the main countries during this period.

CHRONOLOGICAL TABLES

THE RISORGIMENTO AFTER THE ACCESSION OF PIUS IX

15 June 46	Pius IX (Pio Nono) elected Pope. Major liberal concessions including a political amnesty; modification of press censorship; formation of Civic Guard and establishment of a Council of State.
	Charles Albert (in Piedmont) embarks on anti-Austrian

	policy. D'Azeglio advocates end of Papal misrule in his publication *Ultimi casi di Romagna*.
47	Misgovernment in Naples exposed by Settembrini in *Protests of the People of the Two Sicilies*; Austrian occupation of Ferrara (17 July); protest by Pio Nono helped secure subsequent withdrawal.
	Imprisonment of Manin and Tommaseo after pleas for unity at Venice Scientific Congress.
21 Oct 47	Charles Albert of Piedmont dismisses reactionary ministers.
12 Jan 48	Revolt in Sicily. A provisional independent government proclaimed.
10 Feb 48	Constitution proclaimed in Naples by Ferdinand II.
4 Mar 48	Charles Albert proclaims constitution in Piedmont.
14 Mar 48	Pius IX grants constitution in Rome.
17 Mar 48	Daniele Manin leads revolution in Venice.
18 Mar 48	Uprising in Milan: Radetzky evacuates city.
20 Mar 48	Revolt in Parma.
22 Mar 48	Republic proclaimed in Venice.
24 Mar 48	Sardinia declares war on Austria.
8 Apr 48	Piedmontese troops defeat Austrians at Gioto.
13 Apr 48	Sicily declares independence from Naples.
25 Apr 48	Papacy joins war against Austria.
29 Apr 48	Pius IX withdraws support from nationalist movement.
30 Apr 48	Further Austrian reverse at Pastrengo.
15 May 48	Collapse of Naples revolt.
29 May 48	Battle of Curtatone; Austrians defeat Tuscany.
22 July 48	Battle of Custozza. Major victory for Radetzky. Sardinian troops driven from Milan and remainder of Lombardy.
9 Aug 48	Armistice of Vigevano between Sardinia and Austria.
11 Aug 48	Sardinian troops expelled from Venice.
15 Nov 48	Assassination of Count Rossi, Premier of Papal States.
24 Nov 48	Pius IX escapes to Gaeta.
7 Feb 49	Flight of Grand Duke of Tuscany to Gaeta.
9 Feb 49	Mazzini proclaims republic in Rome.
12 Mar 49	Sardinia ends truce with Austria.
23 Mar 49	Battle of Novara; major Austrian victory.
	Abdication of Charles Albert; accession of Victor Emanuel II.
25 Apr 49	French troops land in Papal States.
15 May 49	Troops from Naples occupy Palermo.
4 July 49	French troops enter Rome. Pius IX restored.

2

6 Aug 49	Peace of Milan concludes Austria-Sardinia conflict.
28 Aug 49	Venice finally surrenders to Austrians.
11 Oct 50	Cavour appointed Minister in Piedmont; era of rapid economic development.
6 May 52	Tuscan constitution abolished by Leopold II.
4 Nov 52	Cavour appointed Prime Minister of Piedmont.
26 Jan 55	Piedmont joins allies in Crimean War.
May 55	General La Marmora joins allies in Crimea.
15 Aug 57	Garibaldi forms Italian National Association for unification of Italy under the leadership of Piedmont.
14 Jan 58	Orsini bomb plot to assassinate Napoleon III.
20 July 58	Plombières negotiations between Cavour and Napoleon III.
19 Jan 59	Treaty of Alliance between France and Sardinia.
19 Apr 59	Austrian ultimatum to Sardinia; rejected by Sardinia on 26 Apr.
29 Apr 59	Austrian troops enter Sardinia.
3 May 59	France declares war on Austria (for military details of the campaign, see p. 171).
11 July 59	Peace of Villafranca. Austria cedes Parma and Lombardy. Tuscany and Modena restored. Venice to stay Austrian. Resignation of Cavour.
10 Nov 59	Peace of Villafranca confirmed by Treaty of Zurich.
20 Jan 60	Return to power of Cavour.
24 Mar 60	Sardinia cedes Savoy and Nice to France.
2 Apr 60	First 'Italian' Parliament met at Turin.
5 May 60	Garibaldi's famous expedition sails for Sicily.
11 May 60	Garibaldi's landing.
27 May 60	Fall of Palermo to Garibaldi.
22 Aug 60	Garibaldi lands on the mainland.
7 Sep 60	Naples falls; flight of Francis II.
11 Sep 60	Sardinia invades Papal States.
18 Sep 60	Papal forces defeated at Castelfidardo by Garibaldi.
21 Oct 60	Naples and Sicily vote to unite with Sardinia.
26 Oct 60	Victor Emanuel proclaimed King of Italy by Garibaldi.
4 Nov 60	Umbria votes for union with Sardinia.
13 Feb 61	Garibaldi receives surrender of Francis II of Naples at Gaeta.
18 Feb 61	Victor Emanuel proclaimed King by Italian Parliament.
17 Mar 61	Formal proclamation of the Kingdom of Italy.
6 June 61	Death of Cavour.
29 Aug 62	Garibaldi captured at Aspromonte in the attempt to secure Rome.

8 Apr 66	Secret military alliance between Italy and Prussia.
24 June 66	Italians defeated at Battle of Custozza.
4 July 66	Cession of Venezia announced by Napoleon III.
20 July 66	Battle of Lissa. Destruction of Italian fleet.
12 Aug 66	Italians sign armistice with Austria.
3 Oct 66	Treaty of Vienna between Austria and Italy.
21 Oct 66	Venezia votes for union with Italy.
27 Oct 67	Garibaldi's march on Rome.
28 Oct 67	French forces arrive at Civita Vecchia.
3 Nov 67	Garibaldi defeated at Battle of Mentana.
20 Sep 70	Italian troops enter Rome.
2 Oct 70	Rome finally incorporated into Kingdom of Italy.

THE UNIFICATION OF GERMANY

7 June 40	Accession of Frederick William IV of Prussia.
3 Feb 47	Frederick William IV summons United Diet.
17 Mar 48	Uprising in Berlin: Frederick William IV grants constitution.
31 Mar 48	The *Vorparlament* meets at Frankfurt.
2 May 48	Prussia invades Denmark over Schleswig-Holstein question.
18 May 48	German National Assembly meets at Frankfurt.
22 May 48	Berlin meeting of Prussian National Assembly.
26 Aug 48	Treaty of Malmo between Denmark and Prussia.
5 Dec 48	Dissolution of Prussian National Assembly.
23 Jan 49	Prussia advocates union of Germany without Austria.
27 Mar 49	German National Assembly offers title 'Emperor of the Germans' to an unwilling Frederick William IV.
3 May 49	Revolt in Dresden suppressed by Prussia.
6 June 49	National Assembly moves to Stuttgart.
18 June 49	Troops dissolve Stuttgart assembly.
23 July 49	Baden rebels surrender to Prussia.
31 Jan 50	Liberal constitution granted in Prussia.
20 Mar 50	German Parliament summoned to Erfurt by Frederick William IV.
29 Apr 50	Erfurt Parliament opened.
2 July 50	Peace of Berlin between Prussia and Denmark.
28 Nov 50	Convention of Olmütz. Prussia subordinated to Austria and recognised Frankfurt Diet.
23 Dec 50	Inconclusive Dresden conference.
4 Apr 53	Oldenburg and Hanover join Zollverein.

11 Dec 59	Appointment of Albert von Roon as Prussian Minister of War.
2 Jan 61	Death of Frederick William IV; succeeded by William I.
22 Sep 62	Bismarck appointed Minister-President of Prussia.
29 Sep 62	Bismarck's 'Blood and Iron' speech.
7 Oct 62	Prussian military budget rejected by Diet.
8 Feb 63	Prussian alliance with Russia to crush Polish revolt.
30 Mar 63	Schleswig incorporated into Denmark.
1 Oct 63	German Diet votes for action against Denmark.
15 Nov 63	Death of Frederick VII of Denmark.
24 Dec 63	Saxon and Hanoverian troops enter Holstein.
16 Jan 64	Ultimatum to Denmark from Austria and Prussia.
1 Feb 64	Austro-Prussian forces invade Schleswig.
18 Apr 64	Danes defeated at Battle of Duppel.
25 June 64	Failure of London conference to settle Schleswig-Holstein question.
30 Oct 64	Peace of Vienna. Denmark cedes Schleswig-Holstein and Lauenburg to Austria and Prussia.
14 Aug 65	Convention of Gastein. Austria receives Holstein; Prussia given Schleswig and purchases Lauenburg.
4–11 Oct 65	Biarritz conversations between Bismarck and Napoleon III.
8 Apr 66	Prussian secret military alliance with Italy.
7 June 66	Holstein invaded by Prussia and subsequently annexed.
12 June 66	Secret treaty between Austria and France.
14 June 66	German Diet votes to mobilize against Prussia.
15 June 66	Prussian forces invade Saxony, Hesse and Hanover.
20 June 66	Italian declaration of war on Austria.
29 June 66	Hanover defeated by Prussia at Battle of Langensaza.
3 July 66	Battle of Sadowa-Koniggratz. Major Austrian defeat.
26 July 66	Peace preliminaries between Austria and Prussia at Nikolsburg.
13 Aug 66	Prussian peace signed with Württemburg, Baden and Bavaria.
23 Aug 66	Peace of Prague signed. Austria excluded from Germany. Prussia absorbs Frankfurt, Hanover, Hesse and Nassau. Formation of Prussian-dominated North German Confederation.
19 July 70	French declaration of war on Prussia (for details of the campaign, see p. 173).
2 Sep 70	Surrender of Napoleon III at Sedan.
18 Jan 71	Proclamation of German empire at Palace of Versailles.
10 May 71	Peace of Frankfurt. Alsace-Lorraine ceded by France.

THE DECLINE OF THE OTTOMAN EMPIRE

28 July 48	Russian invasion of Danube principalities to suppress revolts.
1 May 49	Convention of Balta Liman. Joint 7-year Russo-Turkish occupation of Danubian principalities.
19 Apr 53	Russia claims protectorate over Christian subjects within the Ottoman Empire.
2 July 53	Russia invades Danubian principalities.
4 Oct 53	Turkey declares war on Russia.
28 Mar 54	Britain declares war on Russia (for military details of Crimean War, see p. 171).
18 Feb 56	Major reform edict in Ottoman Empire.
30 May 56	Treaty of Paris; neutralization of the Black Sea; Russia cedes Bessarabia.
19 Aug 58	Moldavia united with Wallachia.
8 Nov 58	Frontiers of Montenegro determined.
23 Dec 58	Deposition of Serbian King Alexander Karageorgevic.
23 Dec 61	Union of Moldavia and Wallachia (as Romania) agreed by Sultan.
15 June 62	Rising by Serbs in Belgrade; Turkish bombardment of the city.
2 Sep 66	Revolt in Crete against Turks; union with Greece proposed.
16 July 75	Bosnia and Herzegovina rise in revolt against Ottoman rule.
12 Dec 75	Reforms promised by Sultan.
31 Jan 76	Andrassy Note accepted by Sultan.
9–16 Mar 76	Bulgarian massacres by Turks.
30 June 76	Serbia declares war on Turkey.
2 July 76	Montenegro joins the war.
31 Aug 76	Sultan Murad V deposed: accession of Abdul el Hamid II.
31 Oct 76	Russian ultimatum forced Ottoman Empire to accept armistice.
23 Dec 76	Constitution proclaimed in Ottoman Empire, promised parliamentary government and freedom of worship.
15 Jan 77	Convention of Budapest.
28 Feb 77	Peace treaty between Serbia and Ottoman Empire.
12 Apr 77	Turks reject London Protocol.
24 Apr 77	Russia invades Ottoman Empire (for details, see p. 173).
16 May 77	Romania joins war against Turks.
10 Dec 77	Plevna falls to Russian army.

14 Dec 77	Serbia joins war against Turks.
20 Jan 78	Adrianople falls to Russians.
28 Jan 78	Rebellion in Thessaly.
31 Jan 78	Russo-Turkish armistice.
2 Feb 78	Greek declaration of war on Turks.
3 Mar 78	Preliminary Treaty of San Stefano, unacceptable to Austria and Britain.
13 July 78	Treaty of Berlin signed (for details of territorial changes, see p. 166)
29 Apr 79	Prince Alexander of Battenburg becomes Alexander I of Bulgaria.
26 Nov 80	Montenegrin occupation of Duicigno accepted by Turks.
3 July 81	Greece obtains Thessaly.
18 Sep 85	Disturbances in Eastern Rumelia.
11 Nov 85	Serbian invasion of Bulgaria.
17 Nov 85	Bulgarians defeat Serbs at Slivnitza.
3 Mar 86	Treaty of Bucharest signed between Bulgaria and Serbia.
8 May 86	Greece blockaded by major powers over continued agitation in Eastern Rumelia.
4 Sep 86	Stambulov becomes Regent in Bulgaria.
6 Oct 88	Germany granted concession to construct the Baghdad Railway.
6 Mar 89	Abdication of King Milan of Serbia.
15 July 95	Assassination of Stambulov.
1 Oct 95	Armenians massacred by Turks.
23 Oct 95	British Navy despatched to the Dardanelles.
7 Feb 96	Revolt of Crete against Turks.
3 July 96	Self-government for Crete agreed by Abdul Hamid II: insurrection continues.
6 Feb 97	Crete proclaims union with Greece.
18 Mar 97	Great powers blockade Crete.
7 Apr 97	Turks declare war on Greece.
12 May 97	Greek reverse on Thessaly. Powers aid Greece.
19 May 97	Greek-Turkish armistice.
16 Dec 97	Peace of Constantinople signed between Greece and Turkey.
Oct 98	Visit of Kaiser Wilhelm to Syria and Palestine.
6 Oct 1908	Bosnia-Herzegovina annexed by Austria-Hungary. Provokes major crisis.
May 12	Dodecanese occupied by Italy.
8 Oct 12	First Balkan War begins (for details, see p. 174).
30 May 13	First Balkan War ended by Treaty of London.
1 June 13	Pact between Serbia and Greece.

29 June 13	Second Balkan War begins (for the campaign, see p. 175).
10 Aug 13	Treaty of Bucharest ends Second Balkan War.
14 Dec 13	Von Sanders arrives in Constantinople at the head of the German military mission.

NATIONALISM IN THE HABSBURG MONARCHY

12 Mar 48	Revolution in Vienna.
13 Mar 48	Resignation of Prince Metternich.
15 Mar 48	Hungarian Diet accepts reforms of Mar 47.
25 Apr 48	Constitution, including responsible government, granted to Austria.
15 May 48	Second rising in Vienna.
17 May 48	Ferdinand flees Vienna to Innsbruck.
2 June 48	Pan-Slav Congress meets at Prague.
17 June 48	Czech rising suppressed by Austrians.
12 Aug 48	Ferdinand I returns to Vienna.
7 Sep 48	Abolition of serfdom in Austria.
24 Sep 48	Louis Kossuth proclaimed President of the Committee for the National Defence of Hungary.
6 Oct 48	Third rising in Vienna.
31 Oct 48	Government in full control again in Vienna.
2 Dec 48	Abdication of Ferdinand I: accession of Franz Joseph.
4 Mar 49	Proclamation of an Austrian constitution.
7 Mar 49	Austrian Assembly dissolved.
14 Apr 49	Hungarian Diet proclaims independence with Kossuth as leader.
13 Aug 49	Battle of Vilagas. Hungarians defeated by Austrians, aided by Russians.
31 Dec 51	Austrian constitution abolished.
21 Aug 61	Dissolution of the Hungarian Diet.
17 Feb 67	*Ausgleich* agreed. Hungarian Diet opened.
8 June 67	Franz Joseph crowned King of Hungary.
20 Nov 73	Croats granted self-government within the Dual Monarchy.
12 Dec 92	Pan-Slav congress in Cracow.
29 Oct 93	Resignation of Taaffe.
8 Sep 95	Badeni ministry attempts to pacify Czech agitation.
28 Nov 97	Badeni resigns over language policy.
10 Jan 1900	New attempt to resolve Czech question with appointment of von Koerber ministry

BIOGRAPHICAL NOTES ON MAJOR FIGURES

AZEGLIO, Massinio Taparelli d' (1798–1866)
Italian statesman; leading figure in Risorgimento. Born at Turin, a son-in-law of Manzoni. Active in 1848. His autobiography, *I Miei Ricordi*, gives a full account of his activities.

BALBO, Cesare (1789–1853)
Italian statesman. Born at Turin. Prime Minister in the first constitutional Piedmontese ministry. Published a biography of Dante in 1839.

BISMARCK, Otto Edward Leopold von (1815–98) (Prince Bismarck, Duke of Lauenburg)
Prusso-German statesman. Architect of German unification. Born at Schön-hausen (in Brandenburg), 1 April 1815. Studied law and agriculture at Göttingen, Berlin and Greifswald. By 1847, active as ultra-royalist in Prussian Parliament. In 1851 was a member of new Diet at Frankfurt. In 1859, appointed Minister to St Petersburg; in 1862, Ambassador to Paris. Recalled in same year to be Foreign Secretary. Created a Count in 1866. In 1871, made a Prince and Chancellor of the German Empire. Resigned as Chancellor, March 1890. Died at Friedrichsruh, 30 July 1898.

CAVOUR, Camillo Benso di (1810–61)
Italian statesman. Architect of Italian unification. Born at Turin. Retired from army in 1831 because of his liberal views. In 1847 with Balbo (q.v.) he set up *Il Risorgimento*. Held ministerial office under d'Azeglio (q.v.). In 1852, succeeded d'Azeglio as Prime Minister. Architect of Piedmont economic and diplomatic policies. Resigned in 1859 in protest at Peace of Villafranca (see p. 3). Returned to power in 1860, secretly encouraging Garibaldi. Died 6 June 61.

CRISPI, Francesco (1819–1901)
Italian statesman. Born at Ribera in Sicily. Joined the revolution in 1848, forced to flee to France. Organizer of 1859–60 events. From 1887–90, and again in 1894, Prime Minister. Forced to resign by Italian disaster at Adowa.

DEAK, Francis (1803–76)
Hungarian statesman. Born in Söjtör, Zala. Practised at the bar. Entered Hungarian Diet in 1832. Minister of Justice in 1848. Played a major role in creating the *Ausgleich* in 1867.

ENVER PASHA (1881–1922)
Young Turk leader in the 1908 revolution. Turkish Minister of War in 1914. After Turkish surrender, fled to Russia. Killed in an uprising in Turkestan.

GARIBALDI, Giuseppe (1807–82)
Italian patriot. Born at Nice, 4 July 07. In 1834, became involved with 'Young Italy' movement. Condemned to death for his part in an attempt to seize Genoa. Escaped to South America. Active as guerrilla fighter in Rio Grande area of Brazil. Returned to Europe. In 1849, joined the revolutionary government in Rome. Forced to retreat when French besieged Rome. Went to New York, before returning to Europe in 1854. Active in 1859 war. His most famous exploit, the landing with 1000 men at Marsala, occurred on 11 May 60. Entered Naples, 7 Sep 60. Attempted to march on Rome in 1862. Captured at Aspromonte (28 Aug). Died 2 June 82.

GIOBERTI, Vincenzo (1801–52)
Italian politician and philosopher. Born in Turin. In exile after 1833. His philosophical works (published in Brussels) included *Introduzione allo studio della filosofia* (1839), *Del Bello* (1841) and *Del buono* (1842). His major fame resulted from his publication *Del primato civile e morale degli Italiani* (1843). Prime Minister for 10 weeks in 1848 on his return to Italy. In 1851 he published his major defence of liberalism (*Rinnovamento civile d'Italia*). Died in Paris.

JELLACIC, Count Josef (1801–59)
Hungarian soldier and politician. Born at Petrovaradin. Military career as devoted upholder of Habsburg power. As Governor of Croatia, played major role in suppressing 1848 risings.

KATKOV, Mikhail Nikiforovic (1818–87)
A Russian journalist who became Professor of Philosophy at Moscow. Edited the *Moscow Gazette* after 1861. The Polish insurrection of 1863 made him a leading advocate of Pan-Slavism.

KOLLAR, Jan (1793–1852)
Czech poet and nationalist. A Hungarian Slovak, he was a Protestant pastor at Pest before becoming Professor of Archaeology at Vienna.

KOSSUTH, Louis (1802–94)
Hungarian nationalist. Leader of the Hungarian revolution in 1848. Born at Monok, near Zemplin. In 1832, a deputy to the Diet at Pressburg. Imprisoned in 1837. In 1840, on his release, edited *Pesti Hirlap*. Effective leader of the opposition in the Diet in 1847. In 1848, demanded independent government for Hungary. Appointed Provisional Governor of Hungary. Fled to Turkey after Magyars defeated at Temesvar on 9 Aug 49. Imprisoned; but released in Sep 1851. Lived mainly in England, attempting to plan further Hungarian risings. He retired after the *Ausgleich* of 1867.

MANIN, Daniele (1804–57)
Venetian statesman. Born in Venice, of Jewish ancestry. Achieved fame as

President of the Venetian Republic in 1848. Escaped to Paris when Venice capitulated (24 Aug 1849). Died in Paris of heart disease.

MASARYK, Tómas (1850–1937)
Born at Hodonin, in Moravia. Architect of Czech nationalism. Became first President of Czechoslovakia in 1918, holding office until 1935.

MAZZINI, Giuseppe (1805–72)
Italian patriot. Born at Genoa, 22 June 05. Strongly influenced by romanticism. Joined the Carbonari in 1829. Betrayed in 1830 and imprisoned at Savona. Released in 1831. Organized the 'Young Italy' movement. Banished from France in 1832. Organized abortive invasion of Savoy in 1834. In 1837, came to live in London. Active with Garibaldi in the 1848 revolutions. Organized repeated risings in Mantua (1852), Milan (1853), and Genoa (1857). Founder of the republican 'European Association' and the Society of the Friends of Italy. Died at Pisa, 10 Mar 72.

ORSINI, Felice (1819–58)
Italian conspirator. Born at Meldola in the Papal States. Entered the world of secret societies. Sentenced to the galleys in 1844. In 1848, elected to the Constituent Assembly in Rome. Continued to agitate for risings in Genoa and Modena. Deported to England in 1853, where he became close ally of Mazzini (q.v.). Achieved fame for the assassination attempt on Napoleon III (14 Jan 58). Ten persons killed, 156 wounded in the outrage. Orsini was guillotined on 13 Mar 58.

PALACKY, Frantisek (1798–1876)
Czech nationalist. Active in Prague politics. Most distinguished and well known of historians of Bohemia.

PASIC, Nikola (c. 1846–1926)
Serb nationalist and politician. Born at Zajeĉar. Condemned to death in 1883 for the part he played in the plot against King Milan (the Revolution of Zaitchar). Pardoned on accession of King Peter. Prime Minister of Serbia in 1891, again in 1906, and for long periods after 1908.

PIUS IX (Giovanni Maria Mastai Ferretti) (1792–1878)
Born at Sinigaglia. In 1827, made Archbishop of Spoleto. In 1832, became Bishop of Imola. Created a Cardinal in 1840. Elected Pope in 1846 on the death of Gregory XVI, beginning his reign with a series of reforms. Era of reforming zeal ended when his First Minister, Count Rossi, was assassinated (15 Nov 48). On 24 Nov, Pius IX escaped to Gaeta. After he returned to Rome in 1849, Pius IX was a staunch conservative. His period as Pope saw the bull *Ineffabilis Deus* (1854), the declaration of the Immaculate Conception, the *Syllabus Errarum* (1864), the encyclical *Quanta Cura*, and the Vatican Council

11

of 1869–70. It was this council which proclaimed the doctrine of Papal Infallibility.

RADETZKY, Johann Joseph (1766–1858)
Soldier. Born at Trebnitz (near Tabor) in Bohemia. First major military service against Turks in 1788. In 1831, appointed Commander-in-Chief in Lombardy. Held Verona and Mantua in 1848 against the revolutionaries. Triumphant victory at Custozza enabled him to re-enter Milan. Destroyed Sardinian army at Novara, Mar 49. Ruled Lombardy-Venetia until 1857. Died at Milan.

STAMBULOV, Stephan Nikolov (1854–95)
Bulgarian statesman. Born at Trnova. Active in the 1875–6 rising. Headed the regency, 1886. Prime Minister, 1887–94. Dominated Bulgarian politics. Assassinated in 1895.

VENIZELOS, Eleutherios (1864–1936)
Greek statesman. Born in Crete. Studied law in Athens. Leader of Liberal Party in Crete. Prominent in the revolt of 1896. Having first served under Prince George, led guerrilla warfare from the Therisso mountains. Went to Athens in 1909. Became Prime Minister, 1910–15. Promoted Balkan League. Led Greece during First World War. Defeated in 1920 elections. But Prime Minister again (1924, 1928–32, 1933). Died in Paris, 1936.

VICTOR EMANUEL I of Sardinia (1759–1824)
King of Sardinia, 1802–21. Vigorous anti-liberal. He abdicated in 1821, after a rising against him, in favour of his brother, Charles Felix.

VICTOR EMANUEL I of Italy (1820–78)
The first King of a united Italy. Born 14 Mar 1820, the son of Charles Albert. Became King of Sardinia, 23 Mar 49. Appointed Cavour (q.v.) as Prime Minister in 1852. Proclaimed King of Italy in Feb 61. Entered Rome, 22 Sep 70. Reigned as a sincere constitutional monarch. Known as *Ré Galantuomo*. Succeeded in 1878 by his son, Humbert I.

A NOTE ON MAJOR BOUNDARY CHANGES 1848–1918

AUSTRIA-HUNGARY

The main additions of territory to the Habsburg monarchy were the incorporation of Cracow (6 Nov 46), together with the occupation of Bosnia-Herzegovina (1876). On 6 Oct 1908, Bosnia-Herzegovina was formally annexed. The territories of Lombardy and Parma were surrendered by Austria-Hungary at the Peace of Villafranca (11 July 59). Venezia voted for union with Italy on 21 Oct 66.

BELGIUM

The independence of Belgium was proclaimed on 18 Nov 30. By the Treaty of London (19 Apr 39) Luxembourg was created a Grand Duchy. The province of Limburg was divided. Luxembourg became fully independent in 1890.

BULGARIA

By the Treaty of Berlin (13 July 78) Bulgarian independence was established. Disturbances in Eastern Rumelia (from 18 Sep 85) led to this province becoming united with Bulgaria. Bulgaria ceded the southern Dobrudja to Romania as a result of the Balkan Wars, but was compensated by gains from Turkey in Thrace. In 1915, Bulgaria's entry into the war on the German side resulted in the seizure of much Serb territory; in 1916, the Dobrudja was retaken. All these gains were forfeited in 1918.

DENMARK

By the Peace of Vienna (30 Oct 64), Denmark ceded Schleswig-Holstein and Lauenburg to Austria and Prussia. By the Convention of Gastein (14 Aug 65), Austria received Holstein, Prussia was granted Schleswig and also purchased Lauenburg. Holstein was invaded by Prussia on 7 June 66 and subsequently annexed.

FINLAND

From 1809 to 1917, Finland was an autonomous Grand Duchy, having been ceded to Russia by Sweden. Finland proclaimed independence in 1917.

FRANCE

On 24 Mar 60, France received Savoy and Nice from Piedmont-Sardinia. By the Peace of Frankfurt (10 May 71) France ceded Alsace-Lorraine (except for the territory of Belfort and the department of Meurthe-et-Moselle) to Germany.

GERMANY

No territorial changes after 1870 except for the acquisition of Alsace-Lorraine from France (see above).

GREECE

The independence of Greece was recognized on 16 Nov 28. Its independence was guaranteed by the London Conference (3 Feb 30). At independence, Greece was comprised of the Morea, Euboea, the Cyclades Islands and the mainland south of Arta and Thessaly. In 1864, Britain ceded the Ionian Islands. Thessaly and Arta were ceded by Turkey on 3 July 81. Greece acquired Macedonia and western Thrace in 1913, together with Crete and virtually all the Aegean Islands except the Dodecanese (in Italian hands).

ITALY

The Italian Kingdom was formally proclaimed on 17 Mar 61 (though 1860 was the really crucial year). Venezia voted for union with Italy on 21 Oct 66. Italian troops entered Rome on 20 Sep 70 and Rome was finally incorporated into the kingdom on 2 Oct 70. Italy acquired the Dodecanese in May 1912.

MONTENEGRO

Although nominally under Ottoman rule Montenegro always enjoyed *de facto* independence. On 8 Nov 58, the frontiers of Montenegro were determined— though these boundaries were expanded in 1878 and again in 1913.

THE NETHERLANDS

For the loss of Belgium and Luxembourg see under Belgium (above).

NORWAY

From 1814 to 1905, Norway was part of Sweden, having formerly formed part of the Danish Crown. Norway became independent in Nov 05, though under Sweden it had always been administered separately.

PORTUGAL

There were no territorial changes between 1848 and 1918.

ROMANIA

On 19 Aug 58, the principalities of Moldavia and Wallachia were united. This union was agreed by the Sultan on 23 Dec 61. Romania's independence was recognized in 1878, when southern Bessarabia was ceded to Russia. In compensation, Romania acquired all except the southern Dobrudja from Turkey (the southern part was acquired in 1913 from Bulgaria). This latter province was lost again in 1918, but Bessarabia was re-acquired from Russia. These losses were only temporary, for Romania was greatly enlarged when the Habsburg Empire disintegrated.

RUSSIA

Prior to 1848, Russian territorial expansion had been considerable. In the three partitions of Poland (1772, 1793 and 1795) Russia had acquired large tracts of territory. In 1774 and 1791, Russia also received large amounts of territory from the Ottoman Empire, and Georgia was acquired in 1801; much of the Azerbaijan came under Russian control in 1813. After 1815 Russia acquired Guria in 1829.

Further expansion continued after 1848: Mingelia was acquired in 1857 and Abkhazia in 1864. The Kars region was acquired in 1878. Russian expansion in Central Asia included the annexation of Tashkent (1865), Samarkand and Bukhara (1868), Khiva (1873), Askahabad (1881) and Merv (1885).

SERBIA

On 5 Nov 17, Serbia was granted partial autonomy under Turkish suzereignty. Her frontiers were enlarged in 1833. Full independence was granted in 1878 (when Niš was added). In 1913, Serbia acquired the Sanjak of Novi-Bazar and major areas of Macedonia.

SPAIN

There were no territorial changes during the period 1848–1918.

SWEDEN

Sweden had acquired Norway in 1814 (and lost Finland in 1809). Norway became independent in 1905.

SWITZERLAND

No major territorial changes occurred. In 1815 the cantons of Geneva and Valais (previously independent) were added. In 1857, Neuchâtel (until this date an anomalous fief of the Prussian crown) was added.

2 HEADS OF STATE

AUSTRIA

EMPEROR

Ferdinand I, succeeded his father	2 Mar 35–2 Dec 48 (abdic.)
Francis Joseph I, m. Elizabeth of Bavaria, succeeded his uncle	2 Dec 48–21 Nov 16
Karl, m. Zita of Bourbon-Parma, succeeded his great-uncle	21 Nov 16–11 Nov 18 (deposed)

BELGIUM

Belgium declared itself independent of Holland on 18 Nov 30.

KING

Regency (Baron van Surlet van Chokier)	25 Feb 31–21 July 31
Leopold I (formerly Leopold of Saxe-Coburg), m. (i) Charlotte of Great Britain (ii) Louise of Orleans, elected	21 July 31–10 Dec 65
Cabinet government	10 Dec 65
Leopold II, m. Marie of Austria, succeeded his father	17 Dec 65–17 Dec 1909
Albert, m. Elizabeth of Bavaria, succeeded his uncle	17 Dec 09–20 Aug 14 (deposed)

GOVERNOR-GENERAL

von der Goltz (German)	20 Aug 14–22 Nov 18

KING

Albert, reinstated	22 Nov 18–

BULGARIA

Bulgaria was created an independent kingdom by the Treaty of Berlin in 1878. A provisional government was formed on 21 Aug 86.

PRINCE

Alexander, Prince of Battenberg, elected	29 Apr 79–21 Aug 86 (deposed) 7 Sep 86 (abdic.)
Ferdinand of Saxe-Coburg-Gotha, m. (i) Marie-Louise of Parma (ii) Eleonore of Reuss Köstritz, elected	7 Oct 87–3 Oct 1918 (abdic.)

DENMARK

KING

Christian VIII, m. (i) Charlotte of Mecklenburg-Schwerin (ii) Caroline of Schleswig-Holstein-Sonderburg-Augustenburg, succeeded his cousin	8 Dec 39–20 Jan 48
Frederick VII, m. (i) Caroline of Mecklenburg-Strelitz (ii) Louise Christine Rasmussen, succeeded his father	20 Jan 48–15 Nov 63
Christian IX, m. Louise of Hesse-Cassel, formerly Prince Christian of Schleswig-Holstein-Sonderburg – Glücksburg, and appointed heir by the Treaty of London on 8 May 52	15 Nov 63–29 Jan 06
Frederick VIII, m. Louise of Sweden, succeeded his father	29 Jan 06–14 May 12
Christian X, m. Alexandrine of Mecklenberg, succeeded his father Frederick VIII	14 May 12–

FRANCE

KING

Louis-Philippe of Orleans, m. Marie-Amélie of Sicily, elected	9 Aug 30–24 Feb 48 (abdic.)

17

Provisional government of the Second Republic   24 Feb 48–10 Dec 48

PRESIDENT

Louis Napoleon Bonaparte, m. Eugénie de Mon-
tijo, elected   10 Dec 48–2 Dec 52

EMPEROR

Louis Napoleon Bonaparte   2 Dec 52–4 Sep 70
                                                       (deposed)

Provisional government of the Third Republic
by the Committee of Public Defence   4 Sep 70–12 Feb 71

Government by the National Assembly   12 Feb 71–15 Mar 71

Government by the Paris Commune   15 Mar 71

PRESIDENT

Louis Adolphe Thiers	31 Aug 71–24 May 73
Maurice MacMahon	24 May 73–30 Jan 79
Jules Grévy	30 Jan 79–3 Dec 87
Marie-François Sadi-Carnot	3 Dec 87–24 June 94 (murdered)
Jean Casimir Périer	27 June 94–16 Jan 95
François Felix Faure	16 Jan 95–18 Feb 99
Emile Loubet	18 Feb 99–18 Feb 1906
Clement Armand Fallières	18 Feb 06–18 Feb 13
Raymond Poincaré	18 Feb 13–

GERMANY

The German Confederation of 1815 was formed on 9 June 15 and included 39 states, one of which was Austria (q.v.). The other 38 were:

(a) A group of 7 small states sharing one place in the Federal Diet—Hesse-Homburg (joined in 1817—the original Confederation had 38 states), Liechtenstein, Lippe-Detmold, Reuss-Greiz, Reuss-Schleiz, Schaumburg-Lippe, Waldeck.

(b) A group of 6 small states sharing one place in the Federal Diet—Anhalt-Bernburg, Anhalt-Dessau, Anhalt-Kothen, Oldenburg, Schwarzburg-

Rudolstadt, Swarzburg-Sondershausen. (The Anhalts had become one by 1864.)

(c) Hohenzollern-Hechingen and Hohenzollern-Sigmaringen, which were ruled by a branch of the reigning Prussian house of Hohenzollern and became part of Prussia in 1849.

(d) The four free towns which shared one seat in the Federal Diet—Hamburg, Bremen, Frankfurt, Lübeck.

(e) The Thuringian duchies sharing one place in the Federal Diet—Saxe-Coburg, Saxe-Gotha, Saxe-Meiningen, Saxe-Weimar, Saxe-Altenburg. (Saxe-Gotha became extinct as a duchy in 1826 and its territory was divided between Saxe-Coburg and Saxe-Meiningen, the former then being known as Saxe-Coburg-Gotha.)

(f) A group of 14 larger states with one place each:

1 *Prussia*
KING

Frederick William III, m. Louise of Mecklenburg-Strelitz, succeeded his father	16 Nov 1797–7 June 40
Frederick William IV, succeeded his father	7 June 40–9 Oct 58 (became insane)
Regency (William, brother of Frederick William IV)	9 Oct 58–2 Jan 61
William I, m. Augusta of Saxe-Weimar, succeeded his brother	2 Jan 61–9 Mar 88
Frederick III, m. Victoria of Great Britain, succeeded his father	9 Mar 88–15 June 88
Wilhelm II, m. Augusta of Schleswig-Holstein, succeeded his father	15 June 88–9 Nov 18 (abdic.)

2 *Bavaria*
KING

Maximilian I (formerly Elector of Bavaria), m. (i) Wilhelmine of Hesse-Darmstadt (ii) Caroline of Baden, created first King	1 Jan 06–13 Oct 25
Ludwig I, m. Therese of Saxe-Hildburghausen, succeeded his father	13 Oct 25–20 Mar 48 (abdic.)
Maximilian II, m. Marie of Prussia, succeeded his father	20 Mar 48–10 Mar 64
Ludwig II, succeeded his father	10 Mar 64–8 June 86 (became insane)

19

Regency (Leopold, uncle of Ludwig II)	10 June 86–1912
Otto I, succeeded his brother, though already insane	13 June 86–5 Nov 13 (deposed)
Regency (son of Otto I)	1912–5 Nov 13
Ludwig III, m. Maria Theresa of Austria-d'Este, succeeded his cousin	5 Nov 13–7 Nov 18 (deposed)

3 *Saxony*

KING

Frederick Augustus I (formerly Frederick Augustus III, Elector since 1763)	11 Dec 06–Oct 13
Kingdom ruled by Prussia and Russia	Oct 13–Jan 15
Frederick Augustus I, reinstated	Jan 15–5 May 27
Anton Clement, succeeded his brother	5 May 27–6 June 36
Frederick Augustus II (having shared throne since 1830), m. Caroline of Austria, succeeded his uncle	6 June 36–9 Aug 54
Johann, m. Amalie Augusta of Bavaria, succeeded his brother	9 Aug 54–29 Oct 73
Albert, m. Caroline of Holstein-Gottorp-Wasa, succeeded his father	29 Oct 73–19 June 02
George, m. Maria Anna of Portugal, succeeded his brother	19 June 02–15 Oct 04
Frederick Augustus III, m. Luisa Maria d'Austria Toscana, succeeded his father	15 Oct 04–13 Nov 18 (abdic.)

4 *Hanover*

Ruled by the sovereign of Great Britain as King of Hanover until the accession of Queen Victoria, who could not succeed to the throne of Hanover where the Salic Law was in force.

KING

Ernest Augustus, Duke of Cumberland, m. Frederika of Mecklenburg-Strelitz, succeeded his brother (William IV of Great Britain)	6 June 37–18 Nov 51
George, m. Marie Alexandrine of Saxe-Altenburg, succeeded his father	18 Nov 51–7 Sep 66 (deposed when Prussia annexed Hanover)

5 *Württemberg*
KING

Frederick II (formerly Duke since 1797, then Elector since 1803), m. Augusta of Brunswick-Wolfenbüttel, created King	1 Jan 06–30 Oct 16
Wilhelm I, m. (i) Caroline Augusta of Bavaria (ii) Catharine Pavlovna of Russia (iii) Pauline of Württemberg (his cousin), succeeded his father	30 Oct 16–25 June 64
Charles, m. Olga Nicholaevna of Russia, succeeded his father	25 June 64–6 Oct 91
Wilhelm Carl, m. Carlotta of Schaumburg-Lippe, succeeded his cousin	6 Oct 91–9 Nov 18 (deposed)

6 *Baden*
GRAND DUKE

Charles Ludwig Frederick, m. Stephanie Beauharnais	1811–8 Dec 18
Ludwig, succeeded his brother	1818–30 Mar 30
Leopold I, m. Sophia of Sweden, succeeded his half brother, being the son of a morganatic marriage	1830–4 Apr 52
Regency (Frederick I, whose elder brother retained title of Grand Duke, but did not reign because of mental illness), m. Louise of Prussia, succeeded his father. He then assumed title of Grand Duke by patent in 1856	24 Apr 52–28 Sep 07
Frederick William, m. Hilda of Nassau, succeeded his father	28 Sep 07–

7 *Hesse-Cassel*
ELECTOR

William I (formerly Landgraf since 1785)	1805–27 Feb 21
William II, m. Augusta of Prussia, succeeded his father	1821–20 Nov 47
Frederick William, m. Gertrude Lehmann (created Princess of Hanau), succeeded his father	20 Nov 47–7 Sep 66 (deposed on annexation of Hesse-Cassel by Prussia)

21

8 *Hesse-Darmstadt*

GRAND DUKE

Ludwig I (formerly Landgraf as Ludwig X since 1790) .	1806–30
Ludwig II, m. Wilhelmine of Baden, succeeded his father	6 Apr 30–5 Mar 48
Co-regency (Ludwig II with his son, following insurrection on 5 Mar 48)	5 Mar 48–16 June 48
Ludwig III, m. Mathilde of Bavaria, succeeded his father	16 June 48–13 June 77
Ludwig IV, m. Alice of Great Britain, succeeded his uncle	13 June 77–13 Mar 92
Ernst-Louis, m. (i) Victoria of Saxe-Coburg-Gotha (ii) Elenore of Solms-Hohensolms-Lich, succeeded his father	13 Mar 92–

9 *Holstein and Lauenberg*

Ruled by the sovereign of Denmark (q.v.) until 15 Nov 63. On the death of King Frederick VII of Denmark and the failure of his direct male line, the Salic Law in Holstein prevented the accession of the new Danish King Christian IX. The state was claimed by Frederick, hereditary Duke of Holstein.

DUKE

Frederick of Holstein, m. Adelaide of Hohenlohe-Langenburg	18 Nov 63–30 Oct 64
Treaty of Vienna imposed joint Prussian and Austrian rule, after the defeat of Denmark by the two powers.	30 Oct 64–14 Aug 65
The convention of Gastein imposed Austrian rule in Holstein, Prussian in Lauenberg	14 Aug 65–8 June 66
Annexed by Prussia (q.v.)	8 June 66–

10 *Brunswick*

DUKE

Charles (fled on outbreak of rioting on 8 Sep 30)	16 June 15–2 Dec 30 (declared unfit to govern)

William I (having headed a provisional govern-

ment since 25 Apr 31), succeeded his brother   25 Apr 31–18 Oct 84
Brunswick then became the property of the King of Hanover on William's death; Prussia had already deposed him.

Regency (Prince Albrecht of Prussia, m. Maria of Saxony)	21 Oct 85–13 Sep 06
Regency (Duke Johann of Mecklenburg, m. Elizabeth of Stolberg-Rossia)	28 May 07–
Duke Ernst Augustus, m. Victoria of Prussia	1914–

11 *Nassau*
DUKE

William, m. (i) Louise of Saxe-Altenburg (ii) Pauline of Württemberg	9 Jan 16–20 Aug 39
Adolf, m. (i) Elizabeth of Russia (ii) Adelheid of Anhalt-Dessau, succeeded his father	20 Aug 39–23 Aug 66 (deposed on annexation by Prussia)

12 *Mecklenburg-Schwerin*
GRAND DUKE

Paul Frederick, m. Alexandrine of Prussia	up to 7 Mar 42
Frederick Francis II, m. (i) Augusta of Reuss-Schleiz (ii) Anne of Hesse (iii) Marie of Schwarzburg-Rudolstadt, succeeded his father	7 Mar 42–15 Apr 83
Frederick Francis III, m. Anastasia of Russia, succeeded his father	15 Apr 83–10 Apr 97
Frederick Francis IV, m. Alexandra of Great Britain, succeeded his father	10 Apr 97–

13 *Mecklenburg-Strelitz*
GRAND DUKE

Charles Frederick (formerly Duke)	1815–6 Nov 16
George, m. Marie of Hesse-Cassel, succeeded his father	6 Nov 16–6 Sep 60
Frederick William I, m. Augusta of Cambridge, succeeded his father	6 Sep 60–30 May 04
Adolf Frederick, m. Elizabeth of Anhalt, succeeded his father	30 May 04–24 Feb 18

23

14 *Luxembourg*

Luxembourg separated from Holland on 23 Nov 90.

GRAND DUKE

Adolf William of Nassau, m. Adelaide of Anhalt   23 Nov 90–17 Nov 05
William, m. Maria of Braganza, succeeded his
   father   17 Nov 05–25 Feb12

GRAND DUCHESS

Marie Adelaide, succeeded her father (Regency
   by Maria of Braganza)   25 Feb 12–14 Jan 19
               (abdic.)

The German Empire was established on 18 Jan 71 with King William I of Prussia as Emperor. From then until 9 Nov 1918 the Kings of Prussia were Emperors of Germany (*see* Prussia).

GREAT BRITAIN

QUEEN

Victoria, m. Albert of Saxe-Coburg-Gotha, succeeded her uncle   20 June 37–22 Jan 01

KING

Edward VII m. Alexandra of Schleswig-
   Holstein-Sonderburg-Glücksburg, succeeded
   his mother   22 Jan 01–7 May 10
George V, m. Mary of Teck, succeeded his father   7 May 10–20 Jan 36

GREECE

KING

Otto of Bavaria, elected (acceded on 5 Oct 32
   under regency)   7 May 32–22 Oct 62
               (deposed)

PRESIDENT

A. G. Bulgaris   23 Oct 62–30 Mar 63

KING

George of Schleswig-Holstein-Sonderburg-Glü-
  cksburg, elected, m. Olga of Russia (acceded
  on 6 June 63)   30 Mar 63–18 Mar 13
Constantine XII, m. Sophia of Prussia, suc-
  ceeded his father   18 Mar 13–11 June 17
                                                      (abdic.)

HUNGARY

The Austrian Emperors ruled Hungary as Emperors until the Dual Monarchy
on 12 June 67, when they became separately Emperors of Austria and Kings of
Hungary. The Emperor Karl renounced his power in the government of
Hungary on 13 Nov 1918.

THE KINGDOM OF ITALY

The Kingdom of Italy was formed on 17 Mar 61.

KING

Victor Emanuel of Savoy, m. Marie Adelaide of
  Ranieri   17 Mar 61–9 Jan 78
Umberto I, m. Margharita of Savoy, succeeded
  his father   9 Jan 78–29 July 00
Victor Emanuel III, m. Elena of Montenegro,
  succeeded his father   29 July 00–

The Italian states before unification:
  1 *Piedmont-Savoy-Sardinia*, called the *Kingdom of Sardinia*

KING

Victor Emanuel I, succeeded his brother after the
  French occupation   20 May 14–2 Mar 19
                                                      (abdic.)

Charles Felix, m. Cristina of Naples, succeeded

25

his brother. Ruled with his cousin Charles Albert as regent in his absence, returning to the country on 21 Mar 21	2 Mar 19–23 Mar 21
Rising, then a provisional government established	23 Mar 21

HEAD OF MILITARY GOVERNMENT

Charles Felix	10 Apr 21–18 Oct 21

KING

Charles Felix, reinstated	18 Oct 21–27 Apr 31
Charles Albert, m. Teresa of Austria, succeeded his cousin	27 Apr 31–23 Mar 49 (abdic.)
Victor Emanuel II, m. Marie Adelaide of Ranieri, succeeded his father	23 Mar 49–17 Mar 61

Sardinia became part of the Kingdom of Italy with Victor Emanuel II as King on 17 Mar 61.

2 *Lombardy*

Ruled by Austria (q.v.) until 1859. Annexed to the Kingdom of Sardinia on 5 June 59 (q.v.).

3 *Veneto*

Including small states of Venezia, Friuli, Padua, Polesine di Rovigo and Verona:

(a) Venezia

Ruled by the d'Este family as part of the Austrian Empire (q.v.) until 1848.

Provisional revolutionary government	23 Mar 48–13 Aug 48
Republic proclaimed	13 Aug 48

HEAD OF REPUBLIC

Daniele Manin, G. B. Cavedalis and L. Graziani	13 Aug 48–5 Mar 49

PRESIDENT

Daniele Manin	5 Mar 49–27 Aug 49
Returned to Austria (q.v.)	27 Aug 49
Ceded to France (q.v.)	24 Aug 66

Annexed to the Kingdom of Italy (q.v.)   4 Nov 66

(b) Friuli
Ruled by the d'Este family as part of the Austrian Empire (q.v.) until 1866. On 24 Aug 66 Friuli was annexed to the Kingdom of Italy (q.v.) except for Gorizia and Trieste which belonged to the Emperor of Austria until 1918.

(c) Padua
Ruled by the d'Este family as part of Austria until 1848.
Annexed to the Kingdom of Sardinia (q.v.)   14 June 48
Retaken by Austria (q.v.)   15 June 48
Annexed to the Kingdom of Italy (q.v.)   14 July 66

(d) Polesine di Rovigo
Ruled by the d'Este family as part of Austria until 1866, then on 10 July 66 it was annexed to the Kingdom of Italy (q.v.)

(e) Verona
Ruled by the d'Este family as part of Austria until 1866, and then on 16 Oct 66 it was annexed to the Kingdom of Italy (q.v.)

4 *Parma*, including *Piacenza* and *Fidenza*
(The events of 1848–9 occurred in all three states; the dates actually apply to Parma, so the events occurred in Piacenza and Fidenza two or three days sooner or later.)

DUCHESS

Marie Louise of Austria, m. (i) Napoleon I of
    France (ii) Adam von Neipperg (iii) Carlo
    Renato di Bombelles   11 Apr 14–14 Feb 31
                                             (renounced throne)

Revolution in Parma, followed by provisional
    government   11 Feb 31

DUCHESS

Marie Louise, restored by Austrians   13 Mar 31–17 Dec 47
DUKE

Charles Louis of Bourbon (grandson of Philip of
    Bourbon who had been Duke of Parma from
    1749–65), m. Maria Theresa of Savoy, reigned
    as Carlo II   18 Dec 47–20 Mar 48
                                             (deposed)

27

Revolution, installing a provisional government | 20 Mar 48–10 June 48

Unity with the Kingdom of Sardinia (q.v.) | 10 June 48–18 Aug 48

DUKE

Carlo II, restored by Austrians | 18 Aug 48–14 Mar 49 (abdic.)

Provisional government | 16 Mar 49–22 Mar 49

Joined with the Kingdom of Sardinia (q.v.) | 22 Mar 49

DUKE

Carlo III, m. Louise de Berry, succeeded his father | 4 Apr 49–26 Mar 54 (murdered)

Roberto, succeeded his father under the regency of his mother | 27 Mar 54–9 June 59 (deposed)

Government by commission for Victor Emanuel of Sardinia | 9 June 59

United with the Kingdom of Sardinia (q.v.) | 18 Mar 60

5 Lucca

Under Austrian occupation until 1817.

DUCHESS

Marie Louise de Bourbon, m. Louis of Bourbon (son of Philip of Bourbon, Duke of Parma) | 7 Dec 17–13 Mar 24

DUKE

Charles Louis of Bourbon, m. Maria Teresa of Savoy, succeeded his mother | 13 Mar 24–5 Oct 47 (renounced throne)

Union with the Grand Duchy of Tuscany (q.v.) | 5 Oct 47

6 Tuscany

Under French occupation until 20 Apr 1815.

GRAND DUKE

Ferdinand III of Lorraine, reinstated	20 Apr 15–18 June 24
Leopold II, m. (i) Maria Anna of Saxony (ii) Marie Antoinette of Bourbon, succeeded his father	18 June 24–7 Feb 49 (deposed)
Provisional government	8 Feb 49–18 Feb 49
Proclamation of the Republic of Tuscany. No president	18 Feb 49
Municipality of Firenze established	12 Apr 49

PRESIDENT

Bett. Ricasoli	12 Apr 49–17 Apr 49

GRAND DUKE

Leopold II, reinstated	17 Apr 49–27 Apr 59 (deposed)
Provisional government	27 Apr 59
Victor Emanuel II of Sardinia recognized	28 Apr 59
United with the Kingdom of Sardinia (q.v.)	22 Mar 60

7 *Modena, Reggio nel Emilia* and *Guastalla*

DUKE

Francis IV of Austria d'Este, Duke of Modena-Brisgau, m. Marie of Savoy	13 Apr 15–5 Feb 31 (deposed)
Rising, installation of a provisional government	4 Feb 31

DUKE

Francis IV, restored	9 Mar 31–21 Jan 46
Francis V, m. Adelgonda of Bavaria, succeeded his father	21 Jan 46–21 Mar 48 (deposed)

Rising, installation of a provisional government 21 Mar 48

Proclamation of unity with the Kingdom of
    Sardinia in Modena and Reggio nel Emilia 29 May 48

Proclamation of unity with the Kingdom of
    Sardinia in Guastalla 16 June 48

DUKE

Francis V, restored 10 Aug 48–20 Aug 59
                          (deposed)

Reggio nel'Emilia annexed to the Kingdom of
    Sardinia. Provisional government in Modena
    by commissioners for Victor Emanuel II 14 June 59

Modena and Guastalla annexed to the Kingdom
    of Sardinia 18 Mar 60

   8 *Massa e Carrara*
DUCHESS

Maria Beatrice Cybo of Austria d' Este, restored
    after French occupation, m. Archduke Fer-
    dinand of Austria 4 May 14–14 Nov 29

DUKE

Francis IV of Austria d'Este, Duke of Modena-
    Brisgau, succeeded his mother 14 Nov 29–21 Jan 46
Francis V, m. Adelgonda of Bavaria, succeeded
    his father 21 Jan 46–27 Apr 59
                          (deposed)
Victor Emanuel II of Sardinia recognized 27 Apr 59

Formal annexation to the Kingdom of Sardinia 18 May 60

   9 *Papal States*
   (a) Ferrara
Ruled by the Pope (*see* the Papacy) since 18 Aug 15 restoration.
      Rising–provisional government 7 Feb 31
      Taken by Austria 6 Mar 31
      Pope reinstated 15 Mar 31

Taken by Austria	17 July 47
Pope reinstated	Dec 47
Taken by Austria	14 July 48
Provisional government	Nov 48
United with the Republic of Rome under a triumvirate	9 Feb 49
Pope reinstated	20 May 49
Provisional government	12 June 59
Annexed to the Kingdom of Sardinia (q.v.)	18 Mar 60

(b) Bologna

Pope restored to power	18 July 15
Rising–provisional government	4 Feb 31
Pope restored	20 Mar 31
Citizen government with no president	15 July 31
Pope restored	28 Jan 32
Taken by Austria	15 July 48
United with the Republic of Rome under a triumvirate	9 Feb 49
Pope restored	16 May 49
Provisional government	12 June 59
Annexed to the Kingdom of Sardinia (q.v.)	25 Mar 60

(c) Imola

Pope restored to power	19 July 15
Rising–provisional government	5 Feb 31
Union with the United Italian Provinces. No president	4 Mar 31
Pope restored	21 Mar 31
Provisional government	23 Jan 49
Pope restored	26 May 49
Provisional government	12 June 59
Union with the Kingdom of Sardinia	12 Mar 60

(d) Faenza

Pope restored to power	9 June 15
Rising. Union with the United Italian Provinces. No president	5 Feb 31
Pope restored	22 Mar 31
Union with the Republic of Rome under a triumvirate	Jan 49
Pope restored	18 May 49
Provisional government	13 June 59
Union with the Kingdom of Sardinia	18 Mar 60

(e) Forli

Pope restored to power	9 June 15

Rising. Union with the United Italian Pro-
vinces. No president   5 Feb 31
Pope restored   24 Mar 31
Citizen government. No president   15 July 31
Pope restored   21 Jan 32
Union with the Republic of Rome under a
triumvirate   9 Feb 49
Pope restored   26 May 49
Provisional government   13 June 59
Union with the Kingdom of Sardinia   13 Mar 60

(f) Cesena
Pope restored to power   9 June 15
Rising–provisional government   5 Feb 31
Union with the United Italian Provinces.
No president   4 Mar 31
Pope restored   24 Mar 31
Rising–provisional government   1 Jan 32
Union with the Republic of Rome under a
triumvirate   9 Feb 49
Pope restored   26 May 49
Provisional government   13 June 60
Union with the Kingdom of Sardinia   25 Mar 60

(g) Rimini
Pope restored to power   18 July 15
Rising–provisional government   6 Feb 31
Pope restored   25 Mar 31
Rising–provisional government   29 Mar 49
Pope restored   15 July 49
Union with the Kingdom of Sardinia   18 Mar 60

(h) Ravenna
Pope restored to power   18 July 15
Rising–provisional government   6 Feb 31
Pope restored   23 Mar 31
Rising–provisional government   24 Jan 49
Pope restored   26 May 49
Provisional government ruling for Victor
Emanuel II   13 June 59
Formal annexation to the Kingdom of
Sardinia   18 Mar 60

(i) Pesare
Pope restored to power   7 May 15
Occupation by Victor Emanuel II   12 Sep 60
Formal annexation to the Kingdom of

	Sardinia	17 Dec 60
(j)	Camerino	
	Pope restored to power	7 May 15
	Formal annexation to the Kingdom of Sardinia	17 Dec 60
(k)	Urbino	
	Pope restored to power	7 May 15
	Rising. Union with the Republic of Rome under a triumvirate	11 Feb 49
	Pope restored	1 July 49
	Occupation by Victor Emanuel II	11 Sep 60
	Formal annexation to the Kingdom of Sardinia	17 Dec 60
(l)	Ancona	
	Pope restored to power	25 July 15
	Rising–provisional government	4 Feb 31
	Pope restored	27 Mar 31
	Union with the Republic of Rome under a triumvirate	10 Feb 49
	Pope restored	25 May 49
	Formal annexation to the Kingdom of Sardinia	29 Sep 60
(m)	Perugia	
	Pope restored to power	1814
	Rising–provisional government	14 June 59
	Pope restored	20 June 59
	Formal annexation to the Kingdom of Sardinia	14 Sep 60
(n)	Spoleto	
	Pope restored to power	22 Mar 15
	Formal annexation to the Kingdom of Sardinia	17 Oct 60
(o)	Viterbo	
	Pope in power since 1461.	
	Occupied by Victor Emanuel II of Italy	12 Sep 70
(p)	Benevento	
	Pope restored to power	25 May 14
	Formal annexation to the Kingdom of Sardinia	27 Oct 60
(q)	Rome	
	Pope restored to power	18 July 15
	Roman Republic under a triumvirate: Armellini, Montecchi and Saliceti	5 Feb 49

Triumvirate: Mazzini, Saffi, Armellini   29 Mar 49

10 *Sicily*

Ruled from Naples 1815–48. (*See* Kingdom of the Two Sicilies.)

DUKE

Ferdinand II, deposed   12 Jan 48
Provisional government established

PRESIDENT

Ruggiero Settimo   12 Jan 48–15 May 49

DUKE

Ferdinand II, reinstated   15 May 49
(*See* Kingdom of the Two Sicilies)

11 *Kingdom of the Two Sicilies* (Naples and Sicily)

KING

Ferdinand of Bourbon, reinstated as King Ferdinand I (22 Dec 16), after French occupation,
  m. Maria Caroline of Austria   2 June 15–15 Mar 21
Provisional government under Marchese di Cir-
  cello   15 Mar 21–15 May 21

KING

Ferdinand I, reinstated   15 May 21–4 Jan 25
Francesco I, m. (i) Marie Clementine of Austria
  (ii) Isabella of Spain, succeeded his father   4 Jan 25–8 Nov 30
Ferdinand II, m. Marie Christine of Savoy,
  succeeded his father   8 Nov 30–22 May 59
Francesco II, succeeded his father   22 May 59–21 Oct 60
                                                     (deposed)
Formal annexation to the Kingdom of Sardinia   17 Dec 60

LUXEMBOURG

Luxembourg separated from Holland on 23 Nov 90.

GRAND DUKE

Adolf William of Nassau, m. Adelaide of Anhalt   23 Nov 90–17 Nov 05
William, m. Maria of Braganza, succeeded his
    father   17 Nov 05–25 Feb 12

GRAND DUCHESS

Marie Adelaide, succeeded her father (Maria of
    Braganza as regent)   25 Feb 12–14 Jan 19
                                 (abdic.)

MONACO

PRINCE

Florestan I, m. Mille Rouiller, succeeded his
    brother   2 Oct 41–25 June 56
Charles III, m. Antonietta de Merode, succeeded
    his father   26 June 56–10 Sep 89
Albert I, m. Alice, dowager Duchess of Rich-
    elieu, succeeded his father   10 Sep 89–

MONTENEGRO

PRINCE

Peter Njegos   Since 1813

PRINCE-BISHOP

Peter Njegos   1830–52
Danilo, succeeded his father   1852–60 (murdered)
Nicholas I, succeeded his father   1860–

THE NETHERLANDS

KING

William II, of Holland and Luxembourg, m.
    Anna Pavlovna of Russia, succeeded his father   7 Oct 40–17 Mar 49

William III, m. (i) Sophie of Württemburg (ii)
    Emma of Waldeck, succeeded his father   17 Mar 49–23 Nov 90
Luxembourg separated from Holland   23 Nov 90
Regency (Emma of Waldeck)   23 Nov 90–31 Aug 98

QUEEN

Wilhelmina, m. Henry of Mecklenburg-
    Schwerin, succeeded her father   31 Aug 98–

NORWAY

Norway became independent under a provisional government on 7 June 1905.

KING

Haakon VII, formerly Prince Carl of Denmark,
    m. Maud of Great Britain, elected to the
    throne   18 Nov 1905–

NORWAY AND SWEDEN

Norway became independent of Denmark and united to Sweden by the Treaty of Kiel on 4 Nov 14.

KING (Sweden)

Charles XIII, succeeded his brother   6 June 09–21 Aug10
Charles XIV (formerly Jean-Baptiste Bernad-
    otte), m. Eugenie de Marseilles, elected to the
    throne by Parliament   21 Aug 10–8 Mar 44
Oscar I, m. Josephine of Leuchtenberg, suc-
    ceeded his father   8 Mar 44–8 July 59
Regency (Prince Charles, because of illness of
    King Oscar)   25 Sep 57–8 July 59
Charles XV, m. Louise of Orange-Nassau, suc-
    ceeded his father   8 July 59–18 Sep 72
Oscar II, m. Sophie of Nassau, succeeded his
    brother   18 Sep 72–8 Dec 1907
Norway became independent under a pro-
    visional government   7 June 05

THE PAPACY

POPE

Pius IX, consecrated	21 June 46–7 Feb 78
Leo XIII, consecrated	3 Mar 78–20 July 1903
Pius X, consecrated	9 Aug 03–20 Aug 14
Benedict XV, consecrated	6 Sep 14–22 Jan 22

PORTUGAL

QUEEN

Maria de Gloria   26 May 34–15 Nov 53

KING

Pedro V, succeeded his mother, under his father's
    regency   15 Nov 53–16 Sep 55
Luis I, m. Maria Pia of Savoy, succeeded his
    brother under his father's regency   1 Nov 61–19 Oct 89
Carlos I, m. Maria Amalia of Bourbon-Orleans,
    succeeded his father   19 Oct 89–1 Feb 08
Manuel II, succeeded his father   1 Feb 08–5 Oct 10
                      (deposed)

Republic proclaimed   5 Oct 10

PRESIDENT

Teofilo Braga   5 Oct 1910–
                            19 June 11
Braachamp   19 June 11–24 Aug 11
Manuel de Arriaga   24 Aug 11–7 Aug 15
Bernardino Machado   7 Aug 15–

ROMANIA

Romania became independent of Turkey on 22 May 77.

Karel I (formerly Prince Karl of Hohenzollern-
  Sigmaringen), m. Elizabeth of Wied, elected   1866–14 Mar 81

KING

Karel I, elected   14 Mar 81–10 Oct 14
Ferdinand, m. Marie of Saxe-Coburg-Gotha,
  succeeded his uncle   10 Oct 14–20 July 27

RUSSIA

TSAR

Nicholas I, m. Charlotte of Prussia, succeeded
  his brother Constantine   7 Dec 25–2 Mar 55

(NOTE: Constantine had previously renounced the succession in favour of
Nicholas. The news of his brother Alexander's death did not reach him until 7
Dec 25 when he proclaimed Nicholas as Tsar. The same news reached
Nicholas on 9 Dec 25, and he proclaimed Constantine but was persuaded to
receive the allegiance of the St Petersburg garrison on 26 Dec 25 and put down
the brief rising by Constantine's supporters (the 'Decembrists'). *The Times*
said, 'The Empire is in the strange position of having two self-denying
Emperors and no active ruler.')

Alexander II, m. Marie of Hesse-Darmstadt,
  succeeded his father   2 Mar 55–1 Mar 81
                                                 (assassinated)
Alexander III, m. Marie of Denmark, succeeded
  his father   1 Mar 81–1 Nov 94
Nicholas II, m. Alexandra of Hesse-Darmstadt,
  succeeded his father   1 Nov 94–16 July 18
                                                 (murdered)

SERBIA

Serbia became independent of Turkey by the Treaty of Berlin on 13 July 78.

KING

Milan IV Obrenovitch (formerly Prince), created King	6 Mar 82–6 Mar 89 (abdic.)
Alexander I Obrenovitch, m. Draga Mascin	6 Mar 89–10 June 03 (murdered)
Provisional government	11 June 03

KING

Peter, m. Zorka of Montenegro, elected	15 June 03–16 Aug 21

SPAIN

QUEEN

Isabella, m. Francisco de Assis, her cousin, succeeded her father	29 Sep 33–30 Sep 68
Regency (Mother of Isabella)	29 Sep 33–12 Oct 40
Provisional government under Francesco Serrano	17 Sep 68–16 Nov 70

KING

Amedeo of Savoy, elected (acceded 3 Dec 70)	16 Nov 70–11 Feb 73 (abdic.)
Republican government with no president	11 Feb 73–31 Dec 74

KING

Alfonso XII, m. (i) Maria de las Mercedes (ii) Marie-Christine of Austria, succeeded his mother after the republic	31 Dec 74–25 Nov 85

REGENT

Marie-Christine of Austria (her infant stepdaughter, Maria de las Mercedés being Queen in name)	25 Nov 85–17 May 02

KING

Alfonso XIII (born 17 May 86), m. Princess Ena
of Battenburg, succeeded his half-sister. His
mother acted as Regent until 1902 although
Alfonso XIII became King at birth   18 May 86–

SWEDEN

Sweden and Norway became separate kingdoms on 7 June 1905.

KING

Gustav V, m. Victoria of Baden, succeeded his
father, Oscar II   8 Dec 1907–

SWITZERLAND

Federal state was formed in 1848 with an annually elected President. The first
President was elected to take office in 1849.

1849	Jonas Furrer	1867	Constantin Fornerod
1850	Henri Druey	1868	Jakob Dubs
1851	Josef Munzinger	1869	Emilio Welti
1852	Jonas Furrer	1870	Jakob Dubs
1853	Wilhelm Näff	1871	Karl Schenk
1854	Frederic Frey-Herosée	1872	Emilio Welti
1855	Ulric Ochsenbein	1873	Pierre Ceresole
1856	Jakob Stämpfli	1874	Karl Schenk
1857	Constantin Fornerod	1875	Johan Jakob Scherer
1858	Jonas Furrer	1876	Emilio Welti
1859	Jakob Stämpfli	1877	Joachim Heer
1860	Frederic Frey-Herosée	1878	Karl Schenk
1861	Martin Knüsel	1879	Bernard Hammer
1862	Jakob Stämpfli	1880	Emilio Welti
1863	Constantin Fornerod	1881	Numa Droz
1864	Jakob Dubs	1882	Simeone Bavier
1865	Karl Schenk	1883	Louis Ruchonnet
1866	Martin Knüsel	1884	Emilio Welti

1885	Karl Schenk	1902	Josef Zemp
1886	Adolf Deucher	1903	Adolf Deucher
1887	Numa Droz	1904	Robert Comtesse
1888	Wilhelm Hertenstein	1905	Marc Ruchet
1889	Bernard Hammer	1906	Louis Forrer
1890	Louis Ruchonnet	1907	Eduard Müller
1891	Emilio Welti	1908	Ernest Brenner
1892	Walter Hauser	1909	Adolf Deucher
1893	Karl Schenk	1910	Robert Comtesse
1894	Emil Frey	1911	Marc Ruchet
1895	Josef Zemp	1912	Louis Forrer
1896	Adrian Lachenal	1913	Eduard Müller
1897	Adolf Deucher	1914	Artur Hoffman
1898	Eugène Ruffy	1915	Giuseppe Motta
1899	Eduard Müller	1916	Camille Decoppet
1900	Walter Hauser	1917	Edmond Schultess
1901	Ernest Brenner	1918	Emil Ador

TURKEY

SULTAN

Mahmud II, succeeded his brother	28 July 08–1 July 39
Abd-el-Medjid, succeeded his father	1 July 39–25 June 61
Abd-el-Aziz, succeeded his brother	25 June 61–30 May 76 (deposed)
Murad V, succeeded his uncle	30 May 76–30 Aug 76 (deposed)
Abd el Hamid II, succeeded his brother	30 Aug 76–27 Apr 09 (deposed)
Mehemed V, succeeded his brother	27 Apr 09–3 July 18

3 PARLIAMENTS

ALSACE-LORRAINE

After the Franco-Prussian War the legislative power was given to the German Imperial Parliament and the executive power to the Emperor. In Oct 74 a state council was set up with advisory powers. From 1877 the Emperor might enact laws for Alsace-Lorraine if the German Bundesrath (upper house) and the state council agreed on them, without the consent of the German Reichstag (lower house). The Reichstag still had to give consent to any amendment of its own previous laws. From 4 July 79 the state council might initiate legislation. A Statthalter was appointed to exercise the powers of the Imperial government. He governed through a cabinet of secretaries of state and 4 departmental heads. The cabinet countersigned the Emperor's acts and was assisted by an advisory council of state.

The state council had to be called every year. It had 58 members, of whom 34 were chosen by elected provincial councils, 4 by municipal councils, 20 by commune electors. They sat for three years, but were only elected simultaneously if the council had been dissolved by the Emperor. The house sent 15 representatives to the German Reichstag. In 1879 the Statthalter sent non-voting delegates to the German Bundesrath.

AUSTRIA

On 22 July 48 a parliament met with power to enact a constitution. It had 383 indirectly elected members and represented all nationalities in the empire except the Italians and Hungarians. It had one chamber and no executive; it drafted laws which the Emperor could enact if he wished. It was dissolved on 4 Mar 49, with the proclamation of a new constitution.

The new constitution provided for a Reichstag with a ministry responsible to it, and a Reichsrat, or imperial council, of 21 members nominated by the Emperor. This last was the only institution that was in fact created; it had limited powers at first but its authority was increased and ministers became responsible only to the Emperor. The constitution was revoked on 31 Dec 50.

The Patent of 5 Mar 60 added 38 members to the Reichsrat from each provincial Diet. The Diploma of 20 Oct 60 recognized the authority of the provincial Diets and laid down that the Reichsrat was only to deal with matters common to the whole Empire and that otherwise the Emperor would legislate in co-operation with the provincial Diets concerned.

The Patent of 26 Feb 61 provided for a Reichsrat of 334 deputies elected from each provincial diet, and an upper house of peers.

The *Ausgleich* of June 67 provided that the Reichsrat should be a parliament for the Austrian half of the new Dual Monarchy (Austria-Hungary). This was confirmed by the constitution of 21 Dec 67 which provided for a bicameral legislature, the executive power being exercised by the Emperor through responsible ministers. He had power to appoint the ministers and all officials, to create peers, to summon and dissolve both houses. All his acts had to be countersigned by the ministers, but he had appointed them and they were his servants, not the servants of parliament. His assent was necessary before a bill became law, and he could refuse it even if the bill was passed by both houses.

The lower house sat for a 6-year term. Its members were originally chosen by the provincial diets, but in 1868 a law provided for direct election of representatives from those provinces where the diet refused to name any. On 2 Apr 73 election superseded nomination by the diets altogether, and the number of deputies was raised from 203 to 353. By 1896 there were 425. Voters were of five classes: large landowners, cities, chambers of commerce, rural communes and the general class. There was a constituency for each class in each district. The house was obliged to meet annually. It had power to legislate for the Austrian half of the Dual Monarchy, but the execution of the laws was left to the provincial diets. Bills were passed through committees set up by 'bureaux' within the house; a joint committee was appointed by both houses to deal with the public debt.

The upper house had 81 nobles, princes and bishops, and 94 members nominated for life, with no limit to the number of new nominations. Both houses had the same rights and powers, except that the budget and bills on recruitment must go first to the lower house.

The competence of both houses was limited by the extensive list of matters which came within the competence of the provincial diets and might not be considered in the central parliament.

AUSTRIA-HUNGARY
(THE DUAL MONARCHY)

There was a deliberative body with two delegations, one from Austria and one from Hungary and each of 60 members of whom 20 were chosen by the upper house of each parliament and 40 by the lower. The body was re-elected annually. The proposals of both governments were put before both delegations at once, but they debated separately and only met in common session if they had failed three times to agree in their separate votes. The Hungarian delegation tended to have a unity which the Austrian did not; Hungarian delegates were chosen by majority votes in each house, with Magyars in the majority. Austrian delegates were chosen from the several provinces and did not necessarily have any common interest.

The body had little legislative power; it voted supplies and administered the laws made in the Austrian and Hungarian parliaments. The ministers for common affairs were not responsible to it or to any legislative body.

BADEN

The constitution was granted in 1818 and provided for a bicameral parliament. Both chambers must be summoned at least every other year and had specified competence to deal with all taxes, loans, expenditure and laws regarding the freedom and the property of citizens. Any other measure could be enacted by royal ordinance. The crown controlled the execution of laws and all administration, except that parliament voted the funds.

In 1871 the upper house had 11 hereditary members, 2 by virtue of office, 8 nominated, 8 chosen to represent the landowners and 2 the universities.

The chamber of deputies had 22 members elected from the chief towns and 41 for country districts. There was one member for each 22,500 inhabitants.

BAVARIA

The constitution was granted in 1818, and provided for a bicameral parliament. The King shared executive power with his ministers, who had to countersign all his acts. They were responsible to him and not to parliament. The two chambers were the Reichsrath (upper chamber) which in 1871 was composed of 51 hereditary members, 13 nominated and 8 by virtue of office: the Chamber of Deputies had 154 elected members, one for each 31,000 of the population, returned from electoral districts which sent between one and four members each. The franchise was for all men paying direct state taxes.

Parliament controlled the budget and taxation. Members of both houses had a limited right to interpellate ministers and to question and debate policies; but they might not debate matters outside their competence or issue public addresses.

BELGIUM

The constitution of 7 Feb 1831 provided for a bicameral parliament. The King might dissolve both chambers, but an election must be held within 40 days. He might initiate legislation, but all his acts must be countersigned by his ministers.

The senate sat for an 8-year term and consisted of half the number of members in the lower house. Until September 1893 they were elected by the same electorate; after that the senators were partly elected directly, by all voters over 30, and partly indirectly by the provincial councils. Proportional representation was introduced for both houses in 1899. The senate's term was 8 years, half retiring every 4.

The lower house was directly elected for a 4 year term, half retiring every 2.

BRUNSWICK

The constitution was granted in 1832 and amended in 1851. It provided for a single-chamber parliament which had (1871) 21 members representing the landowners or those most heavily taxed, 10 for the towns, 12 for the country districts, and 3 for the clergy. There was one deputy for each 6600 inhabitants. Members sat for a 6-year term (4 years from 1888) and the parliament had to be called at least every 2 years. All statutes amending the constitution, changing an organic institution or affecting financial, military, criminal or private civil laws required the parliament's consent. On other matters it need only be consulted. Ministers were responsible to the Crown and not to the parliament.

Parliament had some right to initiate laws and to debate estimates of expenses, although it might not refuse to vote them. The house elected a permanent committee which consented to many laws when the house was not in session and might call the parliament if the constitution was violated.

BULGARIA

The constitution of 17 Apr 79 was revised in May 93. It provided for a National Assembly elected by manhood suffrage, 1 deputy for every 10,000 people until 1893 when the proportion was changed to 1 for every 20,000. The term was 5 years (3 until 1893). Every literate male Bulgarian over the age of 30 might be a deputy. The house met for annual sessions from October to December.

All legislative and financial measures had to be debated and voted by the assembly and then submitted to the king for sanction and promulgation. The ministers were appointed by the King and responsible to the assembly. There was also a Great Assembly of elected members—1 for every 10,000 of the population—which was convoked for special purposes, for example to effect a change in the constitution.

Executive power was shared by the King and the cabinet of ministers.

DENMARK

The constitution of June 49 was amended in 1855, 1863 and 1866. It provided for a bicameral parliament composed of the Landsthing or upper house and the Folkething or chamber of deputies. The Landsthing had 66 members, 12 of them nominated for life by the Crown and the rest indirectly elected by the taxpayers of the country districts, by deputies of taxpayers in the cities, and by deputies for the rest of the electorate. The Folkething had about 100 members directly elected by all men over 25 not in private service and not receiving public charity. There was one deputy for every 16,000 people. The Landsthing's term was 8 years, the Folkething's 3. Both houses had to meet at least annually and share legislative power, although money bills had to be passed first to the lower house. Ministers had free access to both houses, but voted only in the chamber of which they were members. Executive power was shared by the King and a council of responsible ministers.

FRANCE

The Parliamentary Commission of 1830 revised the Constitutional Charter of June 1814. Both houses gained the right to initiate laws; the Sovereign lost his power to suspend laws. The sessions of the chamber of peers were made public. The term for the chamber of deputies was altered again to 5 years; the age of electors was lowered to 25.

In 1831 the tax qualification for electors was lowered to 200 francs (100 for some professional classes). This doubled the size of the electorate to about 150th of the population.

On 4 Nov 48 the constitution framed by the National Constituent Assembly provided for a single chamber of 750 members (including those from the colonies and Algeria) to be elected directly by secret ballot on electoral district *scrutin de liste* for a 3-year term. The electors were all men over 21 with 6 months fixed residence and fully possessed of civil rights. It provided for ministers but did not specify their functions. It did specify that executive power was to be vested in a president who should be elected for four years by the whole electorate. He had power to propose laws and to negotiate and ratify treaties with the assembly's consent.

On 31 May 50 the 6 months fixed residence qualification for electors was altered to 3 years, which reduced the electorate by one-third.

In Mar 52 the President's powers were extended; ministers became responsible to him and not to the assembly, which was divided into two chambers, and lost the power to initiate and promulgate laws, which passed to the President. The two chambers were the Legislative Body and the Senate. The Senate consisted of *ex-officio* members and others appointed by the Head of State for life. It exercised executive power in conjunction with the Head of State and acted as a presidential (later imperial) council. The Legislative Body had 251 members elected for 6 years on manhood suffrage. On 8 Sep 69 a *senatus-consulte* measure gave the Legislative Body the right to elect its own officials and re-established a cabinet system, although ministers were responsible to the Emperor and not the assembly, and might not be members of either house. On 20 Apr 70 a *senatus-consulte* measure was passed and approved by plebiscite on 8 May 70 which laid down that the Senate should be a legislative chamber working in conjunction with the Legislative Body and not an imperial council. Both houses might initiate laws, and ministers were no longer solely dependent on the Emperor. The constitution might only be amended with the approval of the people.

On 8 Feb 71 (after the Franco-Prussian war and the abdication of the Emperor) a National Assembly of 758 members was chosen by manhood suffrage; it was the only legal representative of national sovereignty and the only government. A. Thiers was elected President of France on 31 Aug 71 but he was responsible to the assembly and his powers lasted only for the assembly's duration. Ministers were responsible also to the assembly, the President acting as the chief executive.

The Constitution of the Third Republic, 1875, came into force on 8 Mar 76 when the National Assembly resigned its functions to a new parliament.

This provided for a bicameral legislature, with executive power vested in a President. He might dissolve the lower house with the consent of the upper, provided that an election followed; he might refuse to promulgate laws until they had been reconsidered, and might initiate laws concurrently with the two houses. Every action of his must be counter-signed by a minister, and the ministry was responsible to the assembly. Ministries were created by executive decree; parliament might only influence the decision by declining to vote for

47

financial provision. The President chose the Prime Minister, and this was not merely a formality since there was seldom one party with a clear majority to lead the government. The Prime Minister selected the ministers. The President presided over a Council of Ministers, which made decisions on all exercise of the President's powers. He did not preside over the Council of the Cabinet, which discussed policy and acted as a link between the government and parliament.

The Senate had 300 members—75 of them designated by the assembly and the rest indirectly elected from the departments according to their population. The term was 9 years, one-third retiring every 3 years. The Senate itself filled by co-option any vacancy arising on the death of a designated member. In 1884 this was amended, and vacancies so arising were to be filled by election in the normal way.

The Chamber of Deputies was elected by universal male suffrage from single member districts, reapportioned after each 5-yearly census. In 1875 there were 533 deputies, 597 by 1910, 602 by 1914. The term was 4 years. The chamber could be dissolved by the President with the Senate's assent but this only happened once in 1877.

Both chambers were obliged to assemble annually in January and continue in session for at least 5 months. Both divided into 'bureaux' for the preliminary discussion of bills; the bureaux on receiving a bill would appoint a committee to scrutinize it, 1 or more members from each bureau. By 1882 the appointment of these *ad hoc* committees was found to be inadequate and a standing committee was appointed (on the army). By 1902 there was provision for 16 standing committees of 33 members each, chosen by the bureaux for the duration of parliament. In 1910 the chamber itself elected standing committee members, 44 for each committee and chosen according to party quotas.

Bills were originated by ministers, approved by the President and Council of Ministers and submitted to parliament as *projets de lois* (government bills) to pass through the bureau committees. Private members' bills (*propositions de lois*) were submitted in writing for scrutiny by a *commission d' initiative*, who would report whether or not the measure should be considered further. Private members had considerable initiative and right to time. Bills had to pass both houses in the same form; for government bills differences were smoothed out by ministers, for private bills they were tackled by joint committee. Parliament controlled ministers by 'interpellation'—written questions with debate leading to a vote of confidence or no-confidence; in the latter event, the minister must resign. The government might not dissolve the parliament and call a general election to confirm that it still had the confidence of the country, because the lower house could only be dissolved with the consent of the upper. In 1889 multiple candidature was forbidden and secret ballot enforced for general elections.

GERMANY

On 31 Mar 48 a preliminary assembly (Vorparlament) met to make arrangements for the election of a National Assembly; on 7 Apr these were submitted to the Federal Diet which obtained the assent of the state governments. The new assembly met on 18 May with members elected by a variety of franchises in the different states, mostly by indirect election; each state was represented according to size, Austria having 190 representatives, Prussia 159, Bavaria 71, Württemberg 28, Hanover 26, Saxony 24, Baden 20, Hesse-Darmstadt 12, Hesse Cassel 11, Hamburg 3, the rest a total of 62 between them. The assembly's task was to frame a constitution for a united Germany and to bring about the co-operation of state governments, but its members remained divided as to whether it had the authority to do this: whether it should negotiate a constitution with the state governments, leave the state governments to enact a constitution when the assembly had drafted it, or impose a constitution on them by its own power. On 28 June 48 it passed a statute creating a central power with supreme authority, and elected Archduke John of Austria as its head. On 12 July with the consent of the state governments the Federal Diet dissolved and handed its authority to the new central power. The assembly did not publish a constitution until Dec 48 when liberal sentiment was waning, and the state governments would not accept it. The assembly did not survive its conflict with Austria over the composition and leadership of the united Germany; the state governments lost confidence in it and it had dissolved by 18 June 49. Archduke John resigned on 6 Oct 49 and handed his powers to an interim commission.

An adaptation of the assembly's constitution was agreed by a meeting of representatives of the princes in Berlin and submitted to the states for acceptance on 28 May 49. Austria and Bavaria did not accept it. A parliament was elected according to this constitution and met from 20 Mar to 29 Apr 50 (parliament of the Erfurt Union). One chamber represented the states, but only the small states sent deputies; the lower house was elected. It accepted the constitution of 28 May, but only the government of Prussia was strong enough to implement it, and the parliament could not compel Prussia to act.

On 1 May 50 Austria declared that the interim commission to which Archduke John had handed his authority had expired, and that she proposed to summon the Federal Diet in its place on 10 May. The Erfurt parliament had acted without being recognized by Austria; the Federal Diet was reconvened without being recognized by Prussia until the Olmutz agreement was signed on 29 Nov 50 and was held to imply acceptance of the Diet's authority. The Federal Diet continued to operate until 1866, when the Germanic Confederation came to an end with the Austro-Prussian war.

The parliament of the North German Confederation which was formed after the Austro-Prussian war was elected in May 67. There was one federal minister who was responsible to the legislature, and an executive Federal Council composed of nominees of the state governments. The legislature was elected on universal manhood suffrage and had the right to vote the budget.

The imperial constitution of 16 Apr 71 provided for a bicameral parliament. The lower house, the Reichstag, was elected on universal manhood suffrage for 3-year terms (5 after 1888), by direct and secret election. The members were elected from districts which did not over-step state boundaries, but they represented the whole electorate and not their constituents. There was one member for every 100,000 inhabitants of the state or portion of 100,000. It had power to debate government policy and to vote the budget, although many expenses and sources of income were outside its control because of the method of their administration. Bills passed through committees which were set up by 'bureaux', 7 of which were created at the beginning of each session. Representation on the committees was according to party strength. The house could be dissolved by the upper house with the Emperor's consent.

The upper house or Bundesrath was composed of representatives of the member states and free cities. There were 58 members; Prussia sent 17, Bavaria 6, Saxony and Württemberg 4, Hesse and Baden 3, Mecklenbourg-Schwerin and Brunswick 2 and the others 1 each. The members were solely responsible to their governments and not to the Reichstag, in which they might not sit. Its presidency was held by the Chancellor. In practice, bills were normally initiated in the Bundesrath by the Chancellor, worked through the permanent committees, of which there were 7, and presented to the Reichstag for assent; the consent of both houses was necessary before a bill became law, and the Reichstag had the right to question the Chancellor and debate Bundesrath policy, but no vote followed.

The Bundesrath might sit alone, the Reichstag could not. The Bundesrath's standing committees might sit when the house was not in session. Bundesrath members voted *en bloc* for their states, and all the votes could be cast by one representative. The members were appointed by their governments for no fixed term.

There was no responsible imperial ministry; only the Chancellor was answerable to the Reichstag.

GREECE

The constitution of 1844 established a bicameral parliament with a responsible executive. The Senate was nominated by the King and the Chamber of Deputies was elected on universal manhood suffrage. The constitution of November 1864 provided for a single-chamber parliament. There was also provision for a Council of State to which all bills must be referred and which must observe or amend within 10 days. In fact this body was seldom formed.

The single chamber was elected on universal manhood suffrage for 4 years. Candidates needed to be over 30, electors over 21. Sessions were for 3–6 months. No law could be passed except by absolute majority of the house, and half the members must be present to form a quorum. The house had one member for every 12,000 inhabitants until 1905, when there was one for every 16,000. In 1906 the electoral districts were altered to be coterminous with the administrative departments, and junior officers of the army and navy were barred from belonging to the house.

Ministers were responsible to parliament but they were chosen by the King, who had power to sanction laws and to convoke or dissolve the chamber.

HESSE-DARMSTADT

The constitution was granted in 1820 and amended in 1856. It provided for a bicameral legislature, the upper house having (1871) 17 hereditary members, 10 nominated, 2 by virtue of office and 1 representing universities. The lower house had 50 members, one for 16,500 inhabitants. There were 6 representing social classes, 10 for the towns, 34 for the country districts. Election was indirect, the electors being chosen by taxpayers. Members sat for 6 years, half retiring every 3. The Grand Duke held executive power through a cabinet of ministers of state and two department heads. Most legislation was initiated by the government. If a bill was rejected by one house it might be withdrawn and presented again in the next session. If it was again rejected the government might still pass it if the total of affirmative votes at both submissions were greater than the negative.

HUNGARY

Before 1848 Hungary had a parliament of two chambers, the House of Magnates and the House of Deputies; members of the lower house were chosen by county assemblies and by the councils of free cities. The parliament had general legislative power, but any laws passed had to be executed by the local county or free city executives, and the local councils could suspend the operation of any measure they disliked.

All nobles were entitled to sit in the county assemblies, and these assemblies had 1 vote each. The free cities had 1 vote between them.

This parliament did not sit between 1815 and 1825.

51

In 1848 the Emperor, as King of Hungary, agreed to 31 laws of parliamentary reform, providing for a cabinet at Budapest who must countersign the King's acts; an annual parliament; a ministry responsible to the parliament and chosen by the Minister President.

In Mar 49 he revoked his agreement and the laws never operated, although the Hungarians claimed that they were still valid.

In 1867 the laws were brought into operation, and a bicameral parliament sat.

The upper house had about 270 members and was composed of princes, nobility and bishops, and representatives from Croatia, Slavonia and Transylvania. From 1886, no titled magnate might sit unless he paid a land tax of 3000 florins; church officers were also admitted and life members appointed by the King.

The lower house had 453 members including 40 for Croatia. They were elected by specific classes of voters on a property suffrage; voters must be aged 24 and over and Magyar-speaking. The term was 3 years (5 after 1886).

Bills passed through both houses in committees appointed by 'bureaux' or standing committees. Committee reports were considered either by the bureaux or by the whole house.

ITALY

After the Congress of Vienna there were 8 main units: the Kingdom of Sardinia, including Piedmont-Savoy and Genoa; the Kingdom of the Two Sicilies; the Papal States; the Grand-Duchy of Tuscany; the Duchy of Lucca; the Duchy of Parma; the Duchy of Modena; the Austrian territory of Lombardy-Venetia.

In none of these was there any permanent parliament. Legislatures were provided for by constitutions granted in 1820 and 1848, but in both years the grant was to appease a liberal revolt and the constitutions lapsed when the risings were suppressed. These brief parliaments existed in the Two Sicilies and in Piedmont-Savoy in 1820, in Tuscany, Piedmont-Savoy and the Two Sicilies in 1848. The parliament granted in Piedmont-Savoy in 1848 survived, and was adopted by the new Kingdom of Italy in 1861, when the Piedmontese constitution of 1848 became that of the new state.

This provided for 2 houses. The Senate was composed of princes of royal blood over 21, with voting rights at 25, and members appointed by the crown for life and chosen from 21 specific classes, of which the church was originally one but was not represented after 1866. Qualification was by office, by property or by distinction in science, literature or the arts. There was no limit to the number of crown appointees; there had been 78 senators for Piedmont-

Sardinia in 1848, there were 375 for Italy in 1910. Appointment by the King meant in practice appointment by the ruling ministry, the numbers being often augmented for political advantage. The main function of the Senate was as revising body; between 1861 and 1910 the government presented 7570 proposals in the lower house and 600 in the upper; the upper house initiated 40.

The Chamber of Deputies had 508 members chosen simultaneously by direct election. Single-member districts were provided in 1860. The term was 5 years. Suffrage in 1860 was for male literate property holders over 25 paying 40 lire in annual taxes (about 5 % of the population). It was extended in 1882 by lowering the age to 21 and adjusting the property and literacy qualifications. The 508 seats were distributed among 135 districts, each having between 2 and 5 deputies. In 1891 they were distributed again between 508 single-member districts. Manhood suffrage was introduced in 1912.

The King as executive selected the Prime Minister, the selection being seldom an obvious choice because of the lack of a clear majority. The Prime Minister chose the ministers, who initiated legislation but could be prevented from carrying it through by the frequent use of interpellation in the lower house-written question followed by debate and a vote of confidence. Laws might be promulgated by executive decree and ordnance without passing either house; bills which did come before the house were studied by committees set up by 'bureaux'—9 bureaux in the chamber and 5 in the Senate—with committees elected by the bureaux for specific bills and by the whole Chamber of Deputies for the budget. Laws must be passed by both houses. All finance bills were introduced in the chamber and all judicial bills in the Senate. Private members might introduce bills provided they had the support of two-fifths of the Senate and 3 of the 9 bureaux in the chamber. No binding instructions might be given to a member by his constituency; he represented the whole nation and not his own district.

In 1889 the finance ministry and the treasury ministry were separated, but were often held by one minister.

LUXEMBOURG

There was a council of state of 15 members and a chamber of deputies of 48 members elected in 12 cantons for a 6-year term. Half of them retired every 3 years. Both the Grand Duke and the parliament had the right of initiative; the consent of the parliament was necessary for all measures to become law. Election was direct.

MECKLENBURG-SCHWERIN AND MECKLENBURG-STRELITZ

There was no written constitution. Parliament evolved through measures of the sixteenth and seventeenth centuries, the *Vergleich* compact of 1755 and a further compact of 1817. There was a common landtag which might only be summoned by the Grand Duke of Mecklenburg-Schwerin, but which he must summon at least once a year. Either duke might submit measures to it, having given notice to the other of his intention. There was one chamber for each duchy, but sittings were always joint. In 1871 the chamber for Schwerin had 622 members for the knights and 40 for the towns; Strelitz had 62 for knights and 7 for towns. (The principality of Ratzebourg, which formed a large part of Strelitz, was not represented.)

Parliament's consent was needed for laws affecting the various estates of the realm and their members, and the Crown revenues. In laws affecting the Crown domains, the Crown was absolute. In other laws the parliament must be consulted, but its consent was not necessary.

Ministers did not appear in the chamber; the Crown proposed its measures in writing and after debate the chamber sent its acceptance, rejection or amendment. The Crown replied, either accepting or modifying the chamber's vote; this process continued until agreement was reached or seen to be impossible.

MONTENEGRO

According to the Administrative Statute of 1879, executive power was vested in the prince, and legislative power in a State Council of 8 members. Four of them were nominated by the prince, and 4 elected by all men who bore or had borne arms. The prince had the final decision on all measures.

THE NETHERLANDS

The constitution of 1815 was altered in 1848 and 1887. It provided for a bicameral parliament and a responsible ministry. The sovereign enjoyed executive authority, he established the ministries, shared legislative power with the parliament and might dissolve both houses.

The upper house had members elected by the provincial councils from among those holding high offices or paying heavy taxes. The term was 9 years, one-third retiring every 3.

The Chamber of Deputies had one member for every 45,000 of the people, elected for a 4-year term by all male citizens over 23 paying one or more direct tax. Members must be at least 30.

Only the Chamber of Deputies and the ministers might propose legislation or amendments, except on occasions when the State Council suggested measures to the King. The Council was appointed by the King, and all communication between sovereign and parliament was first submitted to it.

If parliament was dissolved, an election must be held within 40 days.

NORWAY

The Swedish parliament recognized the independence of Norway on 16 Oct 1905. The Norwegian parliament had members directly elected by districts returning 1 member each (indirect elections were used until 1906). Every Norwegian male over 25 with a residence qualification might vote. In 1907 women might vote if they or their husbands had paid taxes for 1 year. Members were elected for 3 years.

Parliament sat as a single body which then divided into an upper and lower house by election. Three-quarters of members formed the lower house. Every bill had to be introduced in the lower house and if passed there, then sent to the upper. If a measure passed the lower house twice and not the upper, there was a joint vote. Any measure might be vetoed by the crown, but if it was approved again by 3 successive parliaments it became law.

The ministers formed a Council of State which might not vote in either house, but which was responsible to parliament. Their executive power was shared with the Crown, which also had power to issue provisional ordinances if parliament was not sitting.

Sessions were for 2 months in each year.

PORTUGAL

The Charter of 29 Apr 26 provided a constitution on the British model which was amended in 1852, 1885 and twice in 1895.

The Sovereign had executive power and power to moderate between the 2 legislative chambers, with whom he shared legislative power. The royal veto could not be imposed on a measure which had been passed twice by both houses. The houses met for an annual session of 4 months (before 1885, 3 months). A joint committee dealt with points of dispute between the 2 houses;

55

if it could not agree the matter was referred to the Crown. The House of Peers at first consisted of some hereditary, and some nominated members. In 1885 it was decided that hereditary peers' seats should lapse on the death of the member, and that the house should consist of princes, church dignitaries, 100 peers appointed for life by the King and 50 elected by the Commons for every new parliament. In 1895 the nominated peers were reduced to 90 and the elected membership abolished.

The Commons had members elected from the electoral districts of Portugal, the Azores and Madeira, 35 members representing minorities and 7 for the colonies. Property and educational qualifications applied to candidates and voters. In 1882 the electorate (all male, over 21) was 18 % of the population.

Ministers were responsible to parliament, and there was a Council of State of 12 members nominated for life; this consisted of past and present ministers.

PRUSSIA

The constitution was granted in 1850 and provided for a bicameral parliament. Ministers were to be chosen by the Crown, selected for their individual ability, and responsible to the Crown. They were not collectively responsible for the government's policy; they did not resign on an adverse vote and did not run their departments according to party doctrine. The Ministry of State was required (by ordinances of 1814 and 1817) to meet weekly to discuss all important matters. It had power to advise the King and to make temporary laws or royal ordinances if parliament was not in session during an emergency. Any such laws required the approval of the parliament when it did assemble.

The 2 houses could not be adjourned for more than 30 days (except by the King, who could dissolve them at will) without their own consent. They had power to initiate laws but mainly considered measures submitted by the ministers. The parliament might express its opinion to the ministers but they were not obliged to act on it. The powers of the houses were identical, except that all money bills must first be presented in the lower house. They worked by division into bureaux which appointed committees to consider bills.

The upper house was composed by the King's wish, but must contain members appointed by the Crown for life or in heredity. By an ordinance of 1854 it consisted of princes of the blood, nobles, hereditary members chosen by the crown, life members representing the great offices, universities, churches, cities and large landowners; also an unlimited number of members appointed by the Crown.

The House of Representatives sat for a 3-year term (5 years after 1888) and was chosen by indirect elections, 1–3 deputies from each district, and one elector for every 250 people in the district. Voters were chosen on a 3-tier property basis.

ROMANIA

The constitution of 1866 was amended in 1879 and 1884. It provided for a bicameral parliament with a Senate and a Chamber of Deputies. The Senate was elected for an 8-year term by 2 electoral colleges in each district; the chamber was elected for a 4-year term by 3 colleges. Voters were over 25 and literate. Deputies must be over 25, Senators over 40 with a property qualification. The 3 electoral colleges consisted of (a) all persons with property worth £50 a year, (b) all urban residents with certain professional or property qualifications, and (c) the rest of the taxpayers.

Both houses shared legislative power; executive power was vested in a cabinet of responsible ministers and in the Sovereign, who had a suspensive veto on all measures passed.

By the 1866 constitution deputies were required to belong to certain professions and to have a certain minimum yearly income. The 1884 amendment provided that deputies should be literate Romanians over 25, enjoying civil rights.

RUSSIA

Two legislative bodies had existed since before 1905: the Senate (established by Peter the Great) and the Council of the Empire. Neither body was elected. The constitution of 1905 provided for a parliament (Duma) of 442 members, one from each province, elected by colleges of 5 classes. The Central Asian provinces returned 23 members to the first and second parliaments but were then disfranchised. In 1906 the Council of the Empire was attached to the Duma as an upper house with 196 members, 98 of them nominated by the Tsar and 98 elected by the clergy, the corporations of nobles and other academic, civic and commercial bodies. Both houses had the same powers. The Duma had limited competence. It might not consider the army or navy; all laws must be proposed to a minister who would consider them and prepare his own draft, and ministers were responsible to the Tsar. A preliminary report of all measures must be submitted to the Council of the Empire and the Tsar for approval. A majority vote of the Duma was submitted to the upper house, and in case of disagreement the Tsar could intervene. The Tsar might dissolve parliament and had power to enact measures when the house was not sitting, although he should put those measures before the house at the earliest opportunity.

SAXONY

The constitution was granted in 1831, and afterwards amended. The Assembly of Estates had two houses; the upper house was composed of princes, nobles, officials, crown appointees and members elected to represent specific interests. The lower house had one member for 30,000 population, chosen by direct election and secret ballot. The voters were all men paying a certain land or income tax. The term was 6 years, one-third retiring every 2 years.

The King controlled legislation; all laws required his consent, and the houses would accept or reject a bill in the form in which he chose to present it. His acts must be counter-signed by his ministers, whom he appoints and removes.

In 1871 the upper house had 7 hereditary members, 3 *ex officio*, 12 nominated, 12 chosen to represent the landowners, 3 the universities and 8 the principal towns. The lower house had 35 members for the chief towns and 45 for the rural districts.

A permanent parliamentary committee sat to administer the public debt.

SERBIA

The constitution of June 69 was replaced by a constitution of Jan 89. This was in turn repealed in May 94 and the earlier constitution revived. King Alexander introduced a new constitution in 1901 which was abolished after his assassination in 1903, and the 1889 constitution was then revived.

The 1869 constitution provided for a National Assembly, a Great Assembly (the latter to be summoned for special purposes) and a Senate. The Senate originally nominated members to fill its own vacancies, but during the 1870s it became customary for the prince to nominate the senators, one for each of the seventeen divisions of the country. The Senate sat permanently. The National Assembly sat for a 3-year term; three-quarters of the members were elected, 1 deputy for every 2000 electors, and one-quarter were chosen by the prince, who shared legislative power with the assembly and exercised executive power through a council of five responsible ministers. The electorate consisted of men over 21 paying direct taxes and not being either domestic servants or gipsies.

In 1889 the National Assembly became entirely elected, 1 deputy for 4500 electors, for a 4-year term. The members of the Senate were then 16, half chosen by the assembly and half by the prince. Men over 30 with certain tax or professional qualifications were eligible as members of the National Assembly, which must meet once a year.

SPAIN

In 1820 a constitution drawn up by parliament in 1812 and abolished by Ferdinand VII was restored. It provided for a single-chamber legislature with supreme authority and an executive responsible to it. It was suspended when the absolute authority of King Ferdinand was restored in 1823. A liberal constitution was granted in Oct 33 (the Estatuto Real) but its operation was hindered by civil wars. The republican government of 1868 drew up a constitution which came into effect in June 69. This provided for a bicameral legislature consisting of Senate and Congress. The term of the Congress was 3 years, of the Senate 12 years, a quarter of the members being renewed every 3 years. The Senate was elected by colleges in the municipal districts, 4 senators for each province. Senators must be over 40 and possessing certain civic or professional qualifications. The Congress had 1 deputy for 40,000 inhabitants, elected according to local laws. The houses must meet once a year for at least 4 months. No measure could become law until both bodies had voted on it; financial and military measures must first go to the Congress, and the Congress might vote them even if the Senate disagreed. Both houses could initiate laws. Congress might impeach ministers, who were nominated and dismissed by the King but responsible to parliament. (The monarchy was restored in 1870.) The constitution of June 76 altered the composition of the Senate. Senators belonged by their own right, by nomination from the Crown and by election as before. Elected senators must be half renewed every 5 years. Congress had one deputy for every 50,000 inhabitants, elected by different methods in different districts. In 1890 the franchise was extended to all males over 25 with residence qualifications.

SWEDEN

The constitution of 6 June 09 provided that the King should have all executive power, but all his acts must be made in the presence of the cabinet, who were appointed by him but responsible to parliament, a Diet of the four estates—clergy, nobles, burghers and peasants. The King and the parliament shared legislative power. He might initiate and veto laws, and all laws must have his consent. The parliament had power to impose taxes. In June 1866 the parliament was reorganized into 2 houses. The upper house had 1 member for every 30,000 population and was elected by the provincial and municipal councils. The distribution of members among the constituencies was adjusted every 10 years in proportion to the population. Members must be Swedish and over 35, with certain property qualifications. The term was for 9 years.

The lower house had 1 member for every 10,000 population, elected for a 3-year term by direct or indirect election according to district. The house was renewed as a whole, whereas the upper house was not. All over 21, male, with tax qualifications might vote; all over 25, male, with tax qualifications might sit. Universal manhood suffrage was introduced in 1907. In 1881 electors to the upper house were 0.049 % of the population; to the lower house, 6.2 %.

The houses had to meet annually for a 4 month session. The budget was controlled by annually elected officers. Both houses had to agree on a measure before it could be passed; if they could not, there was a joint vote.

SWITZERLAND

In Sep 43 the 7 Catholic cantons of Switzerland formed an alliance, Sonderbund, which became an armed league in Dec 45. In Nov 47 the Diet ordered its dissolution, and declared war when this was refused; the Bund was dissolved after 19 days' conflict, and the Diet began to draw up a constitution for a new Federation which was put before the people and accepted with $15\frac{1}{2}$ cantons in favour and $6\frac{1}{2}$ against.

It provided for a Federal Assembly consisting of 2 houses; the lower house or National Council and the senate or Council of States.

The National Council was directly elected for a 3-year term, 1 member for every 20,000 people; the Council of States had 2 members for each canton, their term of service and terms of appointment varying according to cantonal custom. The 2 houses sat together for certain purposes: electing officials, exercising pardon, jurisdiction between different federal authorities. Bills might be introduced in either house; in practice they were always introduced in both, except for finance bills which were introduced in the lower house. Bills were referred to committee only by special vote, as most measures originated with and had already been considered and drafted by the executive—the Federal Council.

This was not a cabinet; the members were chosen by the assembly according to cantonal privilege and personal ability and did not represent any party policy. They were not responsible to the assembly and did not resign when their measures were defeated. There were 7 members elected for 3 years, with the President of the State as their chairman, but this did not make him head of the administration or responsible for government policies. Any laws which were not initiated by the Federal Council were referred to it before being sent to committee; their function was to advise on and to administer all legislation.

The constitution of 1848 provided for a referendum as compulsory on matters regarding the constitution and its amendment. In 1874 it was introduced as optional on ordinary laws, which might be suspended for 90 days. If within that time a referendum was requested by 30,000 voters or 8 cantons it would then be held. The people might also initiate a law, if requested by 50,000 voters. Either the people (by initiative) or the houses of the assembly might ask the Federal Council to initiate a law.

TURKEY

The constitution was granted in 1876 and provided for a bicameral parliament. The Sultan had power to convoke and prorogue the parliament and might dissolve the Chamber of Deputies (lower house). He named and dismissed the ministers. The Senate members were nominated by the Sultan for life, and in number must not exceed a third of the Chamber of Deputies. The chamber had one deputy for each 50,000 male inhabitants, elected secretly for a 4-year term. All Turkish men at least 30 years old having civil rights and speaking Turkish might sit. The chamber presented to the Sultan a list of 9 candidates as president and vice-president of the house, and he chose from it.

Laws were initiated by the government; ministers were chosen by the Sultan but responsible to the Chamber of Deputies except in an emergency when the house was not sitting, when their decisions had the force of law without the Assembly's consent, providing the Sultan approved them. Laws had no force otherwise unless approved by both houses and the Sultan.

UNITED KINGDOM

Parliament consisted of 2 houses of legislature, the Lords and the Commons, dating from the time of Edward II, and it had been, except during the period of the Commonwealth, a fundamental principle of the constitution that every lawful Parliament shall consist of an upper and a lower house of legislature.

The upper house consisted of peers who held their seats by virtue of hereditary right, by creation of the Sovereign, by virtue of office—English bishops, by election for life—Irish peers, by election for the duration of a

Parliament—Scottish peers.

The Crown was unrestricted in its power of creating peers, and the privilege was largely used by modern governments to fill the House of Lords. In consequence of certain terms in the Act of Union limiting the right of election of the Scottish representative peers to the then existing peers of Scotland, it was understood that the Sovereign cannot create a new Scottish peerage; and such peerages were in fact never created except in the case of the younger branches of the royal family, though extinct peerages could be revised or forfeited peerages restored. By the Irish Act of Union, the Sovereign was restricted to the creation of 1 new Irish peerage on the extinction of 3 of the existing peerages; but when the Irish peers were reduced to 100, then on the extinction of 1 peerage another could be created.

The lower house of legislature represented, in constitutional theory, all the 'Commons of England'. By the statute of 2 Will. IV. c. 45, commonly called the Reform Bill of 1832, the English county constituencies were increased from 52 to 82, by dividing several counties into separate electoral divisions, and the number of county members was augmented from 94 to 159. In Scotland and Ireland, the county representation remained the same as before. By the Reform Act 56 English boroughs, containing a population in 1831 of less than 2000 each, and returning together 111 members, were totally disfranchised, while 30 other boroughs, containing a population of less than 4000 each, were reduced to sending 1 representative instead of 2. On the other hand, 22 new boroughs, each containing 25,000 inhabitants, received the franchise of returning 2 members, and 20 other new boroughs, each containing 12,000 inhabitants and upwards, that of returning 1 member. In Scotland the town members were increased from 15 to 23, so that the number of representatives became 8 more than the number assigned to Scotland at the union.

The next great change in the constituency of the House of Commons, after the Act of 1832, was made by the Reform Bill of 1867–8. The most important provisions of the new Act as regards England established household suffrage in boroughs and occupation franchise in counties. Clause 3 stipulates that:

Every man shall be entitled to be registered as a voter, and, when registered, to vote for a member or members to serve in Parliament for a borough, who is qualified as follows: (i) Is of full age, and not subject to any legal incapacity; (ii) Is on the last day of July in any year, and has during the whole of the preceding 12 calendar months, been an inhabitant occupier, as owner or tenant, of any dwelling-house within the borough.

The result of the Reform Act of 1868 in enlarging the constituencies was:

Electors of England and Wales

	1868	1866	Increase
Boroughs	1,220,715	514,026	706,689
Counties	791,916	542,633	249,283
TOTAL	2,012,631	1,056,659	955,972

The Reform Acts for Scotland and Ireland, passed in the session of 1868, differed in some important respects from that of England.

The Reform Bill of 1867–8 left in force all the old legal requirements for electors. Under them, aliens, persons under 21 years of age, of unsound mind, in receipt of parochial relief, or convicted of felony and undergoing a term of imprisonment, were not allowed to vote. No one could be a member of Parliament who had not attained the age of 21 years, and no excise, custom, stamp or other revenue officer was eligible. All the judges of the United Kingdom (except the Master of the Rolls in England), priests and deacons of the Church of England, ministers of the Church of Scotland, Roman Catholic clergymen, government contractors, and sheriffs and returning officers for the localities for which they act, were also disqualified. No English or Scottish peer could be elected to the House of Commons, but Irish peers were eligible. No foreigners or persons convicted of treason or felony were eligible for seats in Parliament.

To preserve the independence of members of the House of Commons, it was enacted, by statute 6 Anne, that if any member shall accept any office of profit from the Crown, his election shall be void and a new writ issued; but he is eligible for re-election if the place accepted be not a new office, created since 1705. This provision has been made the means of relieving a member from his trust, which he cannot resign, by his acceptance of the Stewardship of the Chiltern Hundreds, a nominal office in the gift of the Chancellor of the Exchequer.

The union of Ireland with England was carried into effect on 1 Jan 1800, and the Parliament which sat the same month, and which included the members from Ireland, was styled the first Imperial Parliament. The Parliament which assembled 29 Jan 33 was generally styled the first Reformed Parliament.

The powers of Parliament were politically omnipotent within the United Kingdom and its colonies and dependencies. Parliament could make new laws, and enlarge, alter or repeal those existing. The parliamentary authority extended to all ecclesiastical, temporal, civil or military matters, as well as to altering or changing the constitution of the realm. Parliament was the highest court of law, over which no other has jurisdiction.

The executive government of Great Britain and Ireland is vested nominally in the Crown; but practically in a committee of ministers, commonly called the Cabinet, which has come to absorb the function of the ancient Privy Council, or 'the King in Council', the members of which, bearing the title of Right Honourable, are sworn 'to advise the King according to the best of their cunning and discretion', and 'to help and strengthen the execution of what shall be resolved'. Though not the offspring of any formal election, the Cabinet was virtually appointed by Parliament, and more especially by the House of Commons, its existence being dependent on the possession of a majority in the latter assembly. As its acts were liable to be questioned in Parliament, and require prompt explanation, it was essential that the members of the Cabinet should have seats in either the upper or the lower house, where they became identified with the general policy and acts of the government.

WURTTEMBERG

The constitution was granted in 1819, providing for a bicameral legislature. The King had the sole right to initiate legislation for financial purposes, he had considerable emergency powers whether Parliament was sitting or not, and his ordinances need not be submitted to it for approval.

All statutory laws, appropriations and taxes required parliament's consent. Both chambers met annually. The upper chamber in 1871 had 36 hereditary and 9 nominated members. The Chamber of Deputies had 93 members: 1 for each 19,000 inhabitants elected to represent different interests, 13 representing social groups, 63 representing country districts, 7 the principal towns, 9 the church, and 1 the universities. Neither house might communicate with any state official except the ministers, whom they might question. The ministers were not obliged to answer or to give account of their policies. They were appointed by the King and responsible to him.

A standing committee elected by both houses in joint session managed the public debt and watched over constitutional rights.

4 MINISTERS

AUSTRIA

Date of taking office	Prime Minister	Foreign Minister	Finance Minister
8 Oct 09	Klemens Metter-nich	Klemens Metter-nich	Count von Nadsad (since 1837)
20 Mar 48	F. von Kalowrat	K. L. von Ficquelmont	K. F. von Kubau
2 Apr 48			P. von Krauss
19 Apr 48	K. L. von Ficquelmont		
8 May 48		J. P. von Wessenberg-Ampringen	
19 May 48	F. von Pillersdorf		
8 July 48	A. von Dobl-hoff-Dier		
18 July 48	J. P. von Wessenberg-Ampringen		
21 Nov 48	Prince F. von Schwarzenburg	Prince F. von Schwarzenburg	
26 Dec 51			A. von Baumgartner
11 Apr 52	K. F. von Buol-Schauenstein	K. F. von Buol-Schauenstein	
10 Mar 55			K. L. von Brock
17 May 59	Baron von Rechberg und Rothenlöwen	Baron von Rechberg und Rothenlöwen	
23 Apr 60			I. von Plener
4 Feb 61	Anton von Schmerling		
27 Oct 64		A. von Mensdorff-Pouilly	

(continued

AUSTRIA (*continued*)

Date of taking office	Prime Minister	Foreign Minister	Finance Minister
26 June 65	A. von Mensdorff-Pouilly		
27 July 65	R. Belcredi		
30 Oct 66		F. F. von Büsst	J. von Larisch-Mönich
21 Jan 67			F. K. von Becke
7 Feb 67	F. F. von Büsst		

The *Ausgleich*, or establishment of the dual monarchy, occurred 23 June 67. Thenceforward there were ministers for Hungary, ministers for Austria and ministers for common affairs of Austria-Hungary.

MINISTERS FOR AUSTRIA

Date of taking office	Prime Minister	Finance Minister
30 Dec 1867	K. von Auersperg	R. Brestel
24 Sep 68	E. von Taaffe	
15 Jan 70	I. von Plener	
1 Feb 70	L. von Hasner von Artha	
12 Apr 70	A. Potocki	K. von Distler
6 May 70		L. von Holzgethan
6 Feb 71	K. von Hohenwart	
30 Oct 71	L. von Holzgethan	
25 Nov 71	A. von Auersperg	
15 Feb 79	K. von Stremayr	S. von Depretis
12 Aug 79	E. von Taaffe	E. Chertek
16 Feb 80		A. von Kriegs-Au
26 June 80		J. von Dunajewski
4 Feb 91		E. Steinbach
11 Nov 93	A. Windisch-Graetz	I. von Plener
19 June 95	E. von Kielmansegge	E. Bohm von Bawerk
13 Sep 95	K. Badeni	L. von Biliński
30 Nov 97	P. Gautsch von Frankenthurn	E. Bohm von Bawerk
5 Mar 98	F. von Thurn und Hohenstein	J. Kaizl
2 Oct 99	Count Clary-und-Aldringen	S. von Kniaziolucki
21 Dec 99	H. von Wittek	A. von Jorkasch-Koch

(*continued*

AUSTRIA (*continued*)

Date of taking office	Prime Minister	Finance Minister
19 Jan 1900	E. von Kœrber	E. Bohm von Bawerk
26 Oct 04		M. Kosel
1 Jan 05	P. Gautsch von Frankenthurn	
2 May 06	K. von Hohenlohe-Waldenburg-Schillingsfürst	
2 June 06	M. W. von Beck	W. von Korytowsky
14 Nov 08	R. von Bienerth	Baron von Jorkasch-Koch
10 Feb 09		L. von Biliński
9 Jan 11		R. Meyer
28 June 11	P. Gautsch von Frankenthurn	
3 Nov 11	K. von Stürgkh	
19 Nov 11		Count von Zaleski
8 Oct 13		A. Engel von Mainfelden
3 Nov 15		K. von Leth
31 Oct 16	E. von Kœrber	K. Marek
20 Dec 16	H. von Clam-Martinitz	A. B. Spitzmüller
23 June 17	E. Seidler von Feuchtenegg	Baron von Wimmer
25 July 18	M. Hussarek von Heinlein	
27 Oct 18	H. Lammasch	J. Redlich

MINISTERS FOR COMMON AFFAIRS

Date of taking office	Prime Minister	Foreign Minister	Finance Minister
23 June 1867	F. F. von Büsst	F. F. von Büsst	F. K. von Becke
21 May 70			M. von Lonyay
14 Nov 71	J. Andrássy (*d.* 1890)	J. Andrássy	J. Andrássy
15 Jan 72			L. von Holzgethan
17 June 76			J. Andrássy
14 Aug 76			L. F. von Hofmann
8 Oct 79	H. von Haymerle	H. von Haymerle	
8 Apr 80			J. Szlávy

67

(*continued*

AUSTRIA (continued)

Date of taking office	Prime Minister	Foreign Minister	Finance Minister
20 Nov 81	G. Kálnoky	G. Kálnoky	
4 June 82			B. von Kállay
16 May 95	A. Golochowski	A. Golochowski	
14 July 1903			A. Golochowski
24 July 03			S. Burián
24 Oct 06	A. Lexa d' Aerenthal	A. Lexa d' Aerenthal	
17 Feb 12	L. Berchthold	L. Berchthold	
20 Feb 12			L. von Bilińsky
13 Jan 15	S. Burián	S. Burián	
7 Feb 15			E. von Kœrber
2 Dec 16			K. von Hohenlohe-Waldenburg-Schillingsfürst
22 Dec 16	O. Czernin	O. Czernin	S. Burián
16 Apr 18			A. B. Spitzmüller
24 Oct 18	J. Andrássy		
2 Nov 18	L. von Flotow		
4 Nov 18			Baron von Kuh-Chrobak

BADEN

Date of taking office	Prime Minister	Foreign Minister	Finance Minister
19 Dec 46	J. B. Bekk	A. von Dusch (since Nov 43)	F. A. Regenauer (since Nov 44)
9 Mar 48	K. G. Hoffmann		K. G. Hoffmann
14 May 48	Revolutionary council		
1 July 49	F. A. Klüber	L. R. von Kollenberg-Bödigheim	F. A. Regenauer

(continued

BADEN (*continued*)

Date of taking office	Prime Minister	Foreign Minister	Finance Minister
May 56	F. von Stengel		
2 Apr 60	A. Stabel	A. Stabel	V. Vogelmann
2 May 61	F. von Roggenbach		
19 Oct 65		L. von Edelsheim	
27 July 66			K. Mathy
2 Aug 66	R. von Freydorf	R. von Freydorf	
12 Feb 68	J. Jolly		M. Ellstätter

BAVARIA

Date of taking office	Prime Minister	Foreign Minister	Finance Minister
30 Nov 47	L. von Öttingen-Wallerstein	L. von Öttingen-Wallerstein	Baron von Zu-Rhein (since Feb 47)
8 Mar 48			G. von Lerchenfeld
12 Mar 48	Count von Bray-Steinburg	Count von Bray-Steinburg	
14 Nov 48			M. von Weigand
7 Mar 49	L. C. H. von der Pfordten	L. C. H. von der Pfordten	J. Aschenbrenner
23 Mar 59	Baron von Schrenck	Baron von Schrenck	B. von Pfeufer
4 Dec 64	L. C. H. von der Pfordten	L. C. H. von der Pfordten	
1 Aug 66			A. Pfretzschner
1 Jan 67	Prince K. von Hohenlohe-Schillingsfürst	Prince K. von Hohenlohe-Schillingsfürst	

BELGIUM

Date of taking office	Prime Minister	Foreign Minister	Finance Minister
12 Aug 47	C. Rogier	C. de Hoffschmidt de Resteigne	L. Veydt
20 July 48			H. J. W. Frère-Orban
17 Sep 52			C. Liedts
31 Oct 52	H. de Brouckère	H. de Brouckère	
30 Mar 55	P. J. F. de Decker	C. Vilain	E. Mercier
9 Nov 57	C. Rogier	A. de Vrière	H. J. W. Frère-Orban
June 61			V. Tesch
25 Oct 61		C. Rogier	H. J. W. Frère-Orban
3 Jan 68	H. J. W. Frère-Orban	J. van der Stichelen	
2 July 70	Baron J. J. d'Anethan	Baron J. J. d'Anethan	−. Tack
3 Aug 70			V. Jacobs
7 Dec 71	Chev. de Theux de Meylandt	G. B. F. C. d'Aspremont-Lynden	J. E. X. Malou
July 74	J. E. X. Malou		
19 June 78	H. J. W. Frère-Orban	H. J. W. Frère-Orban	Ch. Graux
16 June 84	J. E. X. Malou	Chev. de Moreau	J. E. X. Malou
26 Oct 84	A. Beernaert	Pr. de Chimay	A. Beernaert
1 Nov 92		F. de Mérode	
26 Mar 94	J. de Burlet		P. de Smet de Nayer
26 Feb 96	P. de Smet de Nayer	M. de Favereau	
24 Jan 99	J. Vandenpeereboom		
5 Aug 99	P. de Smet de Nayer		
2 May 1907	J. de Trooz	J. Davignon	J. Liebaert
9 Jan 08	F. Schollaert		J. Renkin
Nov 08			J. Liebaert
14 June 11	M. Levie		
13 July 11	Ch. de Broqueville		
27 Feb 14			A. Burggraf van de Vyvere

(continued

BELGIUM (*continued*)

Date of taking office	Prime Minister	Foreign Minister	Finance Minister
21 Jan 16		E. van Beyens	
30 July 17		Ch. de Broque-ville	
Jan 18		P. Hymans	
3 June 18	G. Cooreman		

BRUNSWICK

Date of taking office	Prime Minister	Foreign Minister	Finance Minister
20 July 48	Baron von Schleinitz		T. J. C. Hantelmann
Apr 62	A. B. C. F. von Campe		Herr von Thielau
66			T. J. C. Hantelmann

BULGARIA

Date of taking office	Prime Minister	Foreign Minister	Finance Minister
1879	T. Burmow		
79	E. Klemens		
1 Apr 80	D. Zankow	D. Zankow	
Dec 80	P. Karavélow	M. Stoilow	M. Cheleskovitch
July 82	L. N. Sobolew		
20 Sep 83	D. Zankow	M. Balabanow	M. Matchevitch
1 July 84	P. Karavélow	J. Tzanow	P. Karavélow
87	V. Radoslavow	G. D. Natchovitch	J. E. Guéchow
12 July 87	K. Stoílow		
31 Aug 87	S. Stambulov	G. Stransky	G. D. Natchovitch
Dec 88			J. Sallabechew
Nov 90		D. Grekow	M. Beltchew

(continued

BULGARIA (*continued*)

Date of taking office	Prime Minister	Foreign Minister	Finance Minister
31 Mar 91			G. D. Natchovitch
94			J. Sallabechew
31 May 94	C. Stoilow	G. D. Natchovitch	J. E. Guéchow
7 Sep 97		C. Stoilow	T. Théodorow
18 Jan 99	T. Ivantchow	T. Ivantchow	M. Tenew
28 Jan 99	D. Grekow		
12 Oct 99	T. Ivantchow	T. Ivantchow	
23 Jan 1901	R. Petrow		
14 Mar 01	P. Karavelow	S. Dánev	P. Karavelow
4 Jan 02	S. Dánev		
15 May 03	R. Petrow	R. Petrow	L. Payakow
14 Nov 06	D. Pétkow	D. Stanciow	
16 Mar 07	P. J. Gúdew		
29 Jan 08	A. Málinow	S. Paprikow	J. Sallabechew
10		A. Málinow	A. Liaptchew
20 Mar 11	S. Dánev		
29 Mar 11	J. E. Guéchow	J. E. Guéchow	T. Théodorow
4 July 13	S. Dánev		
18 July 13	V. Radoslavow	N. Ghenadiev	D. Tontchew
14		V. Radoslavow	
16 June 18	A. Málinov		

DENMARK

Date of taking office	Prime Minister	Foreign Minister	Finance Minister
22 Mar 48	A. G. von Moltke	K. M. Knuth à Soroe	
16 Nov 48		A. G. von Moltke	G. C. E. de Sponnecke
10 Aug 50		C. Reedtz	
28 Jan 52	C. A. Bluhme	C. A. Bluhme	
21 Apr 53	A. S. Oerstedt		

72

(*continued*

DENMARK (continued)

Date of taking office	Prime Minister	Foreign Minister	Finance Minister
12 Dec 54	P. G. Bang	L. N. de Scheel	C. C. C. G. D'Andrae
18 Oct 56	C. C. C. G. D'Andrae		
13 May 57	C. C. Hall	O. G. Michelsen	
7 July 58			A. F. Krieger
10 July 58		C. C. Hall	
6 May 59			C. E. Fenger
3 Dec 59	C. E. Rottwit	B. Finecke	M. Westerhold
24 Feb 60	C. C. Hall	C. C. Hall	C. E. Fenger
31 Dec 63	D. G. Monrad	D. G. Monrad	D. G. Monrad
11 July 64	C. A. Bluhme	C. A. Bluhme	C. G. N. David
4 Nov 65	Count Frijs-Frijsenberg	Count Frijs-Frijsenberg	C. A. Fonnesbech
28 May 70	L. H. C. H. Holstein von Holsteinborg	O. D. von Rosenörn-Lehn	C. E. Fenger
28 June 72			A. F. Krieger
14 July 74	C. A. Fonnesbech		C. A. Fonnesbech
11 June 75	J. B. S. Estrup	F. G. J. Moltke von Bregentved	J. B. S. Estrup
11 Oct 75		O. D. von Rosenorn-Lehn	
92		K. T. T. O. de Reedz-Thott	
7 Aug 94	K. T. T. O. de Reedz-Thott		C. D. de Lüttichau
23 May 97	K. E. Hørring	N. F. Ravn	H. E. Hørring
27 Apr 1900	H. de Sehested	H. de Sehested	H. W. Scharling
24 July 01	J. H. Deuntzer	J. H. Deuntzer	C. F. Hage
14 Jan 05	J. C. Christensen	F. C. O. de Raben-Levetzau	V. Lassen
12 Oct 08	N. T. Neergaard	C. W. de Ahlefeldt-Laurvigen	C. Brun
16 Aug 09	L. von Holstein-Ledreborg		
28 Oct 09	C. T. Zahle	E. J. C. de Scavenius	C. E. C. Brandes

(continued

DENMARK (*continued*)

Date of taking office	Prime Minister	Foreign Minister	Finance Minister
5 July 10	K. Berntsen	C. W. de Ahlefeldt-Laurvigen	N. T. Neergaard
21 June 13	C. T. Zahle	E. J. C. de Scavenius	C. E. C. Brandes

FRANCE

Date of taking office	Prime Minister	Foreign Minister	Finance Minister
Sep 47	G. Guizot	M. Guizot (since Oct 40)	J. G. Humann (since Oct 40)
24 Feb 48	J. C. Dupont	M. Lamartine	M. Goudchaux
8 May 48			M. Garnier-Pages
11 May 48		J. Bastide	M. Duclerc
28 June 48	L. A. Cavaignac		M. Goudchaux
25 Oct 48		L. Bedeau	M. Trouvé-Chauvel
20 Dec 48	O. Barrot	E. Drouin de Lhuys	H. Passy
2 June 49		M. de Tocqueville	
31 Oct 49		A. de Rayneval	A. Fould
10 Apr 51		M. Baroche	
26 Oct 51		M. de Turgot	M. Blondel
3 Dec 51			A. Fould
22 Jan 52	M. de Casabianca		M. Bineau
22 July 52			M. Magne
28 July 52		E. Drouin de Lhuys	
30 July 52	A. Fould		
7 May 55		A. C. Walewski	
24 Jan 60		E. Thouvenel	
23 Nov 60	A. C. Walewski		M. de Forcade la Roquette
14 Nov 61			A. Fould
15 Oct 62		E. Drouin de Lhuys	
23 June 63	M. Billault		
13 Oct 63	M. Rouher		
1 Sep 66		M. de Moustier	

(continued

FRANCE (*continued*)

Date of taking office	Prime Minister	Foreign Minister	Finance Minister
20 Jan 67			M. Rouher
13 Nov 67			M. Magne
18 Dec 68		M. de la Valette	
17 July 69	J. D. F. de la Roquette	Prince H. de la Tour d'Auvergne-Lauraguais	
2 Jan 70	E. Ollivier	Count Daru	L. J. Buffet
14 Apr 70			E. A. Segris
15 May 70		Count Gramont	
9 Aug 70	C. G. M. Cousin-Montauban	Prince H. de la Tour d'Auvergne-Lauraguais	P. Magne
4 Sep 70	J. Trochu	J. Favre	
18 Feb 71	A. Thiers		
25 Feb 71			A. T. Pouyer-Quertier
2 Aug 71		C. de Rémusat	
72			M. de Goulard
7 Dec 72			L. Say
24 May 73	Duc de Broglie	Duc de Broglie	P. Magne
23 May 74	E. L. O. Courtot de Cissey	Duc de Décazes	
20 July 74			M. Bodet
10 Mar 75	L. J. Buffet		L. Say
9 Mar 76	J. Dufaure		
12 Dec 76	J. Simon		
17 May 77	Duc de Broglie		E. Caillaux
23 Nov 77	C. de Grimaudet de la Rochebouet	G. R. M. de Banneville	F. E. du Tilleul
13 Dec 77	J. Dufaure	M. Waddington	L. Say
4 Feb 79	M. Waddington		
29 Dec 79	C. de S. de Freycinet	C. de S. de Freycinet	J. Magnin
23 Sep 80	J. Ferry	M. Barthélemy-Saint-Hilaire	
14 Nov 81	L. Gambetta	L. Gambetta	F. H. R. Allain-Targé

(*continued*

FRANCE (*continued*)

Date of taking office	Prime Minister	Foreign Minister	Finance Minister
31 Jan 82	C. de S. de Freycinet	C. de S. de Freycinet	L. Say
8 Aug 82	C. T. E. Duclerc	C. T. E. Duclerc	P. E. Tirard
29 Jan 83	M. Fallières		
18 Feb 83	J. Ferry	P. A. Challemel-Lacour	
20 Nov 83		J. Ferry	
6 Apr 85	H. Brisson	C. de S. de Freycinet	J. Clamageran
16 Apr 85			M. Sadi-Carnot
4 Jan 86	C. de S. de Freycinet		
13 Dec 86	R. Goblet	E. Flourens	A. Dauphin
30 May 87	M. Rouvier		M. Rouvier
12 Dec 87	P. E. Tirard		P. E. Tirard
2 Apr 88	C. Flocquet	R. Goblet	P. L. Peytral
21 Feb 89	P. E. Tirard	E. Spuller	M. Rouvier
17 Mar 90	C. de S. de Freycinet	A. Ribot	
27 Feb 92	E. Loubet	J. Develle	
6 Dec 92	A. Ribot	A. Ribot	
13 Jan 93		J. Develle	P. E. Tirard
4 Apr 93	C. Dupuy		P. L. Peytral
3 Dec 93	J. P. P. Casimir-Périer	J. P. P. Casimir-Périer	A. L. Burdeau
30 May 94	C. Dupuy	G. Hanotaux	R. Poincaré
27 Jan 95	A. Ribot		A. Ribot
1 Nov 95	L. Bourgeois	M. Berthelot	P. Doumer
29 Apr 96	J. Méline	G. Hanotaux	G. Cochery
27 June 98	E. H. Brisson	T. Delcassé	P. L. Peytral
1 Nov 98	C. Dupuy		
22 June 99	P. M. Waldeck-Rousseau		J. Caillaux
7 June 1902	E. Combes		M. Rouvier
24 Jan 05	M. Rouvier		
13 Mar 06	F. Sarrien	L. Bourgeois	R. Poincaré

(*continued*

FRANCE (*continued*)

Date of taking office	Prime Minister	Foreign Minister	Finance Minister
23 Oct 06	G. Clemenceau	S. Pichon	J. Caillaux
24 July 09	A. Briand		G. Cochery
3 Nov 10			L. L. Klotz
4 Mar 11	A. E. E. Monis	J. Cruppi	J. Caillaux
27 June 11	J. Caillaux	J. de Selves	L. L. Klotz
14 Jan 12	R. Poincaré	R. Poincaré	
18 Jan 13	A. Briand	C. Jonnart	
24 Mar 13	L. Barthou	S. Pichon	C. Dumont
8 Dec 13	G. Doumergue	G. Doumergue	J. Caillaux
9 June 14	R. Viviani	L. Bourgeois	E. Clementael
3 Aug 14		T. Delcassé	A. Ribot
4 Aug 14		G. Doumergue	
27 Aug 14		T. Delcassé	
12 Oct 15		R. Viviani	
29 Oct 15	A. Briand	A. Briand	
20 Mar 17	A. Ribot	A. Ribot	J. Thierry
12 Sep 17	P. Painlevé		L. L. Klotz
17 Nov 17	G. Clemenceau	S. Pichon	

GERMANY

Date of taking office	Prime Minister	Foreign Secretary
At 18 Jan 1871	Otto von Bismarck-Schönhausen	Otto von Bismarck-Schönhausen
17 Mar 90	L. von Caprivi	L. von Caprivi
31 Mar 90		A. Marschall, Fr. von Bieberstein
26 Oct 94	Prince von Hohenlohe-Schillingsfürst	
20 Oct 97		B. von Bülow
17 Oct 1900	B. von Bülow	Baron von Richthofen
17 Jan 06		H. von Tschirschky und Bögendorff
7 Oct 07		W. von Schoen

77

(*continued*

GERMANY (*continued*)

Date of taking office	Prime Minister	Foreign Secretary
27 June 09	T. Bethmann-Hollweg	
28 June 10		A. von Kiderlen-Wächter
11 Jan 13		G. von Jagow
25 Nov 16		A. Zimmermann
14 July 17	G. Michaelis	
7 Aug 17		R. von Kühlmann
25 Oct 17	G. von Herling	
9 Aug 18		P. von Hintze
4 Oct 18	Prince Max of Baden	W. Solf
9 Nov 18	Friedrich Ebert	
20 Dec 18		U. von Brockdorff-Rantzau

GREAT BRITAIN

Date of taking office	Prime Minister	Foreign Minister	Finance Minister
6 July 46	Lord J. Russell	Lord Palmerston	C. Wood
23 Feb 52	Lord Derby	Lord Malmesbury	B. Disraeli
28 Dec 52	Lord Aberdeen	Lord J. Russell	W. E. Gladstone
Feb 53		Lord Clarendon	
8 Feb 55	Lord Palmerston		G. Cornewall-Lewis
26 Feb 58	Lord Derby	Lord Malmesbury	B. Disraeli
12 June 59	Lord Palmerston	Lord John Russell	W. Gladstone
3 Nov 65	Lord John Russell	Lord Clarendon	
6 July 66	Lord Derby	Lord Stanley	B. Disraeli
25 Feb 68	B. Disraeli		G. Ward-Hunt
9 Dec 68	W. E. Gladstone	Lord Clarendon	R. Lowe
June 70		Lord Granville	
9 Aug 73			W. E. Gladstone
20 Feb 74	B. Disraeli	Lord Derby	Sir S. Northcote
2 Apr 78		Lord Salisbury	
28 Apr 80	W. E. Gladstone	Lord Granville	W. E. Gladstone
16 Dec 82			H. C. E. Childers
12 June 85	Lord Salisbury	Lord Salisbury	M. Hicks-Beach
30 Jan 86	W. E. Gladstone	Lord Rosebery	W. V. Harcourt

78

(*continued*

GREAT BRITAIN (*continued*)

Date of taking office	Prime Minister	Foreign Minister	Finance Minister
30 July 86	Lord Salisbury	Lord Iddesleigh	R. H. S. Churchill
3 Jan 87		Lord Salisbury	G. J. Goschen
15 Aug 92	W. E. Gladstone	Lord Rosebery	W. V. Harcourt
5 Mar 94	Lord Rosebery	Lord Kimberley	
25 June 95	Lord Salisbury	Lord Salisbury	M. Hicks-Beach
1 Nov 1900		Lord Lansdowne	
12 July 02	A. J. Balfour		
Aug 02			C. T. Ritchie
5 Oct 03			J. A. Chamberlain
10 Dec 05	H. Campbell-Bannerman	E. Grey	H. H. Asquith
6 Apr 08	H. H. Asquith		D. Lloyd-George
26 May 15			R. MacKenna
10 Dec 16	D. Lloyd-George	A. J. Balfour	A. Bonar Law

GREECE

Date of taking office	Prime Minister	Foreign Minister	Finance Minister
20 Mar 48	L. Conduriotis	J. Colettis (since Aug 44)	–. Korphiotakis (since Sep 47)
7 July 48		C. Coloctronis	T. Mangina
Oct 48	A. Canaris		
29 Nov 49		G. Clarakis	
26 Dec 49	A. Kriezis	–. Londos	D. Christides
2 Aug 50		–. Delijianis	
10 June 51		A. Païkos	
26 May 54	A. Mavrocordatus	P. Argyropoulos	A. Mavrocordatus
55			–. Krestenites
4 Oct 55	A. Bulgaris	R. Rangabis	
July 56			A. Comoundouros
25 June 57	A. Miaulis		
June 59		A. Conduriotis	
July 60			E. Simos
24 Jan 62	Adm. Canaris		

79

(*continued*

GREECE (continued)

Date of taking office	Prime Minister	Foreign Minister	Finance Minister
1 Feb 62	A. Miaulis	A. Conduriotis	E. Simos
7 June 62	Gen Colocotronis		−. Barbogli
Aug 62		N. Dragoumi	
23 Oct 62	T. Zaïmis	A. Diamantopoulos	T. Manghinas
23 Feb 63	−. Balbis	D. Maurocordatus	D. Charalambis
8 Apr 63	D. Kyriaku		
12 May 63	V. Roufos	P. Calligas	M. Kechajas
6 Nov 63	A. Bulgaris	P. Delyannis	−. Dosios
17 Mar 64	Adm. Canaris		D. Christides
28 Apr 64	−. Balbis	P. Calligas	−. Balbis
6 Aug 64	Adm. Canaris	P. Delyannis	−. Sotiropolous
8 Feb 65	V. Roufos		
30 Mar 65	A. Comoundouros	−. Braïtas	A. Comoundouros
28 Oct 65	E. Deligiorgis	E. Deligiorgis	D. Christides
15 Nov 65	A. Bulgaris	A. Bulgaris	A. Bulgaris
25 Nov 65	E. Deligiorgis	E. Deligiorgis	D. Christides
10 Dec 65	V. Roufos	V. Roufos	V. Roufos
16 June 66	A. Bulgaris	E. Deligiorgis	D. Christides
30 Dec 66	A. Comoundouros	C. Trikoupis	E. Kechagyas
1 Jan 68	−. Moraïtinis	P. Delyannis	−. Jannapoulos
6 Feb 68	A. Bulgaris		E. Simos
4 Feb 69	T. Zaïmis		−. Petrali
69			A. Avierinos
22 July 70	E. Deligiorgis		
17 Dec 70	A. Comoundouros	A. Comoundouros	S. Sotiropoulos
9 Nov 71	T. Zaïmis	T. Zaïmis	T. Delyannis
5 Jan 72	A. Bulgaris	A. Bulgaris	−. Mauromichapulos
17 July 72	E. Deligiorgis	−. Spiliotakis	D. Christides
22 Feb 74	A. Bulgaris	T. Delyannis	−. Ulassopoulos
28 Feb 74			−. Papamichaelo-poulos
9 May 75	C. Trikupis		
27 Oct 75	A. Comoundouros	−. Kontastavolos	S. Sotiropoulos
3 Nov 76	E. Deligiorgis	E. Deligiorgis	−. Lerides
13 Dec 76	A. Comoundouros		
10 Mar 77	E. Deligiorgis		
29 May 77	A. Comoundouros	−. Kontastavolos	−. Latiropoulos

80

(continued

GREECE (continued)

Date of taking office	Prime Minister	Foreign Minister	Finance Minister
3 June 77	Adm. Canaris	C. Trikupis	E. Deligiorgis
23 Jan 78	A. Comoundouros		
1 Nov 78	C. Trikupis		
10 Nov 78	A. Comoundouros	T. Delyannis	T. Delyannis
19 Mar 80	C. Trikupis	C. Trikupis	C. Trikupis
25 Oct 80	A. Comoundouros	A. Comoundouros	A. Athanasiades
15 Mar 82	C. Trikupis	C. Trikupis	–. Kalligas
21 July 83		–. Kontastavolos	C. Trikupis
19 Apr 85	T. Delyannis	T. Delyannis	T. Delyannis
9 May 86	C. Trikupis	S. Dragoumis	C. Trikupis
28 Oct 90	T. Delyannis	E. Deligiorgis	C. Karapanos
91			T. Delyannis
21 June 92	C. Trikupis	S. Dragoumis	C. Trikupis
15 May 93	P. Sotiropoulos		
13 June 93	C. Trikupis		
94		–. Stephanou	
22 Jan 95	N. Delyannis		
11 June 95	T. Delyannis	A. G. Skouzès	T. Delyannis
2 Oct 97	A. Zaïmis	A. Zaïmis	E. Streit
10 Nov 98			P. Negris
14 Apr 99	G. N. Theotókis	A. Românos	A. N. Simópoulos
12 Nov			
1901	A. Zaïmis	A. Zaïmis	P. Negris
2 Dec 02	T. Delyannis		
11 July 03	D. G. Rhallis	D. G. Rhallis	D. G. Rhallis
1 Dec 03	G. N. Theotókis		
24 Dec 04	T. Delyannis		
26 June 05	D. G. Rhallis		
21 Dec 05	G. N. Theotókis	A. G. Skouzès	A. N. Simópoulos
5 July 08	D. G. Rhallis	G. Baltazzi	D. Gunaris
28 Aug 09	K. Mavromichalis	K. Mavromichalis	–. Evtaxias
7 Feb 10	S. Dragoumis		
19 Oct 10	E. Venizelos	J. Gryparis	L. Koromilas
12		L. Koromilas	A. N. Diomidis
13		D. Panàs	
14		E. Venizelos	
7 Mar 15	D. Gunaris		

(continued

GREECE (continued)

Date of taking office	Prime Minister	Foreign Minister	Finance Minister
15 Oct 15	A. Zaïmis		
4 Nov 15	S. Skuludis	S. Skuludis	S. Dragoumis
8 Apr 16			D. G. Rhallis
21 June 16	A. Zaïmis	A. Zaïmis	
16 Sep 16	N. Kalojeropulos		
8 Oct 16	S. Lambrós		
26 Apr 17	A. Zaïmis	A. Zaïmis	
27 June 17	E. Venizelos	N. Politis	–. Negrepontis

HANOVER

Date of taking office	Prime Minister	Foreign Minister	Finance Minister
20 Mar 48	A. L. von Bennigsen	A. L. von Bennigsen	J. H. G. Lehzen
28 Oct 50	A. von Munchausen	A. von Munchausen	G. C. C. von Hammerstein-Boxten
22 Nov 51	Baron von Schele		
21 Nov 53	E. C. von Lutcken	E. von Lenthe	E. C. von Lutcken
29 July 55	E. von Kielmansegge	A. von Platen-Hallermund	E. von Kielmansegge
10 Dec 62	W. von Hammerstein		C.A.L.F. Erxleben
21 Oct 65	G. Bacmeister		G. H. G. Dietrichs

HESSE-CASSEL

Date of taking office	Prime Minister	Foreign Minister	Finance Minister
47	F. Schetter	S. F. von Meyer	T. Schweder
17 Mar 48	B. Eberhard		
49			C. G. Wippermann
23 Feb 50	J. D. L. F. Hassenpflug	A. von Baumbach	J. C. Lometsch

(continued

HESSE-CASSEL (*continued*)

Date of taking office	Prime Minister	Foreign Minister	Finance Minister
			J. D. L. F. Hassenpflug
			O. H. I. L. Volmar
7 Sep 51	O. H. I. L. Volmar		G. von Motz
Nov 52	J. D. L. F. Hassenpflug		O. H. I. L. Volmar
16 Oct 55	S. F. von Meyer	S. F. von Meyer	A. von Hanstein-Knorr
7 May 59	Herr von Göddäus	Herr von Göddäus	C. Rohde
21 June 62	K. von Dehn-Rothfelser	K. von Dehn-Rothfelser	K. von Dehn-Rothfelser
63	K. Abee	K. Abee	
25 Oct 65			Herr Ledderhose

HESSE-DARMSTADT

Date of taking office	Prime Minister	Foreign Minister	Finance Minister
5 Mar 48	H. von Gagern	H. von Gagern	Dr Zimmermann (since Mar 44)
May 48	Dr Zimmermann		
July 48	H. K. Jaup		
52	C. F. R. von Dalwigk	C. F. R. von Dalwigk	Baron von Schenk von Schweinsberg

HUNGARY

Date of taking office	Prime Minister	Finance Minister
17 Feb 1867	J. Andrássy	M. Lonyay
21 May 70		C. Kerkapolyi

83

(*continued*

HUNGARY (*continued*)

Date of taking office	Prime Minister	Finance Minister
14 Nov 71	M. Lonyay	
4 Dec 72	J. von Szlávy	
21 Mar 74	E. von Bitto	C. von Ghyczy
2 Mar 75	A. von Wenckheim	C. von Széll
21 Oct 75	S. von Tisza	
11 Oct 78		S. von Tisza
5 Dec 78		J. Szápáry
15 Feb 87		S. von Tisza
9 Apr 89		A. Wekerle
7 Mar 90	J. Szápáry	
17 Nov 92	A. Wekerle	
14 Jan 95	Baron Banffy	
15 Jan 95		L. von Lukács
25 Feb 99	K. von Szell	
27 June 1903	K. Khuen-Héderváry	
3 Nov 03	S. von Tisza	
18 Nov 05	G. Fejérváry-von-Komlos-Keresztes	G. Fejérváry-von-Komlos-Keresztes
8 Apr 06	A. Wekerle	A. Wekerle
17 Jan 10	K. Khuen-Héderváry	L. von Lukács
22 Jan 12	L. von Lukács	J. Teleszky
10 June 13	S. von Tisza	
15 June 17	M. von Esterhazy	G. Gratz
20 Aug 17	A. Wekerle	
16 Sep 17		A. Wekerle
11 Feb 18		A. Popovics
30 Oct 18	J. von Hadik	
31 Oct 18	M. von Károlyi	M. von Károlyi

ITALY

Date of taking office	Prime Minister	Foreign Minister	Finance Minister
20 Mar 1861	B. Cavour	B. Cavour	P. Bastogi

(*continued*

ITALY (*continued*)

Date of taking office	Prime Minister	Foreign Minister	Finance Minister
12 June 61	B. Ricasoli	B. Ricasoli	
4 Mar 62	U. Rattazzi	U. Rattazzi	
31 Mar 62		G. Durando	Q. Sella
9 Dec 62	L. C. Farini	G. Pasolini	M. Minghetti
24 Mar 63	M. Minghetti	E. Visconti-Venosta	
23 Sep 64	A. F. de la Marmora	A. F. de la Marmora	Q. Sella
12 Dec 65			A. Sciajola
28 June 66	B. Ricasoli	E. Visconti-Venosta	
16 Feb 67			A. Depretis
10 Apr 67	U. Rattazzi	P. di Campello	F. Ferrara
July 67			U. Rattazzi
27 Oct 67	L. F. de Menabrea	L. F. de Menabrea	Count Cambray-Digny
9 June 69		M. Minghetti	
12 Dec 69	J. Lanza	E. Visconti-Venosta	Q. Sella
10 July 73	M. Minghetti		M. Minghetti
22 Mar 76	A. Depretis	L. A. Melegari	A. Depretis
14 Dec 77		A. Depretis	A. Magliani
26 Mar 78	B. Cairoli	L. de Corti	F. Seismit-Doda
18 Dec 78	A. Depretis	A. Depretis	A. Magliani
14 July 79	B. Cairoli	B. Cairoli	B. Grimaldi
24 Nov 79			A. Magliani
29 May 81	A. Depretis	P. S. Mancini	
16 June 85		A. Depretis	
6 Oct 85		C. F. Nicolis di Robilant	
4 Apr 87		A. Depretis	
7 Aug 87	F. Crispi	F. Crispi	
26 Dec 88			B. Grimaldi
9 Mar 89			F. Seismit-Doda
19 Sep 90			F. Giolotti
8 Dec 90			B. Grimaldi
7 Feb 91	A. di Rudini	A. di Rudini	J. Colombo

(*continued*

ITALY (continued)

Date of taking office	Prime Minister	Foreign Minister	Finance Minister
15 May 92	J. Giolitti	B. Brin	B. Grimaldi
10 Dec 93	F. Crispi	A. Blanc	S. de Sonnino
14 June 94			P. Boselli
10 Mar 96	A. S. di Rudini	O. Caëtani	A. Branca
14 July 96		E. Visconti-Venosta	
29 June 98	L. Pelloux	F. N. Canevaro	P. Carcano
14 May 99		E. Visconti-Venosta	P. Carmine
24 June 1900	G. Saracco		B. Chimirri
14 Feb 01	G. Zanardelli	G. Prinetti	L. Wollemborg
23 June 03		E. Morin	
3 Aug 03			P. Carcano
3 Nov 03	G. Giolitti	T. Tittoni	P. Rosano
10 Nov 03			L. Luzatti
24 Nov 04			A. Majorana
27 Mar 05	A. Fortis		
27 Dec 05		Marquis de San Giuliano	G. Baccelli
8 Feb 06	S. de Sonnino	F. de Guicciardini	A. Salandra
39 May 06	G. Giolitti	T. Tittoni	F. Massimini
06			P. Lacava
10 Dec 09	S. de Sonnino	F. de Guicciardini	–. Arlotta
30 Mar 10	L. Luzzatti	Marquis de San Giuliano	L. Facta
27 Mar 11	G. Giolitti		
21 Mar 14	A. Salandra		L. Rava
5 Nov 14		S. de Sonnino	E. Daneo
19 June 16	P. Boselli		F. Meda
30 Oct 17	V. E. Orlando		

KINGDOM OF THE TWO SICILIES

Date of taking office	Prime Minister	Foreign Minister	Finance Minister
29 Jan 48	Duc de Serra-Capriola	Duc de Serra-Capriola	Prince Dentice
3 Apr 48	C. Troya	L. Dragonetti	S. Ferretti
10 May 48		C. Troya	G. Manna
15 Mar 48	Prince Cariati	Prince Cariati	P. Ruggiero
50	G. Fortunato	G. Fortunato	P. d'Urso
19 Jan 52	F. Troya	L. Caraffa de Traetto	
56			−. Murena
June 59	C. Filangieri, Duc de Taormina		R. de Liguoro
19 Mar 60	Prince Cassaro		
28 June 60	A. Spinelli	G. de Martino	N. Mauna
29 Sep 60	−. Conforti	−. Casella	

LUXEMBOURG

Date of taking office	Prime Minister	Foreign Minister	Finance Minister
23 Nov 1890	Separated from the Netherlands; at that date the following ministers were in office:		
	P. Eyschen	P. Eyschen	−. Mongenast
1915	−. Loutsch	−. Loutsch	E. Reiffen

MECKLENBURG-SCHWERIN

Date of taking office	Prime Minister	Foreign Minister	Finance Minister
48	L. von Lutzow (since May 40)		T. D. von Levetzow

(continued

MECKLENBURG-SCHWERIN (continued)

Date of taking office	Prime Minister	Foreign Minister	Finance Minister
12 Apr 50	H. von Bülow	H. von Bülow	H. A. Thierri von Brock
29 June 58	G. J. B. von Ortzen	G. J. B. von Ortzen	T. D. von Levetzow
67			A. E. F. L. von Muller
69	H. F. C. von Bassewitz		

MECKLENBURG - STRELITZ

Date of taking office	Prime Minister
37	–. von Ortzen
49	W. von Bernstorff
Oct 62	B. E. von Bülow
68	Fr. von Kardorff A. Piper
69	Fr. von Kardorff A. Piper G. C. C. von Hammerstein-Loxten

MODENA

Date of taking office	Prime Minister	Foreign Minister	Finance Minister
9 Apr – 7 Aug 48	Provisional government under J. Malmusi and J. Minghelli		
10 Aug 48	Council of State	G. Forni	F. Tarabini Castellani
11—13 June 59	Government replaced by Regency		

(continued

MODENA (*continued*)

Date of taking office	Prime Minister	Foreign Minister	Finance Minister
14 June 59	Governor – Victor Emanuel of Sardinia		
27 July 59	–. Farini	–. Farini	–. Farini

MONTENEGRO

Date of taking office	Prime Minister	Foreign Minister	Finance Minister
Ministerial government was established in 1907.			
17 Apr 1907	L. Tomanovitch	L. Tomanovitch	D. Voukotitch
14 Sep 10			P. Yergovitch
23 Aug 11		D. Grégovitch	
12	M. Martinovitch	M. Martinovitch	D. Drlievitch
8 May 13	J. Voukotitch	P. Plamenatz	R. Popovitch
15			–. Mouchkovitch
May 16	A. Radovitch	A. Radovitch	A. Radovitch
Jan 17	M. Tomanovitch	M. Tomanovitch	M. Tomanovitch
13 June 17	E. Popovitch	E. Popovitch	E. Popovitch

NASSAU

Date of taking office	Prime Minister	Foreign Minister	Finance Minister
48	A. Hergenhahn		
11 June 49	F. von Winzingerode		
1 Jan 50			F. Vollpracht
7 Feb 52	Prince A. von Sayn-Wittgenstein-Berlebourg		

(continued

NASSAU (*continued*)

Date of taking office	Prime Minister	Foreign Minister	Finance Minister
59			P. Bertram
64			W. von Heemskerck

THE NETHERLANDS

Date of taking office	Prime Minister	Foreign Minister	Finance Minister
25 Mar 48	Count Schimmel-penninck	Count Schimmel-penninck	Count Schimmel-penninck
17 May 48		A. Bentinck	P. A. Ossewaarde
3 June 48			P. P. van Bosse
21 Nov 48	J. M. de Kempenaer	L. A. Lightenvelt	
30 Oct 49	J. R. Thorbecke	H. van Sonsbeeck	
16 Oct 52		J. P. Pompejus van Zuylen van Nijevelt	
19 Apr 53	F. A. van Hall	F. A. van Hall	E. C. U. van Doorn
5 Jan 54			F. A. van Hall
1 May 54			A. Vrolik
1 July 56	J. J. L. Van der Brugghen	G. d'Endegeest	
18 Mar 58	J. S. Rochussen	J. K. van Goltstein	P. P. van Bosse
22 Feb 60	F. A. van Hall	F. A. van Hall	F. A. van Hall
8 Mar 60		J. P. J. A. van Zuylen van Nijevelt	
14 Jan 61		L. N. van der Goes	
23 Feb 61			J. S. Lotsy
12 Mar 61	J. P. J. A. van Zuylen van Nijevelt	J. P. J. A. van Zuylen van Nijevelt	J. G. H. van Tets van Goudriaan
11 Nov 61		P. Strens	
1 Feb 62	J. R. Thorbecke	A. J. Lucas	G. H. Betz
12 Mar 62		P. van der Maesen de Sombreff	

90

(continued

THE NETHERLANDS (*continued*)

Date of taking office	Prime Minister	Foreign Minister	Finance Minister
2 Jan 64		W. J. C. Huyssen van Kattendyke	
15 Mar 64		E. J. J. B. Cremers	
27 Nov 65			N. Olivier
9 Feb 66	F. van der Putte		P. P. van Bosse
1 June 66	J. P. J. A. van Zuylen van Nijevelt	J. P. J. A. van Zuylen van Nijevelt	A. van Denden
3 June 68	P. P. van Bosse	J. J. van Mulken	P. P. van Bosse
8 June 68		T. M. R. van Limbourg	
12 Nov 70		J. J. van Mulken	
3 Jan 71	J. R. Thorbecke		P. Blussé
18 Jan 71		Baron Gericke van Herwynen	
6 Aug 72	G. de Vries	F. van der Putte	A. van Delden
27 Aug 74	J. Heemskerk	P. J. A. M. van der Does de Willebois	H. J. van der Heim
3 Nov 77	J. K. van der Coppello	Dr van Heeckeren van Hell	J. G. Gleichmann
8 Aug 79	C. T. van Lynden	C. T. van Lynden	S. Vissering
11 June 81			C. T. van Lynden
15 Sep 81		W. F. Rochussen	
22 Apr 83	J. Heemskerk	P. J. A. M. van der Does de Willebois	W. J. L. Grobbée
4 May 85			J. C. Groen
1 Nov 85		A. P. G. van Karnebeek	J. C. Bloem
20 Apr 88	A. E. Mackay	C. Hartsen	K. A. Godin de Beaufort
21 Aug 91	G. van Tienhoven	G. van Tienhoven	N. G. Pierson
21 Mar 94		J. C. Jansen	
9 May 94	J. Roëll	J. Roëll	J. P. Sprenger van Eyk
26 July 97	N. G. Pierson	W. H. de Beaufort	N. G. Pierson
27 July 1901	A. Kuyper	R. Melvil	J. J. I. Harte van Tecklenburg

(*continued*

THE NETHERLANDS (continued)

Date of taking office	Prime Minister	Foreign Minister	Finance Minister
9 Mar 05		A. G. Ellis	
22 Apr 05		W. M. van Weede van Beerencamp	
14 Aug 05	T. H. de Meester	D. A. W. van Tets van Goudriaan	T. H. de Meester
12 Feb 08	T. Heemskerk	R. de Marees van Svinderen	M. J. C. M. Kolkman
29 Aug 13	P. W. A. C. van der Lynden	P. W. A. C. van der Lynden	A. E. J. Bertling
27 Sep 13		J. Loudon	
24 Oct 14			M. W. F. Treub
8 Feb 16			A. van Gijn
22 Feb 17			M. W. F. Treub

NORWAY

Date of taking office	Prime Minister	Foreign Minister	Finance Minister

Norway became independent of Sweden on 7 June 1905. At that date the following ministers were in office:

Since 11 Mar 1905	P. C. H. K. Michelsen	J. G. Lövland	P. C. H. K. Michelsen
06			A. Berge
28 Oct 07	J. G. Lövland		J. M. Helvorsen
08	G. Knudsen	W. Christopherson	G. Knudsen
1 Feb 10	W. Konow	J. Irgens	A. Berge
19 Feb 12	J. Brathé		W. Konow
31 Jan 13	G. Knudsen	N. Ihlen	A. T. Omhalt

PAPAL STATES

Date of taking office	Prime Minister	Foreign Minister	Finance Minister
29 Dec 47	G. Bofondi	G. Ferretti (since July 47)	Mgr Morichini
25 Apr 48			A. Simonetti
3 May 48	Mgr Orioli	G. Marchetti	G. Lunati
8 June 48	Mgr Soglia		
12 Aug 48			I. Lauri
17 Nov 48			G. Lunati
Mar 52	G. Antonelli		A. Galli
1 Dec 54			G. Ferrari

ROMAN GOVERNMENT 1848–9

10 Mar 48	G. Antonelli		
1 May 48	L. Ciacchi		
2 Aug 48	E. Fabbri		
16 Sep 48	Count de Rossi		Count de Rossi
Nov 48	G. Soglia		
15 Nov 48	–. Muzzarelli	T. Mamiani	L. Mariani
11 Dec 48	–. Galletti		
9 Feb 49	C. Armellini ⎫ A. Saliceti ⎬ M. Montecchi ⎭		
29 Mar 49	C. Armellini ⎫ G. Mazzini ⎬ A. Saffi ⎭		
3 July 49	L. Mariani ⎫ A. Calandrelli ⎬ A. Saliceti ⎭		
17 July 49	L. Altieri ⎫ Mgr Della Genga ⎬ Mgr Vannicella- Casoni ⎭		

PARMA

Date of taking office	Prime Minister	Foreign Minister	Finance Minister
44	C. de Bombelles	Chev. L. di Richer (since 1837)	V. Vivenzi
20 Mar 48	Regency under Count de San Vitale		
12 Apr 48	Provisional government under F. de Castagnola		
10 May 48–			
5 Apr 49	Military governments		
6 Apr 49	A. Lombardi (Councillor)	G. Guadagni (Councillor)	M. A. Onesti (Councillor)
17 May 49	H. Salati	V. Cornacchia	A. Lombardini
50			M. A. Onesti
27 Mar 54		J. Pallavichino	A. Lombardini
1 May 59–			
3 May 59	Provisional government		
9 Aug 59	–. Manfredi heads provisional government for Victor Emanuel of Sardinia		

PORTUGAL

Date of taking office	Prime Minister	Foreign Minister	Finance Minister
29 Mar 1848	Marquis de Saldanha (since Oct 46)	J. J. Gomese Castro	A. R. d'O Lopez Branco
19 July 49	Ct de Thomar	Ct de Tojal	–. d'Avila
23 May 51	Duc de Saldanha	J. de Antouquia	F. da Silva
Aug 51			F. Pereira de Mello
4 Mar 52		Viscount d'Almeida Garrett	
17 Aug 52		J. de Antouquia	
6 June 56	Marquis de Loulé	Marquis de Loulé	J. G. Loureiro
14 Mar 57			A. J. D'Avila
16 Mar 59	Duc de Terceira	Duc de Terceira	J. M. do Cazal Ribeiro

(continued

PORTUGAL (*continued*)

Date of taking office	Prime Minister	Foreign Minister	Finance Minister
2 May 60	J. A. d'Aguiar	J. A. d'Aguiar	
1 July 60	Marquis de Loulé	A. J. D'Avila	A. J. D'Avila
21 Feb 62		Marquis de Loulé	
17 Apr 65	Marquis de Sá da Bandeira	A. J. D'Avila	
4 Sep 65	J. A. d'Aguiar	Ct de Castro	A. M. de Fontes Pereira de Mello
9 May 66		J. M. de Casal Ribeiro	
4 Jan 68	A. J. D'Avila		—. Ferreira
22 July 68	Marquis de Sá da Bandeira	Marquis de Sá da Bandeira	C. Bento
17 Dec 68		C. B. da Silva	C. B. da Silva
7 Jan 69	Duc de Saldanha		
11 Aug 69	Duc de Loulé	J. da Silva Mendes Leal	A. J. Braacamp
19 May 70	Duc de Saldanha	Duc de Saldanha	Duc de Saldanha
30 Aug 70	Marquis de Sá da Bandeira	Marquis de Sá da Bandeira	Marquis de Sá da Bandeira
30 Oct 70	Bishop of Vizeu	Bishop of Vizeu	Bishop of Vizeu
30 Jan 71	Ct d'Avila	Ct d'Avila	Ct d'Avila
13 Sep 71	A. M. de Fontes Pereira de Mello	J. d'Andrade Corvo	A. M. de Fontes Pereira de Mello
11 Oct 72			E. de Serpa Pimentel
5 Mar 77	Marquis d'Avila	Marquis d'Avila	C. Bento
29 Jan 78	A. M. de Fontes Pereira de Mello	J. d'Andrade Corvo	E. de Serpa Pimentel
1 July 79	A. J. Braacamp	A. J. Braacamp	H. de Barros Gomes
25 Mar 81	A. Rodriguez Sampaio		L. V. de Sampaio e Mello
5 Apr 81		E. R. Hintze Ribeiro	
22 Oct 83	A. M. de Fontes Pereira de Mello	J. B. Barboza Bucage	E. R. Hintze Ribeiro
9 Feb 86	L. de Castro Pereira Corte Real	H. de Barros Gomes	M. Cyrillo de Carvalho

95

(*continued*

PORTUGAL (continued)

Date of taking office	Prime Minister	Foreign Minister	Finance Minister
20 Feb 86			H. de Barros Gomes
12 Jan 90	S. Pimentel		
13 Oct 90	J. C. d'Abreu de Sousa	J. B. Barboza Bucage	G. de Mello Gouvea
21 May 91		Count de Valbom	M. C. de Carvalho
18 Jan 92	J. Dias Fereira	A. A. de Gouvea	J. Dias Fereira
22 Feb 93	E. R. Hintze Ribeiro	E. R. Hintze Ribeiro	A. M. Fuschini
95		C. Lobo d'Avila	E. R. Hintze Ribeiro
96		L. de Soveral	
7 Feb 97	J. Luciano de Castro	H. de Barros Gomes	F. Ressano Garcia
18 Aug 98		Veiga Beirao	M. A. Espregueira
25 June 1900	E. R. Hintze Ribeiro	J. Arroyo	A. Andrade
01		F. Mattoso	F. Mattoso
28 Feb 03		W. de Lima	A. T. de Souza
20 Oct 04	J. Luciano de Castro	E. Villaça	M. A. d'Espregueira
20 Mar 06	E. R. Hintze Ribeiro		
19 May 06	J. F. Franco	L. Magalhães	E. D. Schröter
2 May 07		L. Monteiro	F. A. Miranda de Carvalho
5 Feb 08	F. J. Ferreira de Amaral	W. de Lima	M. A. d'Espregueira
19 July 08	A. A. de Campos Henriques		
2 Apr 09	S. Tellez		
15 May 09	W. de Lima	C. di Roma du Bocage	P. Azevedo
22 Dec 09	F. A. de Veiga Beirâo		
26 June 10	A. T. de Souza		
5 Oct 10	T. Braga	B. Machado	J. Belvas
2 Sep 11	J. P. Chagas		
11 Nov 11	A. de Vasconcellos	A. de Vasconcellos	S. Pais
16 June 12	D. Leite		V. Ferreira
9 Jan 13	O. Costa	A. Macieira	O. Costa

(continued

PORTUGAL (continued)

Date of taking office	Prime Minister	Foreign Minister	Finance Minister
8 Feb 14	B. Machado Guimarâes	F. Andrade	–. Santos Lucas
7 Dec 14	V. H. de Azevudo		
28 Jan 15	J. P. Continho de Castro	A. L. Vieira Soares	V. M. de Carvalho Guimarâes
14 May 15	J. P. Chagas		
19 May 15	A. Costa		
20 June 15	J. P. de Castro		
30 Nov 15	A. Costa		
16 Mar 16	A. J. d'Almeida	A. L. Vieira Soares	A. Costa
15 Apr 17	A. Costa		
8 Dec 17	S. Pais		

PRUSSIA

Date of taking office	Prime Minister	Foreign Minister	Finance Minister
7 Feb 46	G. A. R. von Rochow (since May 44)	H. von Bülow (since 1842)	F. von Düsberg
19 Mar 48		H. von Arnim-Suckow	L. S. B. Kühne
29 Mar 48	L. Camphausen		D. Hansemann
18 June 48		H. von Armin-Heinrichsdorff	
25 June 48	R. L. von Auerswald		
21 Sep 48	E. von Pfuel		G. von Bonin
8 Nov 48	F. W. von Brandenburg		L. S. B. Kühne
24 Feb 49			R. von Rabe
6 Nov 50	O. von Manteuffel		
19 Dec 50		O. von Manteuffel	
23 July 51			K. von Bodeschwingh
6 Sep 58		A. von Schleinitz	
5 Nov 58	Prince K. von Hohenzollern-Sigmaringen		R. von Patow

(continued

PRUSSIA (continued)

Date of taking office	Prime Minister	Foreign Minister	Finance Minister
12 Oct 61		A. von Bernstorff	
16 Mar 62	Prince A. von Hohenlohe		
17 Mar 62			A. von der Heydt
28 Sep 62	O. von Bismarck-Schönhausen		
1 Oct 62			K. von Bodelschwingh
9 Oct 62		O. von Bismarck-Schönhausen Office dissolved 1871	
2 June 66			A. von der Heydt
20 Oct 69			O. Camphausen
1 Jan 73	A. von Roon		
9 Nov 73	O. von Bismarck-Schönhausen		
30 Mar 78			A. Hobrecht
13 July 79			K. H. Bitter
June 82			A. H. W. von Scholtz
17 Mar 90	L. von Caprivi		
24 June 90			J. von Micquel
26 Oct 94	Prince von Hohenlohe-Schillingsfürst		
17 Oct 1900	B. von Bülow		
6 May 01			Baron von Rheinbaben
27 June 09	T. Bethmann-Hollweg		
28 June 10			Dr. Lentze
14 July 17	G. Michaelis		
5 Aug 17			O. Hergt
25 Oct 17	G. von Hertling		
4 Oct 18	Prince Max of Baden		

(continued

ROMANIA

Romania proclaimed its independence from Turkey on 21 May 1877, which was confirmed at the Congress of Berlin 1878.

Date of taking office	Prime Minister	Foreign Minister	Finance Minister
4 Aug 1876	J. C. Bratianu		
7 Feb 77		–. Ionescu	D. Stourdza
14 Apr 77		M. Cogalnitcheanu	J. Campineanu
22 July 79		B. Boërescu	J. C. Bratianu
19 Apr 81	D. Bratianu		
21 June 81	J. C. Bratianu	E. Statescu	
13 Aug 82		D. Stourdza	G. Lecca
8 Apr 84		J. C. Bratianu	
11 Feb 85		M. Phérékyde	C. Nacou
3 Apr 88	T. Rosetti	P. P. Carp	M. Germani
7 Apr 89	L. Catargi	A. Lahovari	G. Vernescu
16 Nov 89	G. Mano		M. Germani
5 Mar 91	J. E. Florescu	E. Escarcu	G. Vernescu
93	L. Catargi	A. Lahovari	M. Germani
4 Oct 95	D. Stourdza	D. Stourdza	G. C. Cantacuzène
2 Dec 96	–. Aurelian		
31 Mar 97			G. D. Pallade
11 Apr 99	G. C. Cantacuzène	J. Lahovari	G. Manu
7 July 1900	P. P. Carp	A. Marghiloman	P. P. Carp
14 Feb 01	D. Stourdza	D. Stourdza	G. D. Pallade
02		J. C. Bratianu	E. Costinescu
4 Jan 05	G. Cantacuzène	J. Lahovari	T. Ionescu
25 Mar 07	D. Stourdza	D. Stourdza	E. Costinescu
Mar 09	J. C. Bratianu	A. G. Djuvara	
10 Jan 11	P. P. Carp	T. Majorescu	P. P. Carp
10 Apr 12	T. Majorescu		A. Marghiloman
16 Jan 14	J. C. Bratianu	E. Porumbaru	E. Costinescu
9 Feb 18	A. Avarescu		
19 Mar 18	A. Marghiloman	C. Arion	M. Saulescu

RUSSIA

Date of taking office	Prime Minister	Foreign Minister	Finance Minister
6 Mar 47	Count Levachev	K. R. Nesselrode (since 1817)	G. F. P. Vront-schenko (since 1844)
28 Nov 48	Prince Tschernyshchev		
9 Apr 52			P. von Brock
5 Apr 56	Count Orlov		
17 Apr 56		A. Gortschakov	
Apr 58			A. M. Kniayevich
Jan 61	Count D. Bludov		
62			M. von Reutern
Feb 64	Prince P. Gagarin		
5 Mar 72	Count P. Ignatiev		
21 July 78			S. Greigh
2 Jan 80	Count Valuyev		
14 Nov 80			A. A. Abaza
17 Oct 81			N. von Bunge
18 Nov 81	M. von Reutern		
3 Apr 82		N. Giers	
13 Jan 87	N. von Bunge		J. A. Vyshnegradsky
Sep 92			S. J. Witte
27 Jan 95		N. P. Shichkin	
Mar 95		A. Borisovich	
16 June 95	J. N. Durnovo		
Sep 96		N. P. Shishkin	
Sep 96		Count Muraviev	
22 June 1900		Count Lamsdorff	
29 Aug 03	S. J. Witte		
31 Aug 03			E. D. Pleske
10 Apr 04			W. N. Kokovtsov
30 Oct 05			I. P. Shipov
8 May 06	I. L. Goremykin	A. P. Isvolsky	W. N. Kokovtsov
23 July 06	P. A. Stolypin		
28 Sep 10		S. Sazonov	
23 Sep 11	W. N. Kokovtsov		
11 Nov 14	I. L. Goremykin		P. L. Bark

(*continued*

RUSSIA (*continued*)

Date of taking office	Prime Minister	Foreign Minister	Finance Minister
2 Feb 16	B. W. Stürmer		
23 Nov 16	A. F. Trepov	N. N. Pokrovsky	
9 Jan 17	N. D. Golitsin	–. Milyukov	M. I. Tereshchenko
14 Mar 17	G. J. Lvov		
8 May 17		M. I. Tereshchenko	
18 May 17			A. I. Shingaryov
21 July 17	A. F. Kerensky		
6 Aug 17			–. Nekrasov
27 Sep 17			M. W. Bernatskv

SARDINIA

Date of taking office	Prime Minister	Foreign Minister	Finance Minister
Oct 47	H. Asinari di San Marzano	H. Asinari di San Marzano	O. T. de Revel (since Aug 44)
16 Mar 48	Ct C. Balbo	M. L. Pareto	
28 July 48	M. Casati		M. Vicenzo Ricci
4 Aug 48			J. Oytana
19 Aug 48	C. A. de Sostengo	H. Perrone de Saint Martin	O. T. de Revel
23 Aug 48			J. Oytana
Sep 48	– Perrone		
Oct 48	– Pinelli		
16 Dec 48	V. Gioberti	V. Gioberti	M. V. Ricci
21 Feb 49	A. de Chiodo	A. de Chiodo	
23 Feb 49		– Colli	
8 Mar 49		– de Ferrari	
30 Mar 49	– de Launay	– de Launay	G. Nigra
7 May 49	M. T. d'Azeglio	M. T. d'Azeglio	
19 Apr 51			C. B. de Cavour
21 May 52			L. Cibrario
4 Nov 52	C. B. de Cavour	G. Dabormida	C. B. de Cavour
10 Jan 55		C. B. de Cavour	

SARDINIA (*continued*)

Date of taking office	Prime Minister	Foreign Minister·	Finance Minister
31 May 55			J. Lanza
19 July 59	A. Ferraro della Marmora	G. Dabormida	J. Oytana
16 Jan 60	C. B. de Cavour	C. B. de Cavour	F. Z. Vegezzi

SAXONY

Date of taking office	Prime Minister	Foreign Minister	Finance Minister
43	J. T. J. von Kónneritz	H. A. von Zeschau	H. A. von Zeschau (since Sep 30)
16 May 48	A. C. H. Braun	Baron von der Pfordten	R. Georgi
24 Feb 49	G. F. Held	F. F. von Bússt	C. W. d'Ehrenstein
2 May 49	F. von Zschinsky		
19 May 49			J. H. A. Behr
29 Oct 58	F. F. von Büsst		
1 Nov 58			R. von Friesen
20 Aug 66	J. P. von Falkenstein	R. von Friesen	

SERBIA

Date of taking office	Prime Minister	Foreign Minister	Finance Minister
Mar 1877	J. Ristitch	J. Ristitch	—. Jovanovitch

The independence of Serbia, from Turkey, was established by the Treaty of Berlin, 1878.

31 Oct 80	M. Pirotchanatz	T. Miyatovitch	T. Miyatovitch
21 Oct 81		M. Pirotchanatz	

(*continued*

SERBIA (*continued*)

Date of taking office	Prime Minister	Foreign Minister	Finance Minister
15 Mar 83	–. Sobolew		
3 Oct 83	N. Christitch	M. Boguitchevitch	A. Spasitch
18 Feb 84	M. Garaschanin	M. Garaschanin	M. Garaschanin
85			V. Petrovitch
31 Mar 86	N. Christitch		
86	M. Garaschanin	D. Franassovitch	T. Miyatovitch
15 June 87	J. Ristitch	J. Ristitch	M. Vuitsch
1 Jan 88	S. Gruitsch		
27 Apr 88	N. Christitch	T. Miyatovitch	–. Rakitch
5 Mar 89	S. Gruitsch	S. Gruitsch	M. Vuitsch
23 Feb 91	N. Pachitch	M. K. Gjeordjevitch	N. Pachitch
22 Aug 92	J. Avakoumovitch	J. Avakoumovitch	D. Stoianovitch
13 Apr 93	L. Dokitch	A. Nikolitch	M. Vuitsch
5 Dec 93	S. Gruitsch		
24 Jan 94	G. Simitsch		
3 Apr 94	S. Nikolajewitch		
27 Oct 94	N. Christitch	M. Bogitschevitch	V. J. Petrovitch
7 July 95	S. Novakovitch	S. Novakovitch	M. Popovitch
27 Dec 96	G. Simitch		
23 Oct 97	V. Georgievitch	V. Georgievitch	S. D. Pryovitch
98			M. Popovitch
99			V. Petrovitch
12 July 1900	A. S. Yovanovitch	A. S. Yovanovitch	M. Popovitch
20 Mar 01	M. Vuitsch	M. Vuitsch	
20 Oct 02	P. Vélimirovitch	V. Antonitch	M. Radovanovitch
18 Nov 02	–. Zinzar-Markowitch		
11 June 03	J. Awakumovitsch		
11 Feb 04	S. Gruitsch	A. Nikolitch	
10 Dec 04	N. Pachitch		
28 May 05	L. Stojanovitsch	J. Zoujovitch	Dr–. Markovitch
7 Mar 06	S. Gruitsch		
28 Apr 06	N. P. Pachitch	N. P. Pachitch	L. Patchou
7 July 08	P. Velimirovitch	M. G. Milovano-vitch	M. Popovitch
24 Feb 09	S. Nowakovitch		

(*continued*

103

SERBIA (continued)

Date of taking office	Prime Minister	Foreign Minister	Finance Minister
11 Oct 09	N. P. Pachitch		S. M. Protitch
25 June 11	M. G. Milanovitch		
2 July 12	M. Trivkovitch		
12 Sep 12 until 1919	N. P. Pachitch	N. P. Pachitch	L. Patchou

SPAIN

Date of taking office	Prime Minister	Foreign Minister	Finance Minister
4 Oct 47	M. R..Narvaez	P. J. de Pidal	J. de Salamancay Mayol (since Mar 47)
15 June 48			F. de P. Orlando
11 Aug 48			A. Mon
19 Aug 49			J. B. Murillo
15 Jan 51	J. B. Murillo		
May 51		M. P. da Miraflores	
6 Aug 52		D. M. Beltran de Lys	
13 Sep 52	F. Roncali		
14 Apr 53	F. Lersundi		
21 June 53		A. Calderon de la Barca	L. Pastor
19 Sep 53	L. J. Sartorius		
18 July 54	Duc de Rivas	D. Mayans	D. Cantero
30 July 54	Duc de la Victoire	J. F. Pacheco	D. J. M. Collado
30 Nov 54		Sr Luzariaga	
6 June 55		J. de Zabala	J. Bruil
15 July 56	L. O'Donnell	N. P. Diaz	M. Cantero
12 Oct 56	Marshall Narvaez	P. J. de Pidal	M. G. Barzanallana
26 Oct 57	F. Armero y Penaranda		A. Mon
14 Jan 58	G. F. X. Isturiz		
1 July 58	L. O'Donnell	C. Collantes	P. Salaverria
4 Mar 63	Marquis da Miraflores	Marquis da Miraflores	

(continued

104

SPAIN (continued)

Date of taking office	Prime Minister	Foreign Minister	Finance Minister
4 Aug 63			M. M. Lopez
17 Jan 64	L. Arrazola	L. Arrazola	J. B. Trupita
1 Mar 64	A. Mon	J. F. Pacheco	P. Salaverria
16 Sep 64	Marshall Narvaez	A. Llorente	J. G. Barzanallana
11 Dec 64		A. Benavides	
22 Feb 65			A. Castro
11 June 65	L. Arrazola		
21 June 65	L. O'Donnell	M. B. de Castro	M. A. Martinez
28 May 66			C. del Castillo
2 July 66	M. R. Narvaez	E. de Calonge y Fenollet	M. Barzanallano
28 June 67		L. Arrazola	
24 Apr 68	L. G. Bravo Murillo	−. Roncali	M. de Orobio
8 Oct 68	F. Serrano	J. A. de Lorenzana	L. Figuerola
18 June 69	J. Prim	−. Martos	C. Ardanaz
70			L. Figuerola
2 Jan 71	F. Serrano		
25 July 71	R. Zorilla		
5 Oct 71	J. Malcampo y Monje	J. Malcampo y Monje	S. Balaguer y Angulo
6 Oct 71		M. Gomez	
20 Dec 71	P. M. Sagasta		
20 Feb 72		−. de Blas	J. F. Camacho
26 May 72	−. Topete	A. Ulloa	J. de Eludayen
4 June 72	F. Serrano		
14 June 72	R. Zorilla	E. Martos	S. Ruiz Gomez
12 Feb 73	E. Figueras y Moracas	E. Castelar	J. de Echegaray
18 July 73	N. Salmeron y Alonso	S. Soler y Plá	J. Carvajal
9 Sep 73	E. Castelar (emergency government)		
3 Jan 74	F. Serrano	P. M. Sagasta	J. de Echegaray
27 Feb 74	Gen. Zabala		
13 May 74		A. Ulloa	J. F. Camacho
4 Sep 74	P. M. Sagasta		
31 Dec 74	A. Canovas de Castillo (emergency government)		

(continued

SPAIN (*continued*)

Date of taking office	Prime Minister	Foreign Minister	Finance Minister
12 Sep 75	J. Jovellar	–. Casa Valencia	P. Salaverria
27 Nov 75	A. Canovas de Castillo	F. Calderon y Collantes	
15 Jan 77		M. Silvella	J. G. Barzanallana
10 Jan 78			M. de Orovio
7 Mar 79	A. Martinez de Campos y Anton		
16 May 79		C. O'Donnell Abreu	
9 Sep 79	A. Canovas de Castillo		
18 Mar 80		J. de Edluayen	F. Cos-Gayon
8 Feb 81	P. M. Sagasta	A. Aguilar y Correa	J. F. Camacho
9 Jan 83			J. Pelayo Cuesta
13 Oct 83	P. Herrera		
17 Jan 84	A. Canovas de Castillo	J. de Edluayen	F. Cos-Gayon
28 Nov 85	P. M. Sagasta	S. Moret	
Aug 86			L. Puigcerver
14 June 88		A. Aguilar y Correa	V. Gonzalez
5 July 90	A. Canovas de Castillo	C. M. O'Donnell	F. Cos-Gayon
10 Dec 92	P. M. Sagasta	S. Moret	G. Gamazo
95			A. Salvador
24 Mar 95	A. Canovas de Castillo	Duke de Tetuan	J. Navarro Reverter
8 July 97	M. de Azcárraga y Palmero		
30 Sep 97	P. M. Sagasta	P. Gullon	L. Puigcerver
18 May 98		Duc de Almodóvar del Rio	
4 Mar 99	F. Silvela	F. Silvela	R. F. Villaverde
23 Oct 1900	M. de Azcárraga y Palmero	M. Aguilar de Campoo	M. A. Salazar
26 Feb 01	P. M. Sagasta		
6 Mar 01		Duc de Almodóvar del Rio	– Urzaiz

(continued

SPAIN (*continued*)

Date of taking Office	Prime Minister	Foreign Minister	Finance Minister
6 Dec 02	F. Silvela		
20 July 03	R. F. Villaverde		
8 Dec 03	A. Maura y Montomar		
16 Dec 04	M. de Azcárraga y Palmero		
27 Jan 05	R. F. Villaverde		
23 June 05	E. Montero Rios	P. Gullon	J. de Echegaray
20 Dec 05	S. Moret		
6 July 06	J. Lopez Dominguez		J. Navarro Reverter
25 Jan 07	A. Maura y Montomar	M. A. Salazar	G. J. de Osma
08			A. Gonzales Besada
22 Oct 09	S. Moret	J. Perez Caballero	J. Alvarado
9 Feb 10	J. Canalejas	G. Prieto	−. Cobian
12 Nov 12	A. Figueroa y Torres		J. Navarro Reverter
27 Oct 13	E. Dato	Marquis de Lima	Count de Bugallal
10 Dec 15	A. Figueroa y Torres	A. Gimeno	S. Alba
19 Apr 17	M. Garcia-Prieto	J. Alvarado	
11 June 17	E. Dato		
4 Nov 17	M. Garcia-Prieto		
23 Mar 18	A. Maura	E. Dato	A. Gonzales-Besada
9 Nov 18	M. Garcia-Prieto		

SWEDEN

Date of taking office	Prime Minister	Foreign Minister	Finance Minister
43		Baron A. E. von Ihre	S. A. Munthe

SWEDEN (continued)

Date of taking office	Prime Minister	Foreign Minister	Finance Minister
10 Apr 48		Baron Stjerneld	A. P. Sandstroemer
Sep 51			J. A. Gripenstedt
Oct 51			C. O. Palmstjerna
28 May 56			J. A. Gripenstedt
8 Sep 56		E. Lagerheim	
16 Mar 58	Baron L. de Geer	C. R. L. Manderstroem	
Sep 66			C. A. Lagercrantz
23 Aug 67			C. G. D'Ugglas
4 June 68		Ct Wachtmeister	
3 June 70	A. d'Adlercreutz	A. d'Adlercreutz	C. F. Woern
10 Nov 71		B. J. E. de Platen	
17 Dec 72		O. M. de Bjornstjerna	
7 Mar 74	E. H. Carleson		
28 Sep 74			J. G. N. S. Akerheim

Minister of State

11 May 75	Baron L. de Geer		H. L. Forsell
19 Apr 80	A. R. F. Posse		
27 Apr 80		C. F. L. Hoćhschild	
8 Mar 81			O. R. Themptander
13 June 83	C. J. Thyselius		
16 May 84	O. R. Themptander		
25 Sep 85		A. C. A. L. Ehrensvärd	
28 May 86			C. G. A. Tamm
6 Feb 88	D. Gillis, Baron von Bildt		F. von Essen
12 Oct 89	J. G. N. S. Åkerhielm	C. Lewenhaupt	E. Bull
90			F. von Essen
24 Feb 91	E. G. Boström		
95			E. G. Boström
96		L. W. A. Douglas	R. Wersäll
99		C. H. T. A. de Lagerheim	H. H. Wachtmeister

SWEDEN (continued)

Date of taking office	Prime Minister	Foreign Minister	Finance Minister
12 Sep 1900	F. W. von Otter		
5 July 02	E. G. Boström		E. F. W. Meyer
13 Apr 05	J. O. Ramstedt		
2 Aug 05	C. Lundeberg		
7 Nov 05	K. Staaff	E. B. Trolle	J. E. Bisèrt
29 May 06	S. A. A. Lindman		C. J. G. Swartz
11 June 09		A. F. von Taube	
7 Oct 11	K. Staaff	J. J. A. Ehrensvärd	A. T. von Adelswärd
17 Dec 14	H. von Hammars-kjöld	K. A. Wallenberg	A. F. Vennersten
29 Mar 17	K. Swartz	S. A. A. Lindman	M. Carleson
19 Oct 17	N. Edén	J. Hellner	F. W. Thorsson

SWITZERLAND

Head of the government—*see* Head of State.
Head of the Federal Council Finance Department, appointed (as President)
for whole calendar year. They may serve for more than 1 year.

1848	U. Schiess	1871	P. J. Ceresole
1849	J. Munzinger	1872	J. J. Scherer
1851	H. Druey	1873	W. Naeff
1853	J. Munzinger	1876	B. Hammer
1854	H. Druey	1879	S. Bavier
1855	J. Stämpfli	1880	B. Hammer
1856	M. Knüsel	1891	W. Hauser
1857	J. Stämpfli	1900	R. Comtesse
1859	C. Fornerod	1901	W. Hauser
1862	M. Knüsel	1903	R. Comtesse
1864	J. J. Challet-Venel	1910	J. A. Schobinger
1868	V. Ruffy	1911	R. Comtesse
1869	J. J. Challet-Venel	1912	G. Motta (until 1918)

The office of Foreign Minister was held by the President until 1888. Ministers thereafter:

1889   N. Droz
1893   A. Lachenal
1897   A. Deucher (president)
1898   E. Ruffy (president)

Thereafter the office is called 'Head of the Political Department' and reverts once more to the President until:

1915   A. Hoffmann

From 1916 the office is as before.

TURKEY

Date of taking office	Prime Minister	Foreign Minister	Finance Minister
47	M. Reschid (since Sep 46)	M. E. Ali	Sarym Pasha
27 Apr 48	Sarym Pasha		
11 Aug 48	M. Reschid		S. E. Nafiz
27 Apr 50			Haled Effendi
30 Aug 50			S. E. Nafiz
26 Jan 52	Raouf Pasha		
5 July 52	M. Reschid		
4 Oct 52	D. M. Ali	Fuad Effendi	
13 May 53	Moustapha Pasha	M. Reschid	Moukhtar Bey
Oct 53			Mussa Saffeti
29 May 54	M. Kepresli		
3 June 54		Chekib Pasha	
1 July 54		M. Reschid	
23 Nov 54	M. Reschid	M. E. Ali	
4 May 55	M. E. Ali		Moukhtar Pasha
2 July 55		Fuad Pasha	
1 Dec 56	M. Reschid		
31 July 57	Mustafa Naili	M. E. Ali	Hassib Pasha
23 Oct 57	M. Reschid		
11 Jan 58	M. E. Ali	Fuad Pasha	
27 Mar 58			Mussa Saffetti
26 Feb 59			Hassib Pasha
8 Oct 59	M. Kibrisli		
24 Dec 59	Mohammed Ruchdi		

TURKEY (*continued*)

Date of taking office	Prime Minister	Foreign Minister	Finance Minister
4 June 60	M. Kibrisli		Moukhtar Pasha
6 Aug 61	M. E. Ali		Tewfik Pasha
22 Nov 61	M. Fuad	M. E. Ali	
62			Nevres Pasha
6 Jan 63	Yusuf Kâmil		Fazil-Moustapha
3 June 63	M. Fuad		
64			Kiani Pasha
65			Khourchid Pasha
Jan 66			Chirvanzad-Ruchdi
5 June 66	R. Mehemed		
Feb 67	M. E. Ali	M. Fuad	
Mar 68	Miohat Pasha	M. E. Ali	
69	M. E. Ali		Sadik Pasha
19 Aug 70			Fazil Pasha
18 Jan 71			Mohammed Ruchdi
Sep 71	Mahmoud Pasha	Djémel Pasha	
1 Aug 72	Midhat Pasha		Sadik Pasha
15 Sep 72		Khalil-Scherif	
19 Oct 72	Mohammed Ruchdi		
Nov 72		Ahmed-Nunktar	
15 Feb 73	Essad Pasha		
15 Apr 73	Mohammed Ruchdi	Safvet Pasha	
17 Apr 73			Hamdi Pasha
15 May 73		Raschid Pasha	
13 Feb 74	Hussein Arni		Joussouf Pasha
17 May 74		Aarify Bey	
25 Apr 75	Essad Pasha	Raschid Pasha	
23 Aug 75	Mahmud Pasha		
10 May 76	Mohammed Ruchdi	Safvet Pasha	Zuhdi Effendi
22 Dec 76	Midhat Pasha		
20 Jan 77			Joussouf Pasha
5 Feb 77	Edham Pasha	Serber Pasha	
11 Jan 78	Ahmed Hamdi		
5 Feb 78	Ahmed-Nefik		
18 Apr 78	Mehmed Sadik		
May 78	Mohammed Ruchdi		
4 June 78	Safvet Pasha	Safvet Pasha	Zuhdi Effendi

111

(*continued*

TURKEY (continued)

Date of taking office	Prime Minister	Foreign Minister	Finance Minister
Oct 78	Hayreddin Pasha		
28 July 79	Arifi Pasha		
19 Oct 79	Said Pasha	Savas Pasha	Edibb Effendi
13 Feb 80		Assim Pasha	Subhi Pasha
81			Munir Bey
30 Nov 82	Ahmed Nefik	Aarify Pasha	
2 Dec 82	Said Pasha		
83		Assim Pasha	
26 Sep 85	M. Kâmil	Said Pasha	Agob Pasha
86			Zihni Effendi
87			Zuhdi Pasha
88			Zihni Effendi
89			Agob Pasha
15 Mar 91			A. Nazif
Sep 91	Ahmed Cevad	Ahmed Cevad	
94		Said Pasha	
9 June 95	Said Pasha		
Oct 95	M. Kâmil		
Nov 95	Halil Rifat	A. Tewfik	Sabri Bey
97			A. Nazif
98			A. Tewfik
99			Rechad Bey
13 Nov 1901	Said Pasha		
16 Jan 03	M. Ferid		A. Nazif
06			Zia Pasha
22 July 08	Said Pasha		
7 Aug 08	M. Kamil		
31 Mar 09	A. Tewfik		
May 09	H. Hilmi	Rifaat Pasha	Djavid Bey
12 Jan 10	I. Hakki		
4 Oct 11	Said Pasha	Assim Bey	Nail Bey
22 July 12	G. Ahmed Mukhtar		
30 Oct 12	M. Kâmil	Gabriel Effendi	Abdurrahman Bey
23 Jan 13	M. Sevket		
15 June 13	Said Halim	Said Halim	Rifaat Bey
4 Feb 17	M. Talât	A. Nessimi	Djavid Bey

(continued

TURKEY (*continued*)

Date of taking office	Prime Minister	Foreign Minister	Finance Minister
Oct 18	A. Izzet		
Nov 18	A. Tewfik		
10 Mar 19	D. Ferid	D. Ferid	Vassi Pasha
6 Oct 19	Ali Riza		
8 Mar 20	Salih Pasha		
5 Apr 20	D. Ferid		Reshai Bey
21 Oct 20	A. Tewfik	Sefa Bey	

TUSCANY

Date of taking office	Prime Minister	Foreign Minister	Finance Minister
Sep 47	N. des Corsini	N. des Corsini	G. Baldasseroni
late 47		L. Serristori	
2 June 48	Marquis Ridolfi		
16 Aug 48	G. Capponi		
19 Aug 48		G. Giorgini	–. Piovaccari
27 Oct 48	F. D. Guerrazzi	G. Montanelli	P. A. Adami
1 Feb 49		A. Mordini	
21 Feb 49	G. Montanelli		
27 Mar 49	Dictatorship under	F. D. Guerrazzi	
12 Apr 49	Commission at head of government	T. Fornetti	V. Martini
5 May 49	Ct Serristoni (provisional ministry)		
24 May 49	G. Baldasseroni	A. Corsini, duc de Casigliano	G. Baldasseroni
56		G. Baldasseroni	
57		O. Lenzoni	
27 Apr 59	U. Peruzzi V. Malencini A. Danzini }	(provisional ministry)	
11 May 59	Chev. Buoncampagni (provisional ministry)		
1 Aug 59	B. Ricasoli (provisional ministry)		

WURTTEMBERG

Date of taking office	Prime Minister	Foreign Minister	Finance Minister
31 Aug 44	P. F. T. E. von Maucler (since Nov 31)	J. von Beroldingen (since 23)	K. C. G. von Garttner
9 Mar 48	F. von Römer		A. von Goppett
13 May 48		K. L. F. Roser	
28 Oct 49	J. von Schlayer	K. von Wächter-Spittler	J. C. von Herdegen
2 July 50	J. von Linden	C. von Knapp	
6 July 50			J. von Linden
21 Sep 64	K. F. von Varnbüler	K. F. von Varnbüler	A. von Renner
31 Aug 70		A. von Taube	

5 ELECTIONS

RESULTS

AUSTRIA

The calculation of aggregate voting figures for Austria is almost impossible before the elections of 1907, when universal male suffrage was introduced. The results for the last two elections before the dissolution of the Habsburg Monarchy are set out below:

		Votes	% votes	Seats
1907 (14 May)	Christian Social Party	658,198	52·3	94
	Social Democrats	264,431	21·0	28
	German Agrarians	16,656	1·3	−
	German Conservatives	15,260	1·2	1
	German National Party	8,481	0·7	2
	German People's Party	83,073	6·6	15
	German Progressive Party	20,211	1·6	2
	Italian Parties	57,704	4·6	10
	Slovene Parties	57,020	4.5	8
	Others	77,108	6·1	2
		1,258,142		162
1911 (13 June)	Christian Social Party	555,986	45·5	70
	Social Democrats	310,663	25·4	33
	German Agrarians	9,214	0·8	1
	German Conservatives	12,308	1·0	1
	German National Party	26,779	2·2	5
	German People's Party	55,182	4·5	14
	Italian Parties	47,719	3·9	9
	Slovene Parties	53,063	4·3	8
	German Farmers League	15,301	1·2	−
	German Freedom Party	62,789	5·1	15
	Upper Austrian Farmers League	22,009	1·8	−
	Others	53,214	4·4	6
		1,224,227		162

BELGIUM

Between 1848 and 1918, elections were held on the following occasions for the Chamber of Representatives:

13 June 48*	14 June 70	14 June 92*
11 June 50	2 Aug 70*	14 Oct 94*
8 June 52	11 June 72	5 July 96
13 June 54	9 June 74	22 May 98
10 June 56	13 June 76	27 May 1900*
10 Dec 57*	11 June 78	25 May 02
14 June 59	8 June 80	29 May 04
11 June 61	13 June 82	27 May 06
9 June 63	10 June 84	24 May 08
11 Aug 64*	8 June 86	22 May 10
12 June 66	12 June 88	2 June 12*
		24 May 14

Of these 36 elections, only those 8 indicated with an asterisk were general elections for which meaningful figures can be produced. The results of these 8 general elections were as follows:

		Votes	% votes	Seats
1848	Catholic Party	13,122	29·6	26
	Liberal Party	30,806	69·5	82
	Others	383	0·9	—
		44,311		108
1857	Catholic Party	32,503	45·3	38
	Liberal Party	39,280	54·7	70
		71,783		108
1864	Catholic Party	39,750	50·0	53
	Liberal Party	39,576	49·7	63
	Others	240	0.3	—
		79,566		116
1870	Catholic Party	39,705	54·5	73
	Liberal Party	32,448	44·5	51
	Others	720	1·0	—
		72,873		124
1892	Catholic Party	56,199	53·6	92
	Liberal Party	47,518	45·4	60
	Workers' Party	167	0·2	—
	Others	844	0·8	—
		104,728		152

116

		Votes	% votes	Seats
1894	Catholic Party	921,607	51·1	103
	Liberal Party	503,929	28·0	20
	Workers Party	237,920	13·2	28
	Liberal-Workers Party Cartel	94,129	5·2	–
	Daensists	21,849	1·2	1
	Others	23,546	1·3	–
		1,802,980		152
1900	Catholic Party	994,245	48·5	86
	Liberal Party	498,799	24·3	33
	Workers Party	461,095	22·5	32
	Daensists	61,131	3·0	1
	Others	35,744	1·7	–
		2,051,014		152
1912	Catholic Party	1,337,315	51·1	101
	Liberal Party	303,895	11·6	44
	Workers Party	243,338	9·3	39
	Liberal-Workers Party Cartel	679,734	25·9	–
	Daensists	48,716	1·9	2
	Others	8,773	0·3	–
		2,621,771		186

DENMARK

		Votes	% votes	Seats
1884	Conservatives	55,000	38·7	19
	Liberals	80,000	56·3	81
	Social Democrats	7,000	4·9	2
		142,000		102
1887	Conservatives	87,000	38·3	27
	Liberals	132,000	58·1	74
	Social Democrats	8,000	3·5	1
		227,000		102
1890	Conservatives	92,000	39·7	24
	Liberals	123,000	53·0	75
	Social Democrats	17,000	7·3	3
		232,000		102
1893	Conservatives	78,000	34·8	31
	Liberals	63,000	28·1	30
	Social Democrats	20,000	8·9	2
	Moderate Liberals	63,000	28·1	39
		224,000		102
1895	Conservatives	64,000	28·8	25
	Liberals	90,000	40·5	54
	Social Democrats	25,000	11·3	8
	Moderate Liberals	43,000	19·4	27
		222,000		114

		Votes	% votes	Seats
1898	Conservatives	58,000	25·9	16
	Liberals	98,000	43·8	63
	Social Democrats	32,000	14·3	12
	Moderate Liberals	36,000	16·1	23
		224,000		114
1901	Conservatives	51,787	26·0	8
	Liberals	78,319	39·4	76
	Moderate Liberals	23,753	12·0	16
	Social Democrats	38,398	19·3	14
	Others	6,333	3·2	—
		198,590		114
1903	Conservatives	47,286	21·9	12
	Liberals	99,644	46·1	73
	Moderate Liberals	17,167	7·9	12
	Social Democrats	46,646	21·6	16
	Others	5,459	2·5	1
		216,202		114
1906	Conservatives	63,335	21·0	12
	Liberals	93,632	31·1	56
	Moderate Liberals	20,487	6·8	9
	Social Democrats	76,612	25·4	24
	Radicals	38,151	12·7	9
	Others	9,099	3·0	4
		301,316		114
1909	Conservatives	64,189	20·0	21
	Liberals	96,285	30·0	48
	Social Democrats	93,079	29·0	24
	Radicals	51,165	16·0	15
	Others	15,969	5·0	6
		320,687		114
1910	Conservatives	64,904	18·6	13
	Liberals	118,902	34·1	57
	Social Democrats	98,718	28·3	24
	Radicals	64,884	18·6	20
	Others	1,448	0·4	—
		348,856		114
1913	Conservatives	81,404	22·5	7
	Liberals	103,251	28·6	44
	Social Democrats	107,365	29·6	32
	Radicals	67,903	18·7	31
	Others	2,617	0·7	—
		362,540		114

1915   No meaningful figures are obtainable for the election of 15 May 15.

FINLAND

Eight elections to the *Eduskunta* took place between 1907 and 1918, on the following dates:

15–16 Mar 1907	2–3 Jan 11
1–2 July 08	1–2 Aug 13
1–3 May 09	1–2 July 16
1–2 Feb 10	1–2 Oct 17

		Votes	% votes	Seats
1907	Agrarian Union	51,242	5·8	9
	Christian Labour Union	13,790	1·5	2
	Finnish Party	243,573	27·3	59
	Young Finnish Party	121,604	13·6	26
	Social Democrats	329,946	37·0	80
	Swedish People's Party	112,267	12·6	24
	Others	18,568	2·1	—
		890,990		200
1908	Agrarian Union	51,756	6·4	13
	Christian Labour Union	18,848	2·3	1
	Finnish Party	205,892	25·4	48
	Young Finnish Party	115,201	14·2	29
	Social Democrats	310,826	38·4	84
	Swedish People's Party	103,146	12·7	25
	Others	3,772	0·5	—
		809,441		200
1909	Agrarian Union	56,943	6·7	13
	Christian Labour Union	23,259	2·7	1
	Finnish Party	199,920	23·6	48
	Young Finnish Party	122,770	14·5	29
	Social Democrats	337,685	39·9	84
	Swedish People's Party	104,191	12·3	25
	Others	1,703	0·2	—
		846,471		200
1910	Agrarian Union	60,157	7·6	17
	Christian Labour Union	17,344	2·2	1
	Finnish Party	174,661	22·1	42
	Young Finnish Party	114,291	14·4	28
	Social Democrats	316,951	40·0	86
	Swedish People's Party	107,121	13·5	26
	Others	1,034	0·1	—
		791,559		200
1911	Agrarian Union	62,885	7·8	16
	Christian Labour Union	17,245	2·1	1
	Finnish Party	174,177	21·7	43
	Young Finnish Party	119,361	14·9	28
	Social Democrats	321,201	40·0	86
	Swedish People's Party	106,810	13·3	26
	Others	708	0·1	—
		802,387		200

		Votes	% votes	Seats
1913	Agrarian Union	56,977	7·9	18
	Christian Labour Union	12,850	1·8	–
	Finnish Party	143,982	19·9	38
	Young Finnish Party	102,313	14·1	28
	Social Democrats	312,214	43·1	90
	Swedish People's Party	94,672	13·1	26
	Others	1,296	0·2	
		724,304		200
1916	Agrarian Union	71,608	9·0	19
	Christian Labour Union	14,626	1·8	1
	Finnish Party	139,111	17·5	33
	Young Finnish Party	99,419	12·5	23
	Social Democrats	376,030	47·3	103
	Swedish People's Party	93,555	11·8	21
	Others	860	0·1	–
		795,209		200
1917	Agrarian Union	122,900	12·4	26
	Christian Labour Union	15,489	1·6	–
	Finnish Party (and allies)	299,516	30·2	61
	Social Democrats	444,670	44·8	92
	Swedish People's Party	108,190	10·9	21
	Others	1,997	0·2	–
		992,762		200

FRANCE

1848:   *Constituent-Assembly*
The main groups returned in the elections of April 1848 were: Monarchists (c. 300); Moderates/Centre Republicans (c. 500); Socialist Republicans (c. 100).

1849   *(13–14 May) Legislative Assembly*

	Votes	% votes	Seats
Party of Order (Bonapartists)	3,310,000	50·2	500
Constitutional Republicans (Cavaignac)	834,000	12·6	70
Democrats/Socialists/Republicans	1,955,000	29·6	180
Others	495,000	7·5	–
	6,594,000		750

1857	Government	5,471,000	89·2	262
	Opposition	665,000	10·8	5
		6,136,000		267
1863	Government	5,355,000	74·2	250
	Opposition	1,860,000	25·8	33
		7,215,000		283
1869	Government	4,455,000	55·0	200
	Opposition	3,643,000	45·0	92
		8,098,000		292

120

1871:   *National Assembly*
No aggregate votes are available. Monarchists won 415 of the 645 seats.

		Votes	*% votes*	*Seats*
1876	Conservatives	3,202,000	44·3	155
	Republicans	4,028,000	55·7	371
		7,230,000		526
1877	Conservatives	3,639,000	45·6	208
	Republicans	4,340,000	54·4	318
		7,979,000		526
1881	Conservatives	1,789,000	25·9	96
	Republicans	5,128,000	74·1	455
		6,917,000		541
1885	Conservatives	3,420,000	43·9	202
	Republicans	4,373,000	56·1	367
		7,793,000		569
1889	Conservatives	2,915,000	36·5	168
	Republicans	4,353,000	54·6	350
	Boulangists	709,000	8·9	42
		7,977,000		570
1893	Conservatives	1,178,007	16·5	76
	Moderate Republicans	3,187,670	44·6	279
	Radicals	1,443,915	20·2	143
	Ralliés	458,416	6·4	27
	Socialist Radicals	171,810	2·4	10
	Socialists	598,206	8·4	31
	Others	108,596	1·5	—
		7,146,620		566
1898	Conservatives	1,011,398	12·9	65
	Moderate Republicans	3,347,826	42·7	235
	Radicals	1,400,416	17·9	98
	Ralliés	541,576	6·8	35
	Socialist Radicals	748,412	9·5	82
	Socialists	888,385	11·3	57
		7,838,013		572
1902	Radical Socialists	853,140	10·1	75
	Socialists	875,532	10·4	46
	Conservatives	2,383,080	28·3	147
	Liberal Popular Action	385,615	4·6	18
	Left Republicans	2,501,429	29·7	180
	Independent Radicals	1,413,931	16·8	123
		8,412,727		589
1906	Radical Socialist Party	2,514,508	28·5	241
	Socialist Party	877,221	10·0	53
	Independent Socialists	205,081	2·3	18
	Conservatives	2,571,765	29·2	109
	Liberal Popular Action	1,238,048	14·0	69
	Left Republicans	703,912	8·0	52
	Independent Radicals	692,029	7·9	39
	Others	9,924	0·1	—
		8,412,493		581

		Votes	% votes	Seats
1910	Radical Socialist Party	1,727,064	20·4	121
	Socialist Party	1,110,561	13·1	78
	Independent Socialists	345,202	4·1	24
	Conservatives	1,602,209	19·0	112
	Liberal Popular Action	153,231	1·8	11
	Left Republicans	1,018,704	12·1	71
	Independent Radicals	966,407	11·4	67
	Republican Union	1,472,442	17·4	103
	Others	49,953	0·6	—
		8,445,773		587
1914	Radical Socialist Party	1,530,188	18·1	140
	Socialist Republicans	326,927	3·9	27
	Socialist Party	1,413,044	16·8	103
	Conservatives	1,297,722	15·4	73
	Left Republicans	819,184	9·7	57
	Independent Radicals	1,399,830	16·6	96
	Republican Union	1,588,075	18·8	96
	Others	56,086	0·7	—
		8,431,056		592

GERMANY

		Votes	% votes	Seats
1871	Centre Party	700,400	18·0	61
	German Conservatives	549,700	14·1	57
	German People's Party	18,700	0·5	1
	German Reich Party	346,900	8·9	37
	Liberal Reich Party	273,900	7·0	30
	National Liberals	1,176,600	30·2	125
	Progressive Party	342,400	8·8	46
	Social Democrats	124,700	3·2	2
	Danes	18,200	0·5	1
	Guelphs	85,300	2·2	9
	Poles	176,300	4·5	13
	Others	79,100	2·0	—
		3,892,200		382
1874	Centre Party	1,446,000	27·9	91
	German Conservatives	360,000	6·9	22
	German People's Party	21,700	0·4	1
	German Reich Party	375,500	7·2	33
	Liberal Reich Party	53,900	1·0	3
	National Liberals	1,542,500	29·7	155
	Progressive Party	447,500	8·6	49
	Social Democrats	352,000	6·8	9
	Alsace-Lorraine	234,500	4·5	15
	Danes	19,900	0·4	1
	Guelphs	92,100	1·8	4
	Poles	198,400	3·8	14
	Others	46,300	0·9	—
		5,190,300		397

		Votes	*% votes*	*Seats*
1877	Centre Party	1,341,300	24·8	93
	German Conservatives	526,000	9·7	40
	German People's Party	44,900	0·8	4
	German Reich Party	426,600	7·9	38
	National Liberals	1,604,300	29·7	141
	Progressive Party	417,800	7·7	35
	Social Democrats	493,300	9·1	12
	Alsace-Lorraine	200,000	3·7	15
	Danes	17,300	0·3	1
	Guelphs	97,200	1·8	10
	Poles	216,200	4·0	14
	Others	16,100	0·3	—
		5,401,000		397
1878	Centre Party	1,328,100	23·1	94
	German Conservatives	749,500	13·0	59
	German People's Party	66,100	1·1	3
	German Reich Party	785,800	13·6	57
	National Liberals	1,486,800	25·8	109
	Progressive Party	385,100	6·7	26
	Social Democrats	437,100	7·6	9
	Alsace-Lorraine	178,900	3·1	15
	Danes	16,100	0·3	1
	Guelphs	102,600	1·8	4
	Poles	210,100	3·6	14
	Others	14,700	0·3	—
		5,760,900		397
1881	Centre Party	1,182,900	23·2	100
	German Conservatives	830,800	16·3	50
	German People's Party	103,400	2·0	9
	German Reich Party	379,300	7·4	28
	National Liberals	746,600	14·6	47
	Liberal Union	429,000	8·4	46
	Progressive Party	649,300	12·7	60
	Social Democrats	312,000	6·1	12
	Alsace-Lorraine	153,000	3·0	15
	Danes	14,400	0·3	2
	Guelphs	86,700	1·7	10
	Poles	194,900	3·8	18
	Others	15,300	0·3	—
		5,097,800		397
1884	Centre Party	1,282,000	22·6	99
	German Conservatives	861,100	15·2	78
	German People's Party	95,900	1·7	7
	German Reich Party	387,700	6·8	28
	National Liberals	997,000	17·6	51
	Social Democrats	550,000	9·7	24
	Alsace-Lorraine	165,600	2·9	15
	Danes	14,400	0·3	1
	Guelphs	96,400	1·7	11
	Poles	203,200	3·6	16
	Free Thinking Party	997,000	17·6	67
	Others	12,700	0·2	—
		5,663,000		397

123

		Votes	% votes	Seats
1887	Centre Party	1,516,200	20·1	98
	German Conservatives	1,147,200	15·2	80
	German People's Party	88,800	1·2	–
	German Reich Party	736,400	9·8	41
	National Liberals	1,678,000	22·3	99
	Social Democrats	763,100	10·1	11
	Alsace-Lorraine	233,700	3·1	15
	Danes	12,400	0·2	1
	Guelphs	112,800	1·5	4
	Poles	220,000	2·9	13
	Anti-Semites	11,600	0·2	1
	Free Thinking Party	973,100	12·9	32
	Others	47,600	0·6	2
		7,540,900		397
1890	Centre Party	1,342,100	18·6	106
	German Conservatives	895,100	12·4	73
	German People's Party	147,600	2·0	10
	German Reich Party	482,300	6·7	20
	National Liberals	1,177,800	16·3	42
	Social Democrats	1,427,300	19·7	35
	Alsace-Lorraine	101,100	1·4	10
	Danes	13,700	0·2	1
	Guelphs	112,700	1·6	11
	Poles	246,800	3·4	16
	Anti-Semites	47,500	0·7	5
	Free Thinking Party	1,159,900	16·0	66
	Others	74,600	1·0	2
		7,228,500		397
1893	Centre Party	1,468,500	19·1	96
	German Conservatives	1,038,300	13·5	72
	German People's Party	166,800	2·2	11
	German Reich Party	438,400	5·7	28
	National Liberals	997,000	13·0	53
	Social Democrats	1,786,700	23·3	44
	Alsace-Lorraine	114,700	1·5	8
	Danes	14,400	0·2	1
	Guelphs	101,800	1·3	7
	Poles	229,500	3·0	19
	Anti-Semites	263,900	3·4	16
	Free Thinking People's Party	666,400	8·7	24
	Free Thinking Union	258,500	3·4	13
	Bavarian Farmers League	66,300	0·9	4
	Others	62,800	0·8	1
		7,674,000		397
1898	Centre Party	1,455,100	18·8	102
	German Conservatives	859,200	11.1	56
	German People's Party	108,500	1·4	8
	German Reich Party	343,600	4·4	23
	National Liberals	971,300	12·5	46
	Social Democrats	2,107,100	27·2	56
	Alsace-Lorraine	107,400	1·4	10
	Danes	15,400	0·2	1
	Guelphs	105,200	1·4	9

124

		Votes	*% votes*	*Seats*
	Poles	244,100	3·1	14
	Anti-Semites	284,300	3·7	13
	Free Thinking People's Party	558,300	7·2	29
	Free Thinking Union	195,700	2·5	12
	Bavarian Farmers League	140,300	1·8	5
	Farmers League	110,400	1·4	6
	Others	146,800	1·9	7
		7,752,700		397
1903	Centre Party	1,875,300	19·8	100
	German Conservatives	948,500	10·0	54
	German People's Party	91,200	1·0	6
	German Reich Party	333,400	3·5	21
	National Liberals	1,317,400	13·9	51
	Social Democrats	3,010,800	31·7	81
	Alsace-Lorraine	101,900	1.1	9
	Danes	14,800	0·2	1
	Guelphs	94,300	1·0	6
	Poles	347,800	3·7	16
	Anti-Semites	244,500	2·6	11
	Free Thinking People's Party	538,200	5·7	21
	Free Thinking Union	243,200	2·6	9
	Bavarian Farmers League	111,400	1.2	4
	Farmers League	118,800	1·3	4
	Others	97,500	1·0	3
		9,489,000		397
1907	Centre Party	2,179,800	19·4	105
	German Conservatives	1,060,200	9·4	60
	German People's Party	138,600	1·2	7
	German Reich Party	471,900	4·2	24
	National Liberals	1,630,600	14·5	54
	Social Democrats	3,259,000	29·0	43
	Alsace-Lorraine	103,600	0·9	7
	Danes	15,400	0·1	1
	Guelphs	78,200	0·7	1
	Poles	453,900	4·0	20
	Anti-Semites	248,500	2·2	16
	Free Thinking People's Party	736,000	6·5	28
	Free Thinking Union	359,300	3·2	14
	Bavarian Farmers League	75,300	0·7	1
	Farmers League	119,400	1·1	8
	Economic Union	104,600	0·9	5
	Others	219,100	1·9	3
		11,253,400		397
1912	Centre Party	1,996,800	16·4	91
	German Conservatives	1,126,300	9·2	43
	German Reich Party	367,200	3·0	14
	National Liberals	1,662,700	13.6	45
	Social Democrats	4,250,400	34·8	110
	Alsace-Lorraine	162,000	1·3	9
	Danes	17,300	0·1	1
	Guelphs	84,600	0·7	5
	Poles	441,600	3·6	18
	Anti-Semites	51,900	0·5	3

	Votes	% votes	Seats
Bavarian Farmers League	48,200	0·4	2
Farmers League	29,800	0·2	2
Economic Union	304,600	2·5	10
Progressive People's Party	1,497,000	12·3	42
Others	167,100	1·4	2
	12,207,500		397

ICELAND

		Votes	% votes	Seats
1916 (21 Oct)	Home Rule Party	5,333	40·0	12
	Independence Party	1,014	7·6	3
	Hardline Independence	2,097	15·7	7
	Moderate Independence	938	7·0	3
	Farmers Party	1,173	8·8	5
	Independent Farmers	554	4·2	1
	Social Democrats	903	6·8	1
	Others	1,336	10·0	2
				34
1919	Home Rule Party	4,120	29·4	9
	Independence Party	1,563	11·1	7
	Social Democrats	949	6·8	—
	Progressive Party	1,873	13·3	6
	Others	5,528	39·4	12
				34

ITALY

		Votes	% votes	Seats
1895	Ministerial and Opposition Liberals	979,958	80·2	438
	Radical Party	142,356	11·7	47
	Socialist Party	82,523	6·8	15
	Others	16,761	1·4	8
		1,221,598		508
1897	Ministerial and Opposition Liberals	994,083	82·3	437
	Radical Party	51,207	4·2	29
	Socialist Party	108,086	8·9	16
	Republican Party	54,764	4·5	26
		1,208,140		508
1900	Ministerial and Opposition Liberals	935,116	73·7	412
	Radical Party	89,872	7·1	34
	Socialist Party	164,946	13·0	33
	Republican Party	79,127	6·2	29
		1,269,061		508

		Votes	*% votes*	*Seats*
1904	Ministerial and Opposition Liberals	989,929	64·8	415
	Radical Party	128,002	8·4	37
	Socialist Party	326,016	21·3	29
	Republican Party	75,225	4·9	24
	Catholics	8,008	0·5	3
		1,527,180		508
1909	Ministerial and Opposition Liberals	1,144,532	62·6	382
	Radical Party	181,242	9·9	45
	Socialist Party	347,615	19·0	41
	Republican Party	81,461	4·5	24
	Catholics	73,015	4·0	16
		1,827,865		508
1913	Ministerial and Opposition Liberals	2,804,165	55·9	310
	Radical Party	588,193	11·7	73
	Socialist Party	883,409	17·6	52
	Republican Party	173,666	3·5	17
	Catholics	301,949	6·0	29
	Independent Socialists	67,133	1·3	8
	Reformist Socialists	196,406	3·9	19
		5,014,921		508

THE NETHERLANDS

		Votes	*% votes*	*Seats*
1888	Catholic Party	48,922	20·7	25
	Anti-Revolutionary Party	74,048	31·4	27
	Liberal Union	96,157	40·7	46
	Radicals	4,686	2·0	−
	Social Democratic League	2,020	0·9	1
	Others	10,335	4·4	1
		236,168		100
1891	Catholic Party	41,579	20·2	25
	Anti-Revolutionary Party	60,738	29·5	21
	Free Liberal League	86,888	42·2	53
	Radicals	4,409	2·1	1
	Social Democratic League	2,102	1·0	−
	Others	10,230	5·0	−
		205,946		100
1894	Catholic Party	33,454	20·3	25
	Anti-Revolutionary Party	28,274	17·1	15
	Christian Historicals	11,118	6·7	−
	Free Liberal League	82,099	49·8	57
	Radicals	5,151	3·1	3
	Social Democratic Workers	365	0·2	−
	Others	4,433	2·7	−
		164,894		100

127

		Votes	% votes	Seats
1897	Catholic Party	83,826	20·3	22
	Anti-Revolutionary Party	108,581	26·2	17
	Christian Historicals	44,159	10·7	6
	Free Liberal League	126,199	30·5	48
	Radicals	14,863	3·6	4
	Social Democratic Workers	12,312	3·0	3
	Others	23,774	5·7	—
		413,714		100
1901	Catholic Party	61,160	15·7	25
	Anti-Revolutionary Party	106,670	27·4	22
	Christian Historicals	26,233	6·7	10
	Free Liberal League	107,249	27·6	26
	Radicals	28,398	7·3	9
	Social Democratic Workers	36,981	9·5	7
	Others	22,330	5·7	1
		389,021		100
1905	Catholic Party	76,605	13·1	25
	Anti-Revolutionary Party	143,843	24·7	15
	Christian Historicals	62,770	10·8	8
	Free Liberal League	164,376	28·2	34
	Radicals	51,595	8·8	11
	Social Democratic Workers	65,561	11·2	7
	Others	18,638	3·2	—
		583,388		100
1909	Catholic Party	76,087	12·8	25
	Anti-Revolutionary Party	166,270	27·9	25
	Christian Historicals	63,306	10·6	10
	Liberal Union	106,086	17·8	20
	Free Liberal League	33,464	5·6	4
	Radicals	54,007	9·1	9
	Social Democratic Workers	82,855	13·9	7
	Others	13,985	2·3	—
		596,060		100
1913	Catholic Party	111,081	14·5	25
	Anti-Revolutionary Party	165,560	21·5	11
	Christian Historicals	80,402	10·5	10
	Liberal Union	128,706	16·7	22
	Free Liberal League	50,541	6·6	10
	Radicals	56,462	7·3	7
	Social Democratic Workers	142,185	18·5	15
	Others	33,771	4·4	—
		768,708		100

NORWAY

		Votes	% votes	Seats
1882	Liberals	44,803	62·8	83
	Conservatives	26,501	37·2	31
		71,304		114

		Votes	*% votes*	*Seats*
1885	Liberals	57,683	63·4	84
	Conservatives	33,284	36·6	30
		90,967		114
1888	Liberals	37,320	41·6	39
	Moderates	17,745	19·8	24
	Conservatives	34,564	38·6	51
		89,629		114
1891	Liberals	51,780	50·8	63
	Moderates and Conservatives	50,059	49·2	51
		101,839		114
1894	Liberals	83,165	50·4	59
	Moderates and Conservatives	81,462	49·3	55
	Labour	520	0·3	—
		165,147		114
1897	Liberals	87,548	52·7	79
	Moderates and Conservatives	77,682	46·7	35
	Labour	947	0·6	—
		166,177		114
1900	Liberals	127,142	54·0	77
	Conservatives and National Liberals	96,092	40·8	37
	Labour	7,013	3·0	—
	Others	5,163	2·2	—
		235,410		114
1903	Liberals	101,142	42·7	50
	Conservatives and National Liberals	106,042	44·8	63
	Labour	22,948	9·7	4
	Others	6,509	2·8	—
		236,641		117
1906	Liberals	121,562	45·1	73
	Worker Democrats	12,819	4·8	4
	Conservatives and National Liberals	88,323	32·8	36
	Labour	43,134	16·0	10
	Others	3,443	1·3	—
		269,281		123
1909	Liberals	128,367	30·4	46
	Worker Democrats	15,550	3·7	2
	Conservatives and National Liberals	175,388	41·5	64
	Labour	91,268	21·6	11
	Others	12,111	2·8	—
		422,684		123
1912	Liberals and Worker Democrats	195,526	40·0	76
	Conservatives and National Liberals	162,074	33·2	24
	Labour	128,455	26·3	23
	Others	2,848	0·5	—
		488,903		123

129

		Votes	% votes	Seats
1915	Liberals	204,243	33·1	74
	Worker Democrats	25,658	4·2	6
	Conservatives	179,028	29·0	21
	Labour	198,111	32·1	19
	Agrarian League	6,351	1·0	1
	Others	4,279	0·6	2
		617,670		123
1918	Liberals	187,657	28·3	51
	Worker Democrats	21,980	3·3	3
	Conservatives	201,325	30·4	50
	Labour	209,560	31·6	18
	Agrarian League	30,925	4·7	3
	Others	11,074	1·7	1
		662,521		126

RUSSIA

No reliable statistics of voting in Tsarist Russia can be obtained. Various estimates have been made, however, of the relative strengths of different groups in the four Dumas. These are given below:

THE FIRST DUMA

The predominance of the large landowners and upper middle class was made certain by the electoral law of 11 Dec 1905. The actual elections (in Feb–Mar 06) took place in an atmosphere of active police repression. The Bolsheviks boycotted the election (with obvious success in St Petersburg, Poland and the Baltic). The Kadets (Constitutional Democrats) easily emerged as the largest single party.

Composition of the First Duma

The Right (Monarchists, Octobrists, Industrialists, etc.)	44
The Autonomists (Polish League, Lithuanian Circle, Ukrainian Democrats, etc.)	44
Party for Democratic Reform	6
Kadets	179
Labour Group	94
Social Democratic Group	18
Cossack Group	1
Non-party	100

Composition of the Second Duma

The Reactionary Right	10
Octobrists	42
Polish League	46
Muslim Group	30
Party for Democratic Reform	1
Kadets	98
Labour Group	104
Popular Socialists	16
Socialist Revolutionaries	37
Social Democrats	65
Cossack Group	17
Non-party	50
	516

Composition of the Third Duma (First Session)

The Reactionary Right	49
Moderate Right Wing	69
Russian National Group	26
Alliance of 17 October	148
Polish/Lithuanian Group	7
Polish League	11
Progressives	25
Muslim Group	8
Kadets	53
Labour Group	14
Social Democrats	20
Non-party	16
	446

Composition of the Fourth Duma (First Session)

The Reactionary Right	64
Moderate Right	88
Centre Party	32
Alliance of 17 October	99
Polish/Lithuanian Group	6
Polish League	9
Progressives	47
Muslim Group	6
Kadets	58
Labour Group	10
Social Democrats	14
Non-party	5
	438

After the elections to the Fourth Duma, no further elections occurred until after the fall of the Tsarist régime. During 1917, the Provisional Government had been organizing elections to establish a Constituent Assembly. The Bolsheviks allowed these elections to take place on 25 Nov 17. With universal suffrage, the electorate numbered 41,700,000. No reliable figures exist for the results, but the following table gives approximate figures.

Party	Votes cast	Delegates returned
	17,100,000 (Total)	429 (Total)
Bolsheviks	9,600,000	168
Mensheviks	1,400,000	18
Kadets	2,000,000	17
Monarchists	300,000	..
National Minorities	1,700,000	..

At the end of 1917, the Kadets were proscribed. The Constituent Assembly met on 18 Jan 18. It was dissolved by the Bolsheviks a day later after rejecting (237 votes to 136) a Bolshevik motion to recognize the Congress of Soviets as the supreme government authority.

SWEDEN

Elections were held in Sweden after 1887 on the following dates:

29 Mar – 30 Apr 1887	7 – 13 Sep 1902
9 Aug – 29 Sep 87	10 – 16 Sep 05
14 July – 29 Sep 90	6 – 12 Sep 08
2 July – 30 Sep 93	9 – 24 Sep 11
28 June – 29 Sep 96	29 Mar – 7 Apr 14
16 July – 30 Sep 99	5 – 13 Sep 14
	1 – 16 Sep 17

		Votes	% votes	Seats
1887 Mar	Free Traders	76,025	58·6	102
	Protectionists	53,692	41·4	112
		129,717		214
1887 Aug	Free Traders	50,959	53·2	136
	Protectionists	44,915	46·8	85
		95,874		221
1890	Free Traders	60,658	57·3	140
	Protectionists	45,149	42·7	88
		105,807		228
1893	Protectionists	48,963	38·7	86
	Liberals	44,618	35·2	76
	Moderate Free Traders	33,036	26·1	66
		126,617		228

		Votes	% votes	Seats
1896	Protectionists	54,282	38·6	98
	Liberals	53,388	38·0	74
	Moderate Free Traders	32,918	23·4	58
		140,588		230
1899	Liberals	64,145	46·8	93
	Conservatives	72,800	53·2	137
		136,945		230
1902	Social Democrats	6,321	3·5	4
	Liberals	92,503	51·2	107
	Conservatives	81,703	45·3	119
		180,527		230
1905	Social Democrats	20,677	9·5	13
	Liberals	98,287	45·2	109
	Conservatives	98,359	45·3	108
		217,323		230
1908	Social Democrats	45,155	14·6	34
	Liberals	144,426	46·8	105
	Conservatives	118,808	38·5	91
		308,389		230
1911	Conservatives	188,691	31·2	65
	Liberals	242,795	40·2	101
	Social Democrats	172,196	28·5	64
	Others	292	—	—
		603,974		230
1914 (Mar)	Conservatives	286,250	37·7	86
	Liberals	245,107	32·2	71
	Social Democrats	228,712	30·1	73
	Others	125	—	—
		760,194		230
1914 (Sep)	Conservatives	267,124	36·5	86
	Liberals	196,493	26·9	57
	Social Democrats	266,133	36·4	87
	Agrarian Party	1,507	0·2	—
	Others	104	—	—
		731,361		230
1917	Conservatives	182,070	24·7	59
	Liberals	202,936	27·6	62
	Social Democrats	228,777	31·1	86
	Agrarian Party	39,262	5·3	9
	Farmers Union	22,659	3·1	3
	Socialist Left	59,243	8·0	11
	Others	1,037	0·1	—
		735,984		230

133

SWITZERLAND

Figures for elections prior to 1881 and for 1893 were not available.

		Votes	% votes	Seats	
1881	Radicals	169,788	49·1	83	
	Centre	77,687	22·5	26	
	Conservatives	97,976	28·4	36	
				145	
1884	Radicals	186,585	51·0	88	
	Centre	79,818	21.8	22	
	Conservatives	99,319	27·2	35	
				145	
1887	Radicals	173,028	53·9	87	
	Centre	67,747	21·1	24	
	Conservatives	80,099	25·0	34	
				145	
1890	Radicals	215,848	59·4	92	
	Centre	58,068	15·9	19	
	Conservatives	89,342	24·7	36	
				147	
1896	Catholic Conservatives	85,229	23·3	30	
	Democrats	19,946	5·5	9	
	Liberal Conservatives	55,832	15·3	22	
	Radical Democrats	179,113	49·0	83	
	Social Democrats	25,263	6·9	2	(and 1 Independent)
				147	
1899	Catholic Conservatives	76,845	20·9	32	
	Democrats	18,003	4·9	6	
	Liberal Conservatives	56,764	14·2	19	
	Radical Democrats	183,216	50·2	83	
	Social Democrats	35,488	9·7	4	(and 3 Independent)
				147	
1902	Catholic Conservatives	94,031	23·2	34	
	Democrats	15,053	3·7	3	
	Liberal Conservatives	34,928	8·6	19	
	Radical Democrats	205,235	50·7	99	
	Social Democrats	51,338	12·7	7	
	Others	4,481	1·1	5	
				167	
1905	Catholic Conservatives	92,600	22·7	34	
	Democrats	18,028	4·4	5	
	Liberal Conservatives	27,643	6·8	18	
	Radical Democrats	202,664	49·7	104	
	Social Democrats	60,323	14·8	2	
	Others	6,584	1·6	4	
				167	

134

		Votes	% votes	Seats
1908	Catholic Conservatives	81,733	20·6	34
	Democrats	14,414	3·6	4
	Liberals Conservatives	23,597	6·0	16
	Radical Democrats	202,732	51·1	104
	Social Democrats	70,003	17·7	7
	Others	3,982	1·0	2
				167
1911	Catholic Conservatives	76,726	19·3	38
	Democrats	12,610	3·2	5
	Liberal Conservatives	27,062	6·8	13
	Radical Democrats	198,300	49·8	114
	Social Democrats	80,050	20·1	17
	Others	3,608	0·9	2
				189
1914	Catholic Conservatives	71,668	21·2	38
	Democrats	9,069	2·7	3
	Liberal Conservatives	25,142	7·4	14
	Radical Democrats	191,054	56·5	111
	Social Democrats	34,204	10·1	19 ·
	Others	6,805	2·0	4
				189
1917	Catholic Conservatives	84,784	16·5	42
	Democrats	16,818	3·3	4
	Liberal Conservatives	25,188	4·9	12
	Radical Democrats	210,323	41·0	105
	Social Democrats	158,450	30·9	22
	Others	18,025	3·5	4
				189

TURKEY

Elections were held during only two periods between 1848 and 1918. These were the first constitutional period (1876–78), when elections were held in 1876 and 1877, and the second period (1908–20) when elections were held in 1908, 1912 and 1919. No elections were held between 1877 and 1908. No meaningful figures are available for these elections.

UNITED KINGDOM

Overall Result

	Conservatives	Liberals
1847	327[1]	329
1852	331[2]	323
1857	281[3]	373
1859	301	347
1865	298	360
1868	276	382
1874	352	300[4]
1880	238	414[5]

[1] Of this total an estimated 235 were Protectionists and an estimated 90 were Peelites.
[2] Including 45 Peelites.
[3] Including 26 Peelites.
[4] Including 58 Home Rulers.
[5] Including 60 Home Rulers.

Party Strengths in England were:

	Conservatives	Liberals
1847	247	222
1852	251	216
1857	201	266
1859	220	247
1865	225	246
1868	220	243
1874	288	171
1880	203	256

		Votes	% votes	Seats
1885	Conservatives	2,020,927	43·6	249
	Liberals	2,199,998	47·4	335
	Irish Nationalist	310,608	6·9	86
	Others	106,702	2·2	—
				670
1886	Conservative and Liberal Unionists	1,520,886	51·4	394
	Liberals	1,353,581	45·0	191
	Irish Nationalist	97,905	3·5	85
	Others	1,791	0·1	—
				670

		Votes	% votes	Seats
1892	Conservatives	2,159,150	47·0	314
	Liberals	2,088,019	45·1	272
	Irish Nationalist	311,509	7·0	81
	Others	39,641	0·9	3
				670
1895	Conservatives	1,894,772	49·1	411
	Liberals	1,765,266	45·7	177
	Irish Nationalist	152,959	4·0	82
	Independent Labour Party	44,325	1·0	—
	Others	3,730	0·2	—
				670
1900	Conservatives	1,767,958	50·3	402
	Liberals	1,572,323	45·0	184
	Irish Nationalist	91,055	2·6	82
	Labour	62,698	1·3	2
	Others	29,448	0·8	—
				670
1906	Conservatives	2,422,071	43·4	157
	Liberals	2,751,057	49·4	400
	Irish Nationalist	35,031	0·7	83
	Labour	321,663	4·8	29
	Others	96,269	1·7	1
				670
1910 *(Jan)*	Conservatives	3,104,407	46·8	273
	Liberals	2,866,157	43·5	275
	Irish Nationalist	126,647	1·9	82
	Labour	505,657	7·0	40
	Others	64,532	0·8	—
				670
1910 *(Dec)*	Conservatives	2,420,169	46·6	273
	Liberals	2,293,869	44·2	271
	Irish Nationalist	131,720	2·5	84
	Labour	371,802	6·4	42
	Others	17,678	0·3	—
				670
1918	Conservatives	4,144,192	39·6	382
	National Democratic Party	181,331	1·7	9
	Lloyd George Liberals	1,396,590	12·6	127
	Liberal Party	1,388,784	13·0	36
	Labour Party	2,357,524	21·4	62
	Irish Nationalist Party	238,197	2·2	7
	Sinn Fein	497,107	4·6	73
	Others	583,093	4·9	11
				707

THE GROWTH OF THE FRANCHISE

BELGIUM

1848	79,076
1857	90,543
1870	107,099
1892	136,707
1894	2,111,127
1900	2,269,414
1912	2,814,181

DENMARK

1884	322,000
1890	358,000
1898	399,000
1903	416,748
1909	460,553
1913	491,422

FINLAND

1907	1,272,873
1910	1,324,931
1913	1,430,135
1917	1,441,075

FRANCE

1830	94,000	
1831	166,000	
1846	241,000	
1848	8,221,000	(Constituent Assembly)
1849	9,837,000	(Legislative Assembly)
1863	..	
1869	..	
1876	9,961,000	
1885	10,181,000	
1898	10,635,206	
1902	11,058,702	
1910	11,326,828	
1914	11,305,986	

GERMANY

1871	7,975,750
1878	9,124,311
1884	9,383,074
1893	10,628,292
1903	12,531,210
1907	13,352,880
1912	14,441,436

ICELAND

1916	28,529
1919	31,870

ITALY

1895	2,121,185
1900	2,248,509
1904	2,541,327
1909	2,930,473
1913	8,443,205

THE NETHERLANDS

1888	292,613
1891	293,888
1894	299,073
1897	576,598
1901	609,634
1905	752,692
1909	843,487
1913	960,595

NORWAY

1882	99,501
1885	122,952
1888	128,368
1891	139,690
1894	184,124
1897	195,956
1900	426,593
1903	433,448
1906	446,705

1909	760,277
1912	809,582
1915	1,086,557
1918	1,186,602

SWEDEN

1887	274,733
1890	288,096
1899	339,876
1908	503,128
1911	1,066,200
1917	1,123,969

SWITZERLAND

1881	638,589
1884	640,395
1887	650,182
1890	663,438
1896	713,367
1905	779,835
1914	855,142
1917	916,642

UNITED KINGDOM

1831	435,391
1833	652,777
1866	1,056,659
1869	1,995,086
1883	2,618,453
1886	4,380,540
1900	6,730,935
1910	7,709,981
1918	21,392,322

MAJOR CHANGES IN THE ELECTORAL SYSTEM

AUSTRIA

1897   A fifth 'curia' added to the Austrian House of Assembly: all men over 24 granted the vote.

1907   The Estates system abolished. Replaced by universal male suffrage.

BELGIUM

1830   (until 1893) Suffrage confined to men over 25 paying a minimum direct tax.

1877   Secret ballot introduced.

1893   Universal male suffrage (but still some plural voting) introduced.

1899   The d'Hondt system of proportional representation replaced the majority system.

1919   New electoral law. Plural voting abolished. Voting age reduced to 21.

DENMARK

1849   Elections to the Folketing were on a broad franchise—all men over 30, except servants, farm workers and paupers. Elections held in single member constituencies.

1850   Faroe Islands first represented.

1901   Secret ballot introduced, replacing open voting.

1915   Introduction of universal adult suffrage; voting age reduced to 29.

FRANCE

Numerous changes occurred in the electoral system during this period. They are admirably summarized by Campbell as follows:[1]

Date of Law	Type of constituency	No. of ballots	Method of allocating seats
1848	Multi-member	1	Simple majority of the electors voting
1849	Multi-member	1	As in 1848
1852	Single-member	2	1st ballot: absolute majority of electors voting. 2nd ballot: relative majority of votes cast
1871	Multi-member	1	As in 1848
1873	Multi-member	2	As in 1852
1875	Single-member	2	As in 1852
1885	Multi-member	2	As in 1852
1889	Single-member	2	As in 1852

[1] Campbell, P. *French Electoral Systems and Elections since 1789* (London, 1965).

ITALY

1870   (until 1882). Franchise limited to males over 25 who were literate. A 2-ballot single-member constituency system in use.

1882   Voting age reduced to 21. A system of multi-member con-
        stituencies briefly introduced (abandoned in 1891).
1912   All males over 30 enfranchised; illiterates granted the vote if they
        had completed military service.
1919   Adult male suffrage introduced. D'Hondt system of proportional
        representation introduced.

LUXEMBOURG

1868   Introduction of the directly elected parliament (the Chambre des
        Deputés). Franchise restricted to males over 25 paying 30 francs
        a year tax.
1879   Secret ballot introduced.
1902   Tax qualification for franchise reduced to 10 francs.
1918   Franchise extended to all adults over 21. Voting became com-
        pulsory

THE NETHERLANDS

1848   Birth of Dutch parliamentary government. Franchise limited to
        men over 23 with some wealth or property qualification.
1887   Extension of franchise, with doubling of the electorate. In-
        troduction of single-member constituencies, except in major
        cities.
1896   Minimum voting age increased to 25, but suffrage qualifications
        reduced. Multi-member constituencies in the large towns aban-
        doned.
1917   Introduction of universal male suffrage and also a system of
        proportional representation.
1919   Women first granted the vote.

NORWAY

1884   Secret ballot introduced: franchise extended to those paying a
        minimum amount of income tax (as opposed to property
        holders, leasehold farmers and high officials).
1898   All men over 25 enfranchised (except paupers and bankrupts).
1905   Indirect system of election replaced by direct elections in single-
        member constituencies.
1907   Women first granted the vote.
1913   Equal voting rights granted to women.
1914   Bankrupts enfranchised (paupers in 1919).

SWEDEN

1866   Electoral law lays down main features of Swedish system. Unaltered until 1907.

1907   Series of electoral reforms. Property requirement for voting abandoned. Minimum voting age raised from 21 to 24.

SWITZERLAND

1848   All males aged over 20 eligible to vote. Elections in multi-member seats using multiple-ballot system.

1872   Secret ballot introduced.

1900   Abandonment of third ballot; candidates secured election with a plurality at the second ballot.

1919   Hagenbach–Bischoff system of proportional representation introduced.

Note: No women were granted the vote until the 1971 referendum.

6 POLITICAL PARTIES

AUSTRIA

Up to the 1880s, political parties in the Habsburg Monarchy were really only informal groupings of parliamentary notables. There was virtually no constituency organization. The Liberals tended to represent the German-speaking urban middle class, whilst the Conservatives spoke for the nobility, the interests of agriculture and the non-German minorities. The main developments from the 1880s onwards were:

1882	Foundation of Georg von Schonerer's Pan-German League. Extremely anti-clerical and racialist, with a more militant defence of German-speaking interests. Essentially a dissident Liberal Party.
1887	Formation of the Catholic Social Union. Anti-Liberal (and anti-Semitic) with support from lower middle class in Vienna.
1889	Foundation of the Social Democratic Party.
1896	German People's Party founded.
1903	German Radical Party founded.
1905	German Agrarian Party founded.
1910	Union of the Liberal-National parties into the *Deutscher National-verband*.

BELGIUM

Before the advent of the Belgian Labour Party, party politics were dominated by two parties: the Liberals, who formed a national party organization in 1846, and the Conservatives, whose national organization, dating from the 1860s, remained weak until 1921, when the Catholic Union (*Union Catholique Belge*) was established. The Catholics alternated in office with the Liberals from 1830 to 1884– when the party came into power in its own right. The Catholics were divided on the language question, as well as having divisions between a Conservative right-wing and a more democratic left-wing faction.

The Liberals lost ground after 1884 with the rise of the Belgian Labour Party and the extension of the franchise.

The Belgian Labour Party (*Parti Ouvrier Belge*) was founded in 1885 by César de Paepe, rapidly making progress in such cities as Brussels, Ghent, the Liège country and Hainaut province. The Daensists (*Christene Volkspartis*) were formed in 1894 by the Abbé Daens.

BULGARIA

After independence, Bulgarian politics was dominated by the political groupings around Stambulov, Radoslavow and Tonchev. Among other groups active prior to 1914 were:

(1) *The Social Democratic Party* (founded 9 Aug 91). By 1899, its membership was 800. In 1901, this total had risen to 2180 and by 1902 to 2507. An orthodox evolutionary party, its extremist left broke away in 1903, eventually forming the Communist Party in 1918.

(2) *The Democratic Party* was founded in 1895 by P. Karavelow. The governing party from Jan 08 to Mar 11.

(3) *The Radical Party*. Founded in 1906 by N. Tsanow, who broke away from the Democratic Party. It advocated radical tax reforms and protection of co-operative societies.

(4) *The Agrarians Union*. Founded in 1899, and ably led by Stamboulisky. Secured a major increase in influence during the Balkan Wars. Its programme was heavily in favour of the protection of agriculture and allied industries. In 1919 a breakaway group, led by D. Dragyhev, organized a rival, more moderate faction.

DENMARK

The Liberal Party (*Venstre*) exercised a dominant control of the Folketing prior to the First World War, despite repeated secession to both right and left. Founded in 1870, it was split and reunited on several occasions. A traditional Liberal Party, its aims were free trade and a minimum of state control.

The historic opponents of the Liberals were the Right (*Hojre*). From 1875 to 1894, under the leadership of Estrup the main planks in the Conservative programme were the elevation of the Landsting (upper house) to equal authority with the Folketing and the strengthening of national defences. In 1915 the Right was formally constituted as the Conservative People's Party (*Konservative Folkeparti*).

145

Two other important pre-1914 parties were:

(1) *Social Democratic Party.* Founded in 1871, its political outlook was an orthodox evolutionary policy. With strong working-class support, the party assumed office in 1924.

(2) *Radical-Liberal Party.* The party was founded in 1905 as a result of a split in the Liberal Party. Its chief adherents were the small landed proprietors and certain intellectuals. It held office from 1909 to 1910, and again, with Zahle as Prime Minister, from 1913 to 1920. The main planks of its programme were social reform, reduction of armaments, and the establishment of small-holdings.

FINLAND

In the late nineteenth century, the main political party in Finland was the Finnish Nationalist Party. This later split into the Old Finns and the Young Finns. Other developments were:

1899	Foundation of the Finnish Labour Party.
1903	Finnish Labour Party renamed Social Democratic Party.
1906	Formation of the Swedish People's Party representing the Swedish minority.

Other parties contesting elections prior to 1918 were the Christian Labour Union and the Agrarian Union.

FRANCE

Despite the many upheavals in French politics, the development of clear-cut political parties in France was a slow process. Inside the parliament, deputies often belonged to more than one group whilst constituency organization at local level was hardly developed. By 1900, in addition to the Conservative Right and a variety of socialists, other parties contesting elections were:

1898	*Action Française* founded by Henri Vaugeois and Maurice Pujo as a nationalist and anti-Semitic organization. It became Royalist later under the influence of Charles Maurras. It did not believe in democracy, favoured a monarchy without parliament, and with ministers responsible to the King only. It advocated a considerable degree of provincial autonomy, with local assemblies, from which delegates would gather every year in Paris to vote upon and to control common finances.
1901	Formation of the Radical Socialist Party (*Parti Républicain*

Radical et Radical Socialiste), a merger of Radicals and Radical Socialists. *Alliance Républicaine Démocratique* created by Adolphe Carnot.

1905   Foundation of the *Parti Socialiste*–an amalgamation of the *Parti Socialiste de France*, the revolutionary party of Jules Guesde, with the *Parti Socialiste Français*, the reformist party of Jean Jaurès. The union was, however, split on 24–5 Dec 20, at the Congress of Tours.

1906   Formation of the French Socialist Party.

1910   Elections contested by Republican Union.

GERMANY

In the new German Empire, the electoral stage was dominated by three main groups: the Centre Party (*Deutsche Zentrums-partei*), the National Liberals (the *Nationalliberale*) and a small but rapidly-growing Social Democratic Party, formed in 1871. In 1877, the National Liberals split, with the Liberal Union (*Liberale Vereiniging*) breaking away over the tariff question. In addition there were some right-wing German national parties (e.g. the *Deutsche Reichs partei* and the *Deutsche-Konservative*) and the national minority parties of Poles, Danes and Alsatians, these latter first fighting elections after 1874.

Other developments after 1877 were:

1884   Elections contested by the Free Thinking Party (*Freisinnige Partei*), a merger of the Progressive Party and the Liberal Union.

1892   The Free Thinking Party split in this year to form the Free Thinking People's Party (*Freisinnige Volks Partei*) and the Free Thinking Union (*Freisinnige Vereinigung*).

1898   Two farmers parties, the Bavarian Farmers League (*Bayerische Bauernbund*) and the Farmers League (*Bund der Landwirte*) contested the elections.

1907   The Economic Union (*Wirtschafts Vereinigung*) formed.

1912   Progressive People's Party formed from a merger of the Free Thinking Union, the Free Thinking Peoples Party and the German People's Party.

147

ITALY

In Italy, even after 1870, political parties were extremely slow to develop. Politics centred around the groups attached to a particular individual. Although after 1870, deputies could usually be identified with the right, (*Destra*) or left (*Sinistra*), such labels often meant little, whilst the deputies from the south could usually be 'bought' by the government. The impetus to the development of political parties came in 1892, with the formation of the Socialist Party (*Partito Socialista Italiano*, PSI).

Major developments thereafter were:

1898   Dissolution of the Italian Republican Party (originally founded in 1880 and reorganized in 1892) by order of Pelloux. It was subsequently reformed in 1901.

1904   The Vatican began to allow Catholics to vote for moderate candidates—but no national Catholic party formed until 1919, when the Popular Party (*Partito Popolare Italiano*) came into being.

1913   Splits in the Socialist ranks led to the elections being contested by Independent Socialists and by the Reformist Socialist Party.

LUXEMBOURG

From 1868, when the first directly-elected parliament was introduced, the Liberals were the dominant party. They formed every administration until 1915. Major dates in the evolution of national party organizations were:

1896   Formation of the Socialist Party (*Parti Sociale Démocrate*).

1904   The Ligue Liberale formed, first national organization of the Liberals.

1914   Right-wing (*Parti de la Droite*) established rival national organization.

THE NETHERLANDS

The main political parties began to develop party organization after the establishment of the Anti-Revolutionary Party in 1879. The main groupings were:

(1) *The Catholic State Party* (after 1897, the Catholic Electoral League). The Catholic State Party subscribed to the ruling and tenets of the Roman

Catholic Church as expressed, in religious affairs, in the *Quanta Cura* Encyclical and, in social affairs, in the *Rerum Novarum* Encyclical. Including, as it did, Conservatives and Democrats, anti-militarists and Labour leaders, it was anything but homogeneous, and was repeatedly threatened with schism.

(2) *The Anti-Revolutionary Party* (ARP). Established in 1879 as a political organization of orthodox neo-Calvinistic Protestants. Strongly opposed to Liberalism and Socialism, it aims at founding a polity 'based on that traditional national character which the Reformation created and which William the Silent moulded'.

(3) *Christian Historical Union* (*Christelijk-Historische Unie*, CHU). Formed in 1908, from a variety of earlier local groupings; these included the Free Anti-Revolutionaries (founded in 1894), the Christian Historical Electoral Union (founded 1896 and became Christian Historical Party in 1903) and the Friesian Christian Historical Party (originally established in 1898) as a result of the secession from the Anti-Revolutionary Party of its anti-democratic elements. The Christian Historicals constitute the more conservative Protestants, approximating on politico-religious questions to the Anti-Revolutionaries and on economic questions to the Liberals. The Union leans towards Nationalism and Orangism, advocates a strong army and navy, upholds the rights of the Dutch Reformed Church as the national church.

(4) *The Liberal Union* (Liberale Unie).

(5) *The Radicals.* Merged in 1901 as the Liberal Democratic League (*Urijzinnig-Democratische Bond*).

(6) *The Social Democratic Workers Party.*

(7) *The Free Liberal League* (formed 1891), composed of Conservative dissenters from the Liberal Union.

(8) *The Social Democratic League.*

NORWAY

In the second half of the nineteenth century, the main party division lay between the left (the *Venstre*, or Liberals) and the conservative right (the *Hyre*). Generally, the left had the support of the radicals and the peasantry. From 1903 to 1913, the Conservatives fought under the title of *Samlingspartei* (Unionist Party). From 1894, the Norwegian Labour Party (*Norske Arbeiderpartei*) began to capture the working-class vote. By 1912, it was polling over 26% of all votes cast.

Other parties to contest elections were the Free-Thinking Left (*Frisinnide*

149

Venstre) after 1909, the Worker Democrats (after 1906) and the Agrarian League (formed in 1915).

SWEDEN

In the late nineteenth century, the main party divisions in Sweden revolved round the tariff question—the Free Traders, (*Frihardelssinade*) against the Protectionist Right, (*Protektionistiska Hôgermân*). The Swedish Social Democratic Party was originally formed in 1880. By 1914, it had secured 36 % of all votes cast. During the First World War, other parties to begin contesting elections were the Agrarian Party, (*Bondefôrbundet*), the Farmers Union and the Left Socialists. The Left Socialists provided the core of the Swedish Communist Party (established in 1921).

SWITZERLAND

In the last decade of the nineteenth century, the present divisions in Swiss party politics began to appear. Hitherto, Swiss parties had been almost exclusively cantonal affairs.

The first organized group was the Social Democratic Party (founded in 1888). The old left wing formed the Radical Democratic Party in 1894, whilst the right came together the same year as the Popular Catholic Party.

TURKEY

No political parties emerged in time to contest the elections of 1876 or 1877. Under the despotism of Abdul Hamid, a number of illegal opposition groups were formed. Easily the most important was the Committee of Union and Progress. This party dominated the parliaments of the second constitutional period (1908–1920). Only one other party, the Liberals (Ahrar) contested the 1908 elections. The Liberals stood only in Istanbul; all were defeated. After 1913, the Committee of Union and Progress established a virtual dictatorship. In the May 1914 elections, the Committee was the only party to fight. It remained the only party until the 1918 armistice. It dissolved itself at its last party Congress on 14–19 Oct 1918.

UNITED KINGDOM

During the period 1848 to 1918, British politics was dominated by two parties: the Liberals and Conservatives.

Liberal Party: Formed from an amalgamation of the old Whig Party, the Radicals and Reformers. The party placed emphasis on free trade, reduced government spending, Home Rule for Ireland, reform of the House of Lords and modest social and land reform. It had great electoral strength in Wales, Scotland and the nonconformist areas of England. Its working-class base was under threat after 1900 from the newly-formed Labour Party. In 1886 it survived the breakaway of the Liberal Unionists.

Conservative Party: Formed from the old Tory Party. Survived the Peelite split in 1846 over the repeal of the Corn Laws. A party with strong Anglican roots, anti-Home Rule and favoured imperialism more than the Liberals. A strong electoral base in the counties and in the smaller towns, but also with some 'working-class Tory' support in the large cities such as Liverpool and the East End of London.

Other political parties were:

Independent Labour Party. Set up at Bradford in Jan 1893 by Keir Hardie as a party to return more labour men to Parliament. Participated in the formation of the Labour Representation Committee (LRC) in Feb 1900.

Irish Nationalists. Successors to the Irish Home Rule League founded in Dublin in Nov 1873 to win self-government for Ireland. Returned 59 Home Rulers in 1874 election. Under Parnell's leadership after 1880, Irish Nationalists won firm control of all except Ulster (in 1885, 86 Home Rulers were returned). In 1890, Parnell's divorce case split the party. In 1900, the Nationalists reunited under Redmond.

Labour Party. Established in Feb 1900 as the Labour Representation Committee, with Ramsay MacDonald as Secretary. It returned only two MPs in the 1900 election. Through an electoral pact with the Liberals (the Gladstone-MacDonald entente) it secured 29 seats in 1906 and 42 in Jan 10. With the Liberal split in 1916, the way was paved for it to replace the Liberals as the party of the Left.

Liberal Unionist Party. The party of those former Liberals, led by Joseph Chamberlain and the Marquess of Hartington, who broke away, in opposition to Home Rule for Ireland. The party finally merged with the

Conservatives in 1912. Liberal Unionists returned the following members: 1886 (79); 1892 (47); 1895 (70); 1900 (68); 1906 (23); Jan 1910 (31); Dec 1910 (35).

Peelites. The supporters of Peel's Free Trade Policy in 1846. In the vote to repeal the Corn Laws, 112 Tories supported Peel. Mainly, they represented the moderate centre of the old party. Peel himself died in 1850 and in Dec 1852 the Peelites joined the Aberdeen coalition. Their parliamentary representation was: 1847 (89): 1852 (45): 1857 (26).

Scottish Crofters Party. A party of protest at the neglect of the grievances of the smallholders in the Scottish Highlands. Active after the 1884 Reform Act in the elections of 1885 and 1886. (In 1885, 5 Crofters were elected, in 1886, 7). The label had been virtually abandoned by 1892.

7 JUSTICE

AUSTRIA-HUNGARY

In Austria the ordinary judicial authorities were: (i) The Supreme Court of Justice and Court of Cassation (*Oberste Gerichts-und Kassationshof*) in Vienna: (ii) The higher provincial courts (*Oberlandesgerichte*). (iii) The provincial and district courts (*Landes-und Kreisgerichte*), and, in connection with these, the jury courts (*Geschworenengerichte*). (iv) The county courts (*Bezirksgeriehte*). Of these, the third and fourth groups were courts of first instance; the second group consisted of courts of second instance. Courts of first instance acted as courts of inquiry and had summary jurisdiction. Courts of second instance were courts of appeal from the lower courts, and had the supervision of the criminal courts in their jurisdiction. The jury courts tried certain cases where severe penalties were involved, political offences, and press offences. The county courts exercised criminal jurisdiction in the counties and co-operated in preliminary proceedings regarding crime.

In 1892 there were for Austria 68 provincial and 916 county or district courts.

There existed also special courts for commercial, revenue, military, shipping, and other matters.

In case of conflict between different authorities the Imperial Court (*Reichsgerichte*) in Vienna had power to decide. Private persons could in certain cases appeal against the decisions of magistrates to the High Court for Administrative Affairs.

For Hungary with Fiume the judicial authorities were: The Royal Court (*Kuria*) in Budapest, and the Supreme Court of Justice in Zágreb, of the highest instance in all civil and criminal matters. In 1892 there were 11 Royal Courts of Justice, of second instance. As courts of first instance, 65 courts (*Gerichtshöfe*) with collegiate judgeships; 384 county, later called district, courts (*Bezirksgerichte*) with single judges; 10 jury courts (*Geschworenenger-ichte*) for press offences, besides an army special court.

BELGIUM

Judges were appointed for life by the King from lists prepared by the Senate and by the Court. There was one Court of Cassation for the whole kingdom. There were three Courts of Appeal, and there were Assize Courts for criminal cases. The country was divided into 26 judicial arrondissements or districts, in each of which was a court of first instance. In each canton there was a justice of the peace, a police court, and a judge of the peace; there were, in 1892, 212 such cantons. There were, besides, special military, commercial and other tribunals, represented by law. There was trial by jury in all criminal and political cases.

DENMARK

The lowest courts of justice in Denmark were those of the hundred or district magistrates (*herredsfogder* and *Birkedommere*) and town judges (*byfogder*). From these courts an appeal lay to the superior court or court of second instance, in Viborg with 9 judges, and in Copenhagen with 17 judges. The Copenhagen superior court, however, was identical with that of the civic magistrates. The supreme court (*Hojesteret*) or court of final appeal, with a chief justice, 12 puisne judges and 11 special judges sat in Copenhagen.

FRANCE

The courts of first instance in France were those of the Justices of Peace and the Police Court, where all petty offences were disposed of. The Police Correctional Courts pronounced upon all graver cases of misdemeanour (*délits*) including cases involving several years' imprisonment. They had no jury, and consisted of 3 judges. In all general cases, the preliminary inquiry was made in secrecy by an examining magistrate (*juge d' instruction*), who might dismiss the case or send it for trial. The Court of Assizes was assisted by 12 jurors, who decided by simple majority. The highest courts were the 26 Courts of Appeal, composed each of 1 President and 4 Councillors for all criminal cases which had been tried without a jury, and by 1 Court of Cassation which sat at Paris and was composed of a First President, 3 Presidents of Sections, and 45 Councillors, for all criminal cases tried by jury.

For civil cases there was, under the Justice of Peace in each arrondissement, a civil tribunal of first instance, then the Appeal Courts and Courts of

Cassation. For commercial cases there were Tribunals of Commerce and Councils of Experts.

All judges were nominated by the President of the Republic, and could be dismissed by him, and could be removed only by a decision of the Court of Cassation constituted as the *Conseil Supérieur* of the magistracy.

GERMANY

In terms of judicature acts in 1877 and 1879 a uniform system of law courts was adopted throughout the empire not later than 1 Jan 1879, though, with the exception of the *Reichsgerichte*, all courts were directly subject to the government of the special state in which they exercised jurisdiction, and not to the imperial government. The appointment of the judges was also a state and not an imperial function. The empire enjoyed uniform codes of commercial and criminal law, but the civil code of 18 Aug 96 did not come into force until 1 Jan 1900.

The lowest courts of first instance were the *Amtsgerichte*, each with a single judge, competent to try petty civil and criminal cases. *The Landgerichte* exercised a revising jurisdiction over the *Amtsgerichte*, and also a more extensive original jurisdiction in both civil and criminal cases, divorce cases, etc. In the criminal chamber five judges sat, and a majority of four votes was required for a conviction. Jury courts (*Schwurgerichte*) were also held periodically, in which three judges presided; the jury were 12 in number. The first court of second instance was the *Oberlandesgerichte*. In its criminal senate, which also had an original jurisdiction in serious cases, the number of judges was 7. There were 28 such courts in the empire. In Bavaria alone there was an *Oberste Landesgerichte*, with a revising jurisdiction over the Bavarian *Oberlandesgerichte*. The supreme court was the *Reichsgerichte*, which sat at Leipzig. The judges were appointed by the Emperor on the advice of the *Bundesrath*. The court exercised an appellate jurisdiction over all inferior courts, and also an original jurisdiction in cases of treason. It had 4 criminal and 6 civil senates.

ALSACE-LORRAINE

Alsace-Lorraine had an *Oberlandesgericht* at Colmar and 6 *Landgerichte*.

BAVARIA

Bavaria was the only German State which had established an *Oberste Landesgericht*, or appeal court intervening between the *Oberlandesgerichte* and the *Reichsgericht*. This court had its seat at Munich, with a bench of 18 judges.

BREMEN

Bremen contained 2 *Amtsgerichte* and a *Landgericht*, whence appeals lay to the *Hanseatische Oberlandesgericht* at Hamburg.

HAMBURG

The state contained 3 *Amtsgerichte*, a *Landgericht*, and the *Hanseatische Oberlandesgericht* or court of appeal for the Hanse towns and the principality of Lübeck (Oldenburg).

LUBECK

Lübeck contained an *Amtsgericht* and a *Landgericht*, whence the appeal lay to the *Hanseatisches Oberlandesgericht* at Hamburg.

MECKLENBURG-SCHWERIN

The grand-duchy contained 43 *Amtsgerichte*, 3 *Landgerichte*, and 1 *Oberlandesgericht* at Rostock, which was also the supreme court for Mecklenburg-Strelitz. There were also certain special military and ecclesiastical tribunals.

OLDENBURG

Oldenburg contained an *Oberlandesgericht* and a *Landgericht*. The *Amtsgerichte* of Lübeck and Birkenfeld were under the jurisdiction of the *Landgerichte* at Lübeck and Saarbrücken, respectively.

PRUSSIA

Prussia contained 15 *Oberlandesgerichte*. The *Oberlandesgericht* at Berlin was called the *Kammergericht*, and served as an ultimate appeal court for summary convictions; though for all cases the court of final instance was the *Reichsgericht* at Leipzig. The prosecution in all criminal cases was conducted by *Staatsanwälte*, or public prosecutors, paid by the state.

SAXE-WEIMAR

Saxe-Weimar contained two *Landgerichte*, while the district of Neustadt was subject to the jurisdiction of the *Landgericht* at Gera. The *Oberlandesgericht* at Jena was a common court of appeal for the 4 Saxon duchies, Schwarzburg-Rudolstadt, the 2 Reuss principalities, and parts of Prussia.

SAXONY

Saxony had 1 *Oberlandesgericht*, at Dresden, 7 *Landgerichte*, and 103 *Amtsgerichte*. The *Reichsgericht* had its seat at Leipzig.

WURTTEMBERG

In Württemberg there was 1 *Oberlandesgericht* at Stuttgart.

HUNGARY

In Hungary the ordinary judicial authorities were: The Royal Court (*kir. kuria*) in Budapest and the Supreme Court of Justice (Table of Septemvirs), in Zágreb (*Agram*) of the highest instance in all civil and criminal matters; 12 Royal Tables (*Királyi táblak*) of second instance. As courts of first instance, 76 county courts (*törvényszékek*) with collegiate judgeships; 457 district courts (*járásbiróságok*) with single judges; 15 jury courts (*sajtóbiróságok*) for press offences, besides an army special court.

ITALY

In Italy, justice in penal matters was administered in the first instance by the *Pretori*, by the penal tribunals, and by the courts of assize; on appeal, by the penal tribunals, and by the courts of appeal. The highest court was the Court of Cassation, which confined itself to inquiring whether the forms prescribed by law had been observed. The new penal code came into force on 1 Jan 90, abolishing the distinction between crimes and misdemeanours, *crimini e delitti*.

The *Pretori* had jurisdiction concerning all offences, *delitti* punishable by imprisonment or banishment not exceeding 3 months, or by fine not exceeding 300 lire. The penal tribunals had jurisdiction in the first instance in offences punishable by imprisonment or banishment over 3 months, or fines exceeding 300 lire. The courts of assize, which in most cases had juries, had jurisdiction in the first instance in all proceedings concerning crimes brought before them by direct citation, or by sentence of the sections of accusation (*sezioni d'accusa*). They had exclusive jurisdiction concerning offences against the internal and external security of the state, and all crimes of a serious character. Appeal was allowed to the penal tribunals from the sentences of the *Pretori*, and to the courts of appeal from those of the penal tribunals. The courts of cassation had power to annul, for illegality, sentences passed by the inferior courts, and to decide questions of jurisdiction or competency.

Italy was divided, for the administration of justice, into 20 appeals court districts, each of which was subdivided into tribunal districts, and these again into *mandamenti*, each with its own magistracy (*Pretura*).

MONTENEGRO

There were district courts in 4 or 5 of the principal towns. In rural districts justice was administered in the first instance by the local *knezes*, but the *Veliki Sud* or supreme court at Cettinjé had jurisdiction, both appellate and concurrent, over the whole principality, and in the last resort there lay an appeal to the Prince in person.

THE NETHERLANDS

Justice was administered by the High Court of the Netherlands, Court of Cassation (formerly Appeal), 5 Courts of Appeal (formerly Justice), 23 district tribunals, and 106 cantonal courts. Trial by jury was non-existent.

All judges were appointed for life by the King, the judges of the High Court from a list prepared by the Second Chamber. They could be removed only by a decision of the High Court.

NORWAY

For civil justice Norway was divided into 117 (1892) districts, each with an inferior court. Of these 81 were rural courts, divided into 424 circuits. The other courts were in towns. There were 3 superior courts having each 1 chief justice and 2 other justices, and 1 supreme court for the whole kingdom (*Hoiesteret*) consisting of 1 president and at least 6 other justices. There was a court of mediation (*Forliegelseskommission*) in each town and parish (*Herred*), consisting of 2 men chosen by the electors before which, as a rule, civil cases were first brought.

According to the law of criminal procedure of 1 July 87, all criminal cases (not military, or coming under the *Rigsret*—the court for impeachments) were tried either by jury, *Lagmandsret* or *Meddomsret*.

The *Lagmandsret* consisted of 3 judges, 1 president (*Lagmand*), and 10 jurors (*Lagrettemand*). The kingdom was divided into 5 jury districts (*Lagdommer*) each having its chief judge (*Lagmand*). Each district was divided into circuits corresponding, as a rule, to the counties (*Amter*) in which courts were held at fixed times. The *Meddomsret* consisted of the judge and was held in the district of the inferior court, and 2 assistant judges, not professional, summoned for each case. The *Lagmandsret* took cognizance of the higher classes of offences. The *Meddomsret* was for the trial of other offences and was also court of first instance.

The prosecutions were directed by the state advocates (*Statsadvokater*), 13 in number, subordinate to 1 *Rigsadvokat*.

PORTUGAL

Portugal was divided for judicial purposes into *comarcas*; in every *comarca* there was a court of first instance. More than half of the chief towns were seats of such courts. There were 3 courts of appeal (*Tribunaes de Relacao*) at Lisbon, Oporto and Ponta Delgada (Azores) and a Supreme Court in Lisbon.

RUSSIA

The administration of justice was reformed by a law of Nov 64 which instituted assize courts with juries; elective justices of peace with functions similar to those of English magistrates; assemblies of justices of peace, before which appeals from judgements of individual magistrates might be brought; appeal courts for rehearing cases not tried by jury. Above all these courts was the Court of Cassation, which formed part of the Senate. This system never became general throughout the empire. The examining magistrates, who ought on principle to have been irremovable, were very rarely confirmed in their office, and the investigation of criminal cases was entrusted to magistrates temporarily appointed. By law of 20 May 85 the principle of irremovability was restricted; by laws of 9 May 78 and 7 July 89 the assistance of a jury in certain cases was suppressed. A law of 12 July 89 abolished elective justices of peace, putting in their places in the country districts the country chiefs, and in the towns the urban justices; in both cases the appointments being made by the Minister of Justice. Justices of peace had been retained only in the two capitals and in 6 of the largest towns of the empire.

Reformed tribunals, but without juries, were introduced in Poland in 1875, in the Baltic provinces in 1889, in the governments of Ufa, Orenburg, Astrakhan, and Olonets in 1894, and in Siberia in 1897. The reformed system of justice was extended over Turkestan, the provinces of the steppes, the north-eastern districts of Vologda, and the Transcaspian province in 1898 and 1899.

SERBIA

The judges were appointed by the King, but according to the constitution could not be removed against their will; however, when the constitution was suspended on 9 May 94, their irremovability ceased. There were (1892) 22 courts of first instance, a court of appeal, a court of cassation, and a tribunal of commerce.

SWEDEN

The administration of justice was entirely independent of the government. Two functionaries, the chancellor of justice (*Justitie-Kansler*) and the attorney-general (*Justitie-Ombudsman*) exercised a control over the administration. The former, appointed by the King, acted also as a counsel for the Crown; while the latter, who was appointed by the Diet, extended a general supervision over all the courts of law. The kingdom, which possessed one Supreme Court of Judicature, was divided into 3 high court districts and 206 district court divisions, of which 90 were urban districts and 116 country districts in 1892.

In towns these district courts (or courts of first instance) were held by the burgomaster and his assessors; in the country by a judge and 12 jurors (peasant proprietors) the judge alone deciding—unless the jurors unanimously differed from him, in which case their decision prevailed. In Sweden trial by jury only existed for affairs of the press.

SWITZERLAND

The Federal Tribunal (*Bundes-Gericht*), which sat at Lausanne, consisted of 14 members, with 9 supplementary judges appointed by the Federal Assembly for 6 years, the president and vice-president, as such for 2 years. The tribunal had 2 sections, to each of which was assigned the trial of suits in accordance with regulations framed by the tribunal itself. It had original and final jurisdiction in suits between the confederation and cantons; between one canton and another; between the confederation or cantons and corporations or individuals, the value in dispute being not less than 3000 francs; between parties who referred their case to it, the value in dispute being at least 3000 francs; and also in such suits as the constitution or legislation of cantons placed within its authority. There were also many classes of railway suits on which it took decisions. It was a court of appeal against decisions of other federal authorities, and of cantonal authorities applying federal laws. The tribunal also tried persons accused of treason or other offences against the confederation. For this purpose it was divided into four chambers: the Chamber of Accusation, the Criminal Chamber (*Cour d'Assises*), the Federal Penal Court, and the Court of Cassation. The jurors who served in the assize courts were elected by the people.

Each canton had its own judicial system for ordinary civil and criminal trials.

UNITED KINGDOM

ENGLAND AND WALES

The principal courts having criminal jurisdiction were the petty sessional courts, the general or quarter sessions, the courts of oyer and terminer and gaol delivery, more popularly known as 'assizes', and the Central Criminal Court. Two or more justices of the peace sitting in a petty sessional court house, the Lord Mayor or any alderman of the City of London, or any metropolitan or borough police magistrate or other stipendiary magistrate sitting in a court house, constituted a petty sessional court. The courts of quarter sessions were held 4 times a year by the justices of the county. Similar courts could be held at other times, and were then called 'general sessions'. Two justices constituted a court, but usually a larger number attended. Certain boroughs had a court of quarter sessions with similar jurisdiction to the county justices in quarter sessions assembled, in which the recorder of the borough was the judge. The assize courts were held four times a year in various towns throughout the country by 'commissioners' nominated by the Crown. These commissioners were generally judges of the King's Bench Division of the High Court of Justice, but sometimes King's Counsel of good standing were appointed. The trial took place before a single commissioner. The Central Criminal Court was the court of oyer and terminer and gaol delivery for the City of London and a large surrounding district. The sessions of this court were held at least 12 times a year, and more often if necessary. The Recorder and the Common Serjeant, and, if the number of the prisoners made it necessary, the judge of the City of London Court, sat on the first 2 days, after which they were joined by the judges of the High Court on the rota, for whom the more serious cases were reserved. A petty sessional court dealt summarily with minor offences. Cases of a more serious nature were usually investigated by a petty sessional court before being tried at the sessions or the assizes. To every session, assize, and to every sitting of the Central Criminal Court the sheriff cited 24 of the chief inhabitants of the district, of whom not less than 12 and not more than 23 were sworn and constituted a grand jury. The grand jury examined the bill of indictment against the accused person, heard the evidence of witnesses for the prosecution, and if they thought a *prima facie* case for trial was made out they endorsed the bill 'a true bill'. All criminal trials, except those which came before a court of summary jurisdiction, took place before a judge and a petty jury of 12 men. Except on some highly technical point of procedure there was no appeal in criminal cases. No man could be tried again for the same crime after a petty jury had found him 'not guilty'. On a conviction the judge could, if he thought fit, reserve a question of law (but not of fact) for the Court for Crown Cases Reserved. This Court was formed by 5 or more judges of the High Court, and could reverse, amend, or affirm the judgement. The only other method of securing the revision of a sentence was by the Royal prerogative, exercised on the advice of the Home Secretary, by which a sentence could be modified or annulled. Nominally all the judges were appointed by the King, but in practice the Lord Chancellor (who was a Cabinet minister, *ex-officio* president of the House of Lords, and went out with the ministry) and the Lord Chief Justice were appointed on the recommendation of the Prime Minister, and all the other judges on the recommendation of the Lord Chancellor.

SCOTLAND

The High Court of Justiciary was the supreme criminal court in Scotland. It consisted of all the judges of the Court of Session, and sat more or less frequently as the number of cases before it might require in Edinburgh or in the circuit towns. One judge could, and usually did, try cases, but 2 or more presided in cases of difficulty or importance. It was the only competent court in cases of treason, murder, robbery, rape, fire-raising, deforcement of messengers, and generally in all cases in which a higher punishment than imprisonment was by statute directed to be inflicted; and it had moreover an inherent jurisdiction to punish all criminal acts, both those already established by common law or statute, and such as had never previously come before the courts and were not within any statute.

The sheriff of each county was the proper criminal judge in all crimes occurring within the county which inferred only an arbitrary punishment, and if the case was tried with a jury the High Court had no power of review on the merits. Even in cases indicted to the High Court the accused was, under the Criminal Procedure (Scotland) Act of 1887, regularly asked to plead in the sheriff court, and minor objections to the indictment could be wholly or in part disposed of there. Borough magistrates and justices of the peace had jurisdiction in petty cases occurring within the county (burgh), and in a number of minor offences under various statutes.

162

In Ireland persons charged with crime were first brought before the petty sessions court, which consisted of at least 2 ordinary justices of the peace, 1 of whom *might* be a stipendiary—commonly called a resident magistrate. Then if the charge was trifling it might be disposed of; the prisoner, if convicted, had a right of appeal to the quarter sessions or recorder's court (according as it was in a borough or in the county), provided he was fined more than 20 shillings or sentenced to a longer imprisonment than 1 month (Petty Sessions Act, sec. 24). If the charge was of a more serious character it had either to be dismissed or sent for trial to the quarter sessions or recorder's court, or to the assizes as in England. There was this difference, however, between quarter sessions in Ireland and in England: in England they were presided over by an unpaid chairman, who need not be a lawyer and who was elected by his fellow justices of the peace for the county; while in Ireland they were presided over by a paid official, who must be a barrister, whose decision on points of law bound the court, who was appointed by the Crown, and who was also judge of the civil bill court of the county, which corresponded to the English county court. The assizes were presided over by one of the common law judges of the High Court of Justice. In the quarter sessions, recorder's court, and assizes the trial was by jury in all cases save appeals from petty sessions. Under the Crimes Act witnesses and persons suspected of crime might be interrogated before a secret court of inquiry; but admissions then made were not evidence against the persons making them. Prisoners might be convicted before 2 resident magistrates specially appointed to hear cases under the Crimes Act, and in cases where the sentence exceeded a month, convicted persons had a right of appeal to the county chairman at quarter sessions.

8 DEFENCE AND TREATIES

EUROPEAN TREATIES 1848–1914

1849	1 May	Balta-Liman	Russia and Turkey	Agreement regarding Moldavia and Wallachia
	6 Aug	Milan	Sardinia and Austria	Treaty of peace
1850	2 Jul	Berlin	Denmark and the King of Prussia (for Prussia and for the Germanic Confederation)	Treaty of peace
	29 Nov	Olmütz	Austria and Prussia	Affairs of Holstein and Hesse–Cassel
1851	24 May–5 June	Warsaw	Denmark and Russia	Protocol on the Danish succession
1852	8 May	London	Britain, Austria, France, Prussia, Russia, Denmark, Sweden and Norway	Succession to the Crown of Denmark
	20 Nov	London	Britain, Bavaria, France, Greece and Russia	The Greek succession
1854	12 Mar	Constantinople	Britain, France and Turkey	Military aid for Turkey
	9 Apr	Vienna	Britain, France, Austria and Prussia	Maintenance of the integrity of the Ottoman Empire
	10 Apr	London	Britain and France	Military aid for Turkey
	20 Apr	Berlin	Austria and Prussia	Offensive and defensive alliance
	14 June	Boyadji-Keuy	Austria and Turkey	Austrian occupation of the Danubian Principalities
	2 Dec	Vienna	Britain, Austria and France	Treaty of alliance
1855	26 Jan	Turin	Britain, France and Sardinia	Military convention
	3 Feb	Constantinople	Britain and Turkey	Employment of Turkish troops in British service
	21 Nov	Stockholm	Britain, France, Sweden and Norway	Preservation of United Kingdom of Sweden and Norway
1856	30 Mar	Paris	Britain, Austria, France, Prussia, Russia, Sardinia and Turkey	Treaty of peace, with annexation regarding the straits of the Dardanelles and the Bosphorus

	30 Mar	Paris	Russia and Turkey	Limitation of naval forces in the Black Sea
	30 Mar	Paris	Britain, France and Russia	Demilitarization of the Aaland Islands
	14 Apr	Paris	Britain, Austria, France, Prussia, Russia, Sardinia and Turkey	Protocol on avoidance of future conflicts by recourse to the mediation of a third power
	15 Apr	Paris	Britain, Austria and France	Guarantee of independence and integrity of Ottoman Empire
1857	30 Mar – 11 Apr	Kishinev	Britain, France, Austria, Russia and Turkey	Settlement of the Bessarabian frontier
	19 June	Paris	Britain, Austria, France, Prussia, Russia, Sardinia and Turkey	Agreement regarding the Bessarabian Frontier, the Isle of Serpents, and the delta of the Danube
	5 Dec	Constantinople	Britain, Russia and Turkey	Turco-Russian boundary in Asia
1858	20 July	Plombières	France and Sardinia	Secret treaty of alliance
	19 Aug	Paris	Britain, Austria, France, Prussia, Russia, Sardinia and Turkey	Convention regarding United Principalities of Moldavia and Wallachia
1859	11 July	Villafranca	Austria and France	Preliminary peace treaty
	10 Nov	Zurich	Austria, France and Sardinia	Treaties of peace
	10 Nov	Zurich	France and Sardinia	Treaty of alliance
	10 Nov	Zurich	France and Austria	Declaration concerning Italian provinces of Austria to form part of Italian Confederation
1860	23 Jan	Paris	Britain and France	Commercial treaty
	19 Mar	Paris	Britain, Austria, France, Prussia, Russia and Turkey	Prolonged European occupation of Syria
	24 Mar	Turin	France and Sardinia	Annexation of Savoy and Nice to France
1863	13 July	London	Britain, France, Russia and Denmark	Accession of Prince William of Denmark to the Greek throne
	14 Nov	London	Britain, Austria, France, Prussia and Russia	Regarding the Ionian Islands
1864	29 Mar	London	Britain, France, Russia and Greece	Union of Ionian Islands and Kingdom of Greece
	20 June	Constantinople	Turkey and Prince Couza	United Principalities of Moldavia and Wallachia
	30 Oct	Vienna	Austria, Prussia and Denmark	Treaty of peace
1865	14 Aug	Gastein	Austria and Prussia	Convention regarding Schleswig-Holstein and Lauenburg
1866	26 July	Nikolsburg	Austria and Prussia	Preliminary peace treaty
	23 Aug	Prague	Austria and Prussia	Treaty of peace
	3 Oct	Vienna	Austria and Italy	Treaty of peace

165

1867	11 May	London	Britain, Austria, Belgium, France, Italy, the Netherlands, Prussia and Russia	Luxembourg and the Duchy of Limburg
1869	20 Jan	Paris	Britain, Austria, France, Italy, Prussia, Russia and Turkey	Declaration on Greco-Turkish relations
1870	9 Aug	London	Britain and Prussia	Independence and neutrality of Belgium
	11 Aug	London	Britain and France	Independence and neutrality of Belgium
1871	17 Jan	London	Britain, Austria, France, Italy, North Germany, Russia and Turkey	Declaration on binding force of treaties
	28 Jan	Versailles	France and Germanic Confederation	Convention of armistice
	26 Feb	Versailles	France and Germany	Preliminary peace treaty
	13 Mar	London	Britain, Austria, France, Germany, Italy, Russia and Turkey	Navigation of Black Sea and the Danube
	16 Mar	Rouen	France and Germany	Return of occupied areas to French control
	10 May	Frankfurt	France and Germany	Treaty of peace
1873	25 May – 6 June	Schönbrunn	Austria-Hungary and Russia	Co-operation against subversion of peace of Europe
1877	15 Jan	Budapest	Austria-Hungary and Russia	An understanding over the Balkans
	16 Apr	Bucharest	Russia and Romania	Convention regulating passage of Russian troops through Romania
1878	19–31 Jan	Adrianople	Russia, Serbia, Romania and Turkey	Convention of armistice
	19 Feb – 3 Mar	San Stefano	Russia and Turkey	Preliminary peace treaty
	4 June	Constantinople	Britain and Turkey	Defensive alliance with respect to Asiatic provinces of Turkey
	1 July	Constantinople	Britain and Turkey	Conditions of British occupation and administration of Cyprus
	11–12 July	Berlin	Britain and Russia	Declaration regarding the Straits
	13 July	Berlin	Britain, Austria-Hungary, France, Germany, Italy, Russia and Turkey	Settlement of affairs in the East
	14 Aug	Therapia	Britain and Turkey	Concerning British occupation of Cyprus
1879	27 Jan – 8 Feb	Constantinople	Russia and Turkey	Treaty of peace
	21 Apr	Constantinople	Austria-Hungary and Turkey	Concerning occupation and administration by Austria-Hungary of Bosnia-Herzegovina

	7 Oct	Vienna	Austria-Hungary and Germany	Treaty of alliance
1881	24 May	Constantinople	Britain, Germany, Austria-Hungary, France, Italy, Russia and Turkey	Settlement of Greco-Turkish frontier
	16–28 June	Belgrade	Austria-Hungary and Serbia	Treaty of alliance
	18 June	Berlin	Austria-Hungary, Germany and Russia	'The League of the Three Emperors'
	2 July	Constantinople	Greece and Turkey	Settlement of frontier
1882	14 May	Constantinople	Russia and Turkey	Settlement of Russian war indemnity
	20 May	Vienna	Austria-Hungary, Germany and Italy	First treaty of Triple Alliance
	25 June	Therapia	Britain, Austria-Hungary, France, Germany, Italy and Russia	Self-restraint in dealing with affairs of Egypt
1883	10 Mar	London	Britain, Austria-Hungary, France, Germany, Italy, Russia and Turkey	Navigation of the Danube
	22 Mar	Vienna	Austria-Hungary and Germany	Prolonged alliance of 1879 for 5 years
	30 Oct	Vienna	Austria-Hungary and Romania (with accession of Germany and Italy)	Treaty of alliance
1884	27 Mar	Berlin	Austria-Hungary, Germany and Russia	Prolonged alliance of 1881
1885	26 Feb	Berlin	Britain, Austria-Hungary, Belgium, Denmark, France, Germany, Italy, the Netherlands, Portugal, Russia, Spain, Sweden and Norway, and Turkey	General act of conference at Berlin on the African continent
	17 Mar	London	Britain, Austria-Hungary, France, Germany, Italy, Russia and Turkey	Declaration on Egyptian finances, and free navigation of the Suez Canal
	18 Mar	London	Britain, Austria-Hungary, France, Germany, Italy, Russia and Turkey	Convention on finances of Egypt
	29 Apr	London	Britain and Germany	Agreement on spheres of action in Africa
	25 July	–	Britain, Austria-Hungary, France, Italy, Russia and Turkey	Declaration on payment of Egyptian loan
	10 Sep	London	Britain and Russia	Protocol on Afghan frontier
1886	3 Mar	Bucharest	Serbia and Bulgaria	Treaty of peace
1887	12 Feb–24 Mar	London	Britain, Austria-Hungary and Italy	Agreement on the Mediterranean
	20 Feb	Berlin	Austria-Hungary, Germany and Italy	Second treaty of Triple Alliance
	4 May	Madrid	Italy and Spain (with accession of Austria-Hungary)	Mediterranean agreement
	18 June	Berlin	Germany and Russia	'Reinsurance Treaty'

	12–16 Dec	London	Britain, Austria-Hungary and Italy	Second Mediterranean agreement
1888	29 Oct	Constantinople	Britain and Austria-Hungary, France, Germany, Italy, the Netherlands, Russia, Spain and Turkey	Convention on free navigation of Suez Canal
1889	28 Jan– 9 Feb	Belgrade	Austria-Hungary and Serbia	Prolonged treaty of 1881
	14 June	Berlin	Britain, Germany and the United States	Final act of conference on Samoa
1890	1 July	Berlin	Britain and Germany	Cession of Heligoland and colonial agreement
	2 July	Brussels	Britain, Austria, Belgium, Congo, Denmark, France, Germany, Italy, the Netherlands, Persia, Portugal, Russia, Spain, Sweden and Norway, Turkey, United States, Zanzibar (accessions: Abyssinia, Liberia and Orange Free State)	General Act of conference on African slave trade
	5 Aug	London	Britain and France	Declaration on territories in Africa
1891	4 May	Madrid	Spain and Italy (with accession of Austria-Hungary)	Prolonged Mediterranean agreement of 1887
	6 May	Berlin	Austria-Hungary, Germany and Italy	Third treaty of Triple Alliance
	26 June	Paris	Britain and France	Demarcation of spheres of influence in Africa
	9–27 Aug	Paris	France and Russia	Understanding on action if threatened with aggression
1892	13–25 July	Sinaia	Austria-Hungary and Romania (with accession of Germany and Italy)	Second treaty of Alliance
1893	8 July	Berlin	Britain and Germany	Delimitation of Anglo-German boundary in East Equatorial Africa
	12 July	Paris	Britain and France	Agreement on boundaries on the Gold Coast
	31 July	Paris	Britain and France	Protocol on territories in Upper Mekong region
	15 Nov	Berlin	Britain and Germany	Agreement on boundaries in Africa
	15–27 Dec	St Petersburg	France and Russia	Adoption of military convention drawn up in 1892
1894	5 May	Rome	Britain and Italy	Agreement on spheres of influence in Eastern Africa
1896	30 Sep	Sinaia	Austria-Hungary and Romania (with accession of Germany and Italy)	Prolonged treaty of 1892

168

1897	5–17 May	Vienna	Austria-Hungary and Russia	Agreement on Balkan affairs
	18 Sep	Paris	Britain and France	Convention on Tunis
	4 Dec	Constantinople	Greece and Turkey	Treaty of peace
1898	14 June	Paris	Britain and France	Possessions and spheres of influence to West and East of the Niger
	30 Aug	London	Britain and Germany	Agreement over Angola, Mozambique and Portuguese Timor
1899	28 July– 9 Aug	St Petersburg	France and Russia	Modifying convention of 1893
	7 Nov– 2 Dec	Washington	Britain, Germany and United States	Agreement over Samoa
1900	20 Mar		United States, France, Germany, Britain, Italy, Japan and Russia	Exchange of letters with Washington accepting commercial policy of the 'Open Door' in China
	16 Oct	London	Britain and Germany	Agreement over China
	20 Dec	Rome	Austria-Hungary and Italy	Agreement over Albania
	Dec– Nov 1902	Rome	France and Italy	Exchange of letters concerning Morocco and Tripolitania
1901	7 Sep	Peking	Germany, Austria-Hungary, Belgium, Spain, United States, France, Britain, Italy, Japan, the Netherlands, Russia and China	Final protocol for settlement of disturbances in China
1902	4–17 Apr	Bucharest	Austria-Hungary and Romania (with accession of Germany and Italy)	Renewed alliances of 1892 and 1896
	1 June	Berlin	Austria-Hungary and Germany	Protocol continuing treaty of 1879 and protocol of 1883
	28 June	Berlin	Austria-Hungary, Germany and Italy	Fourth treaty of Triple Alliance
1904	31 Mar	Sofia	Bulgaria and Serbia	Treaties of alliance and friendship
	8 Apr	London	Britain and France	Settlement of colonial problems
	2–15 Oct	St Petersburg	Austria-Hungary and Russia	Declaration of neutrality if other at war
	3 Oct	Paris	France and Spain	Convention over Morocco
1906	7 Apr	Algeciras	Britain, Austria-Hungary, Belgium, France, Germany, Italy, Morocco, Portugal, the Netherlands, Russia, Spain, Sweden and United States	General Act of conference on affairs of Morocco
1907	31 Aug	St Petersburg	Britain and Russia	Convention on Persia, Afghanistan and Tibet

1909	9 Feb	Berlin	France and Germany	Declaration on Morocco
	30 Nov – 15 Dec	Vienna-Rome	Austria-Hungary and Italy	Supplementing treaty of Triple Alliance of 1887
1911	4 Nov	Berlin	France and Germany	Convention on Morocco
1912	29 Feb	Sofia	Bulgaria and Serbia	Friendship and alliance
	29 Apr	Varna	Bulgaria and Serbia	Military convention
	16–29 May	Sofia	Bulgaria and Greece	Defensive alliance
	16 July	Paris	France and Russia	Naval convention
	12 Sep – 6 Oct	Lucerne	Serbia and Montenegro	Treaty of alliance
	22 Sep	Sofia	Greece and Bulgaria	Military convention
	15 Oct	Ouchy	Italy and Turkey	Treaty of peace
	28 Oct	Paris	France and Italy	Exchange of notes on Libya and Morocco
	5 Dec	Vienna	Austria-Hungary, Germany and Italy	Fifth treaty of Triple Alliance
1913	5 Feb	Bucharest	Austria-Hungary and Romania (with accession of Germany and Italy)	Renewed previous alliances
	22 Apr – 5 May	Athens	Greece and Serbia	Protocol on conclusion of an alliance
	1–14 May	Salonika	Greece and Serbia	Military convention
	19 May – 1 June	Salonika	Greece and Serbia	Alliance and military convention
	30 May	London	Turkey and Balkan allies	Treaty of peace
	28 July – 10 Aug	Bucharest	Bulgaria, Romania, Greece, Montenegro and Serbia	Treaty of peace
	2 Aug	Vienna	Austria-Hungary, Germany and Italy	Naval agreement
	29 Sep	Constantinople	Turkey and Bulgaria	Treaty of peace
	14 Nov	Athens	Turkey and Greece	Treaty of peace
1914	15 June	London	Britain and Germany	Agreement over Baghdad Railway
	12 Aug	Lisbon	Britain and Portugal	Treaty of Commerce and Navigation
	5 Sep	London	Britain, France and Russia (accessions: Japan and Italy)	Declaration not to conclude a separate peace

PRINCIPAL EUROPEAN ARMED CONFLICTS 1848 – 1914

HUNGARIAN INSURRECTION. *March 1848 – August 1849*
Austria, Hungary, Russia

Revolution in Hungary began 15 Mar 48. Austrian forces invaded Hungary to reassert control 11 Sep 48. Buda fell 4 Jan 49 but was reoccupied by the Hungarians in May. Intervention by Russian forces in June 49. The Hungarians were defeated 9 Aug 49, and surrendered to the Russians at Vilagos 13 Aug 49.

ITALIAN WAR. *March 1848— August 1849*
Austria, Sardinia

Precipitated by revolt in Milan 18–23 Mar 48. Charles Albert of Sardinia declared war on Austria 24 Mar 48, but was defeated by General Radetsky in battles around Custozza 23–5 July 48. An armistice was arranged at Vigevano 9 Aug 48. Renewed fighting in Mar 49, and a further Austrian victory at Novara 23 Mar 49. Charles Albert abdicated, and his son Victor Emanuel made peace by the Treaty of Milan 6 Aug 49.

PRUSSO-DANISH WAR. *March 1848—May 1852*
Prussia, Denmark

The duchies of Schleswig-Holstein declared their independence of Denmark 24 Mar 48, and the Prussian army intervened in support of the rebels in Apr 48. Truce of Malmö signed 26 Aug 48. Fighting broke out again in Apr 49, but a fresh truce was arranged after international pressure 10 July 49. A peace treaty was signed in July 50, and a final settlement, including a Great Powers guarantee of Danish integrity, by the Treaty of London 8 May 52.

TURKISH-MONTENEGRAN WAR. *December 1852—March 1853*
Turkey, Montenegro

Turkey declared war after the seizure of a town in Turkish territory. After diplomatic intervention by Austria in support of Montenegro an armistice was signed 12 Feb 53, and a peace treaty 3 weeks later.

CRIMEAN WAR. *October 1853— March 1856*
Turkey, Russia, Britain, France, Sardinia

Fighting between Turkey and Russia began in Oct 53, and the Turkish fleet was destroyed at Sinope 30 Nov 53. France and Britain declared war on Russia 27 Mar 54. Allied troops landed in the Crimea 14 Sep 54, and besieged Sebastopol. The battle of Balaclava was fought 25 Oct 54, and the battle of Inkerman 5 Nov 54. After a Military Convention 26 Jan 55, 15,000 Sardinian troops joined the allies. The Russians evacuated Sebastopol 8 Sep 55, and under threat of an Austrian declaration of war they accepted peace preliminaries 1 Feb 56. A settlement was made at the Treaty of Paris 30 Mar 56.

ITALIAN WAR. *April — November 1859*
Austria, Sardinia, France

Napoleon III and Cavour made a secret agreement to attack Austria at Plombières in July 58. When war began 26 Apr 59, the Austrians invaded

Piedmont but withdrew into Lombardy, and were defeated at Magenta 4 June and Solferino 24 June 59, battles in which both sides suffered heavy casualties. Napoleon concluded an armistice at Villafranca 11 July 59 without consulting the Sardinians, and a settlement was made at the Treaty of Zurich 10 Nov 59.

ITALIAN REVOLUTION. *April 1860 – February 1861*
France, Naples, Sardinia

In Apr 60 a revolt broke out against Francis II at Palermo. Garibaldi landed in Sicily 11 May 60, and Naples fell to him 7 Sep 60. To forestall Garibaldi, Cavour marched Piedmontese troops into the Papal States 10 Sep 60. Francis II escaped from the last Bourbon stronghold of Gaeta in Feb 61. Garibaldi's conquests were annexed by Sardinia and the Kingdom of Italy was proclaimed at Turin 17 Mar 61.

POLISH INSURRECTION. *January 1863 – August 1864*
Poland, Russia

The insurrection began 22 Jan 63. It was eventually suppressed by the Russians in Aug 64 after a period of guerrilla warfare.

GERMAN-DANISH WAR. *February–October 1864*
Denmark, Prussia, Austria, Saxony, North German states

Prussia and Austria declared war on Denmark 1 Feb 64 after a dispute over the duchies of Schleswig and Holstein. An armistice was arranged 12 May, but a conference at London failed to settle the problem. A further period of successful military action by Prussia in June and July led to the Treaty of Vienna 30 Oct 64. The disputed territories were surrendered to an Austro-Prussian condominium, and became part of Prussia after the Seven Weeks' War of 1866.

SEVEN WEEKS' WAR. *June – October 1866*
Austria, Prussia, Baden, Bavaria, Hanover, Hesse, North German states, Sardinia, Saxony, Württemberg, France

Following a dispute with Austria over Schleswig and Holstein, Prussian troops advanced into Hanover, Saxony and Hesse 15 June 66. The Austrian forces were defeated at Sadowa 3 July 66. Armistice 22 July 66. Preliminary peace at Nikolsburg 26 July 66. Peace of Prague 23 Aug 66 – Austria to be excluded from German affairs. Despite defeats at Custozza 24 June 66 and in a sea battle off Lissa 20 July 66, the Italians received Venetia at the Treaty of Vienna 3 Oct 66.

CRETAN REVOLT. *August 1866—January 1869*
Greece, Turkey, Britain, France

Crete revolt against the Ottoman Empire and to achieve union with Greece. Greek volunteers assisted the rebels, until a declaration of the Great Powers 20 Jan 69 forbade Greece to allow further recruiting of volunteers and the rebellion petered out.

FRANCO-PRUSSIAN WAR. *July 1870— May 1871*
France, Prussia, Baden, Bavaria, North German states, Saxony, Württemberg

Precipitated by the incident of the Ems Telegram, arising out of Prussian support for the candidature of a Hohenzollern prince for the Spanish throne. France declared war 19 July 70. Series of French defeats—at Wörth 6 Aug 70, Vionville 16 Aug 70, Gravelotte 18 Aug 70, culminating in the capitulation of 120,000 men at Sedan 2 Sep 70. A further 173,000 French soldiers surrendered at Metz 27 Oct 70. Despite the efforts of forces hastily organized by Gambetta, Paris surrendered 28 Jan 71, and an armistice was agreed the same day. Revolt of the Paris commune 18 Mar − 28 May 71 suppressed by French government forces. By the Treaty of Frankfurt 10 May 71 France lost Alsace and most of Lorraine, and had to pay 5000 million francs indemnity.

SECOND CARLIST WAR. *April 1872—February 1876*
Spain

Revolt 8 Apr 72 against King Amedeo, who had been chosen as successor to Queen Isabella in Nov 70. The Basque provinces took up the cause of Don Carlos, but his supporters were defeated and signed the Convention of Amorebeita 24 May 72. Amedeo abdicated and left Spain 12 Feb 73. A republic was proclaimed, which led to renewed fighting by the Carlists. Restoration of the monarchy when Alfonso, Isabella's son, was proclaimed King 29 Sep 74. Don Carlos was forced to withdraw from Spain at the end of Feb 76.

BALKAN WARS. *July 1876— March 1878*
Russia, Turkey, Montenegro, Serbia, Romania

Revolts against Turkish rule in Bosnia-Herzegovina in July 75, and in Bulgaria the following May. Serbia and Montenegro declared war on Turkey 1–2 July 76. Russian declaration of war 24 Apr 77. Romania declared war on Turkey 11 May. Plevna fell to the Russians after a lengthy siege 10 Dec 77, and Adrianople was taken 20 Jan 78. Armistice 31 Jan. Treaty of San Stefano 3 Mar; its provision for the creation of a 'Big Bulgaria' was annulled by the Congress of Berlin.

SERBO-BULGAR WAR. *November 1885 – March 1886*
Serbia, Bulgaria

King Milan of Serbia declared war on Bulgaria in pursuit of territorial concessions 13–14 Nov 85. The Serbs advanced to Slivnitsa, but were defeated there 17–19 Nov, and the Bulgars entered Serbia. Diplomatic intervention by Austria, and the pre-war situation was restored at the peace of Bucharest 3 Mar 86.

CRETAN REVOLT. *May 1896 – December 1898*
Crete, Greece, Turkey

Disturbances on Crete in May 96. Greek troops landed in support of the rebels 4 Feb 97. Military and diplomatic intervention by the Great Powers; Cretan autonomy proclaimed 20 Mar 97. The Greeks withdrew from Crete 9 May 97, and the last Turkish soldiers left 14 Nov 98. The revolt was finally suppressed, in Dec 98, after the arrival in Crete of Prince George of Greece, who had been given the post of high commissioner by the Powers.

GRECO-TURKISH WAR. *April – December 1897*
Greece, Turkey

Greek aid to the Cretan rebels led Turkey to declare war on Greece 19 Apr 97. The Greeks were defeated, and forced to make an armistice 19 May. By the Treaty of Constantinople 4 Dec 97, Greece had to pay an indemnity to secure the restoration of Thessaly.

ITALO-TURKISH WAR. *September 1911 – October 1912*
Italy, Turkey

Italy declared war 29 Sep 11 in pursuit of territorial claims in Tripoli and Cyrenaica. Italy proclaimed their annexation 5 Nov 11, and routed the Turks at the end of the month. At the Treaty of Ouchy 15 Oct 12, Turkey surrendered Tripoli and Cyrenaica; contrary to the treaty, Italy retained Rhodes and the Dodecanese which they had occupied in May 12.

FIRST BALKAN WAR. *October 1912 – May 1913*
Bulgaria, Greece, Montenegro, Serbia, Turkey

Alliance of Balkan states against Turkey. War began 1 Oct 12. Ended by Treaty of London 30 May 13. Turkey withdrew from most of her Balkan territory, on the understanding that a new and independent Albania would be created.

SECOND BALKAN WAR. *June — August 1913*
Bulgaria, Greece, Romania, Serbia, Turkey

Friction between victors of First Balkan war. Bulgaria attacked Serbia and Greece 29 June 13. They themselves were invaded by the Romanians and Turks and rapidly defeated. Settlement at the Treaty of Bucharest 10 Aug 13; Turkey concluded peace treaties with Bulgaria 29 Sep 13 and with Greece 14 Nov 13.

PRINCIPAL CAMPAIGNS OUTSIDE EUROPE INVOLVING EUROPEAN POWERS 1848 – 1914

Second Anglo-Sikh War	Apr 1848–Apr 1849
French campaigns against Vietnamese	1851–57
Second Anglo-Burmese War	Feb 1852–June 1853
Russian conquest of Turkestan	July 1852–Jan 1864
Anglo-French War with China	Oct 1856–Oct 1860
British expedition against Persia	Dec 1856–Mar 1857
Indian Mutiny	May 1857–Apr 1859
Franco-Spanish operations in Cochin China	1858–62
Spanish-Moroccan War	Oct 1859–Apr 1860
French expedition to Mexico	Apr 1862–June 1867
Spanish-South American War	Sep 1865–May 1866
British expedition to Abyssinia	Oct 1867–Apr 1868
Cuban revolt against Spain	Oct 1868–Feb 1878
French suppression of Algerian revolt	1871
British campaign against the Ashanti	Oct 1873–Feb 1874
British conquest of Zululand	Dec 1878–July 1879
Second British campaign in Afghanistan	Nov 1878–Apr 1881
First Anglo-Boer War	Dec 1880–Aug 1881
French expedition against Tunisia	Mar 1881–Apr 1882
British suppression of nationalist revolt in Egypt	July–Sep 1882
French establishment of protectorate over Tongking	Dec 1882–Aug 1885
French establishment of protectorate over Madagascar	1883–1885
Anglo-Sudanese War	1884–5
First French War with the Mandinga (West Africa)	1885–6
Third Anglo-Burmese War	Nov 1885–1892
First Dahomey-French War	1889–90

British and Italian operations against Somaliland	1890–1920
German suppression of Wahehe rebellion in German East Africa	1891–3
Second Dahomey-French War	1892
Belgian conquest of East Congo	1892–4
Spanish hostilities with the Riff tribesmen	1893–4
Second French War with the Mandinga	1894–5
French conquest of Madagascar	Mar 1895–Aug 1896
Italo-Abyssinian War	Nov 1895–Oct 1896
British conquest of Ashantiland	1895–1900
British conquest of the Sudan	1896–9
Batetela War against Belgians on the Upper Congo	1897–1900
Third French War with the Mandinga	1898
Spanish-American War	Apr–Dec 1898
French conquest of Chad	1899–1900
Second Anglo-Boer War	Oct 1899–May 1902
Suppression of Boxer Rebellion in China by Belgium, Britain, France, the Netherlands, Spain, Austria, Germany, Italy, Russia, China, Japan and the United States	June 1900–Sep 1901
Portuguese suppression of uprising in Angola	1902
British, German and Italian blockade of Venezuela	Dec 1902–Feb 1903
British expedition to Tibet	Nov 1903–Sep 1904
German suppression of Herero and Hottentot revolts	1903–8
Russo-Japanese War	Feb 1904–Sep 1905
German suppression of rising in Kamerun	1904–5
German suppression of Maji-Maji rebellion in Tanganyika	1905–7
British suppression of Zulu revolt	Mar–Aug 1906
Dutch destruction of Venezuelan fleet	1908
French conquest of Mauretania	1908–9
Spanish-Moroccan War	1909–10

CASUALTIES IN MAJOR EUROPEAN WARS, 1848–1914

CRIMEAN WAR 1853–6

	Effective strength	Killed or died of wounds	Died of disease	Total fatalities	Wounded
France	310,000	20,240	73,375	93,615	47,000
Britain	98,000	4,602	17,580	22,182	13,000
Sardinia	21,000	28	2,166	2,194	..
Turkey	230,000	..	..	35,000	..
Russia	500,000	40,000	60,000	100,000	120,000

ITALIAN WAR 1859

	Total losses[1]
France	19,000
Austria	40,000
Sardinia	7,600

PRUSSO-DANISH WAR 1864

	Total losses[1]
Prussia	2,423
Austria	1,100
Denmark	11,000

SEVEN WEEKS' WAR 1866

	Effective strength	Total losses[1]
Austria	407,000	87,844
Austria's allies	137,000	24,618
Prussia	437,000	22,376
Italy	200,000	11,197

FRANCO-PRUSSIAN WAR 1870

	Total mobilized	Total losses[1]
Prussia	1,494,412	130,000
France	2,000,740[2]	580,000

FIRST AND SECOND BALKAN WARS 1912–13

	Total mobilized	Killed or died of wounds
Turkey	350,000	70,000
Bulgaria	370,000	50,000
Greece	220,000	7,500
Serbia-Montenegro	250,000	33,500
Romania	400,000	1,500

[1] Total losses include missing and prisoners.

[2] Including newly-formed corps and the National Guard of Paris; troops of the line and reserves numbered 935,740.

WORLD WAR I–THE WAR PLANS 1914

THE WEST

Germany: the Schlieffen Plan: devised by Count Alfred von Schlieffen, Chief of the German General Staff 1891–1905, to meet the dangers of a war on 2 fronts. Reversing the policy of his predecessors, Schlieffen decided to defeat France first, concentrating 90% of the German army in the west for a campaign which was to last no more than 6 weeks. While the left wing in Alsace-Lorraine remained on the defensive, Schlieffen planned to use two-thirds of the troops as a massive right wing which, pivoting on Verdun, would sweep through Belgium and Holland, disregarding the political implications of the breach of neutrality this involved. This right wing would swing round behind the French armies (which Schlieffen expected to advance into Alsace-Lorraine), trapping and annihilating them against the Vosges. The plan required very strong central control, which the younger Moltke failed to provide when he attempted to put it into practice in 1914. The plan had been much modified by 1914 so that the left wing no longer played a purely defensive role; but for the inherent difficulties of the plan see *The Schlieffen Plan* by Gerhard Ritter (London, 1958).

France: the French plan, Plan XVII, reflected France's desire to recover Alsace-Lorraine and her faith in the offensive spirit. The plan simply entailed vigorous offensives in Alsace-Lorraine by the First, Second and Third French Armies, while the Fourth and Fifth Armies guarded France's northern frontier. The French optimistically expected that if the Germans did attack they would attempt to do so through the Ardennes, even though the terrain was regarded as highly unsuitable for military operations. When in 1911 General Michel, the Commander-in-Chief designate, began to make plans to strengthen the French left, the likelihood that this would weaken the Alsace-Lorraine offensive led to his replacement by General Joffre.

Britain: from 1905 Staff Conversations had been taking place between British and French military leaders. In 1910 Henry Wilson became Director of Military Operations, and on 20 July 1911 he signed a memorandum with General Dubail to the effect that in the event of war the whole British Expeditionary Force would be employed on the exposed left flank of the French line; the BEF was thus interlocked as a small part of Plan XVII. On the naval side in 1912 the British and French signed an agreement for concentration of their respective naval strengths in the North Sea and Channel, and the Mediterranean.

THE EAST

Here plans were more fluid. The Austrians formed 6 armies; 3 were to operate against Serbia, while the others would advance north-east to co-operate with German forces in cutting off the Russian troops in Russian Poland. The Russians wished to concentrate their forces against the Austrians, but France persuaded them also to mount an offensive against Germany. Four Russian armies were therefore to attack the Austrians in Galicia, while 2 armies advanced into East Prussia.

WORLD WAR I–DECLARATIONS OF WAR (EUROPEAN POWERS AND THE UNITED STATES) CHRONOLOGICALLY

1914	28 July	Austria-Hungary against Serbia
	1 Aug	Germany against Russia
	3 Aug	Germany against France
	4 Aug	Britain against Germany; Germany against Belgium
	5 Aug	Montenegro against Austria-Hungary
	6 Aug	Austria-Hungary against Russia; Serbia against Germany
	9 Aug	Montenegro against Germany; Austria-Hungary against Montenegro
	12 Aug	Britain against Austria-Hungary
	13 Aug	France against Austria-Hungary
	22 Aug	Austria-Hungary against Belgium
	1 Nov	Russia against Turkey
	2 Nov	Serbia against Turkey
	5 Nov	Britain against Turkey; France against Turkey
1915	23 May	Italy against Austria-Hungary
	21 Aug	Italy against Turkey
	14 Oct	Bulgaria against Serbia
	15 Oct	Britain against Bulgaria; Montenegro against Bulgaria
	16 Oct	France against Bulgaria; Serbia against Bulgaria
	19 Oct	Italy against Bulgaria; Russia against Bulgaria
1916	9 Mar	Germany against Portugal
	15 Mar	Austria-Hungary against Portugal
	27 Aug	Romania against Austria-Hungary; Italy against Germany
	28 Aug	Germany against Romania

179

	30 Aug	Turkey against Romania
	1 Sep	Bulgaria against Romania
1917	6 Apr	United States against Germany
	2 July	Greece against Germany, Austria-Hungary, Turkey and Bulgaria
	7 Dec	United States against Austria-Hungary

WORLD WAR I—DECLARATIONS OF WAR (EUROPEAN POWERS AND THE UNITED STATES) BY COUNTRY

Austria-Hungary declared war on: Serbia 28 July 14; Russia 6 Aug 14; Montenegro 9 Aug 14; Belgium 22 Aug 14; Portugal 15 Mar 16

Britain declared war on: Germany 4 Aug 14; Austria-Hungary 12 Aug 14; Turkey 5 Nov 14; Bulgaria 15 Oct 15

Bulgaria declared war on: Romania 1 Sep 16

France declared war on: Austria-Hungary 13 Aug 14; Turkey 5 Nov 14; Bulgaria 16 Oct 15

Germany declared war on: Russia 1 Aug 14; France 3 Aug 14; Belgium 4 Aug 14; Portugal 9 Mar 16; Romania 28 Aug 16

Greece declared war on: Austria-Hungary, Bulgaria, Germany and Turkey 2 July 17

Italy declared war on: Austria-Hungary 23 May 15; Turkey 21 Aug 15; Bulgaria 19 Oct 15; Germany 27 Aug 16

Montenegro declared war on: Austria-Hungary 5 Aug 14; Germany 9 Aug 14; Bulgaria 15 Oct 15

Romania declared war on: Austria-Hungary 27 Aug 16

Russia declared war on: Turkey 1 Nov 14; Bulgaria 19 Oct 15

Serbia declared war on: Germany 6 Aug 14; Turkey 2 Nov 14; Bulgaria 16 Oct 15

Turkey declared war on: Romania 30 Aug 16

United States declared war on: Germany 6 Apr 17; Austria-Hungary 7 Dec 17

A MILITARY AND NAVAL CHRONOLOGY OF WORLD WAR I

1914	2 Aug	Germans invade Luxembourg
	4 Aug	Germans invade Belgium
	5–16 Aug	Germans capture Liège and its forts
	7 Aug	First British troops land in France; the French invade Alsace
	10 Aug	Russian front-Austrians invade southern Russian Poland
	12–20 Aug	Balkan theatre-Austrian invasion of Serbia checked by the battle of the Jadar (16–19 Aug)
	14–24 Aug	The Battle of the Frontiers: French defeated in Lorraine, the Ardennes and on the Sambre; British fall back from Mons
	17–20 Aug	Russian front-Russian armies invade East Prussia and Galicia
	20 Aug	Germans take Brussels
	26 Aug	British fight delaying action at Le Cateau
	26–9 Aug	Russian front-crushing German victory over Russian Second Army in the battle of Tannenberg
	5–9 Sep	Battle of the Marne; the Germans begin retreat to the Aisne
	5–11 Sep	Russian front-Austrian defeat in Galicia in the battle of Rawa Ruska
	8–16 Sep	Balkan theatre-second Austrian invasion of Serbia halted by Serbian counter-attack
	10–14 Sep	Russian front-Russian First Army decisively defeated in Masurian Lakes campaign, and driven from East Prussia
	14–18 Sep	First battle of the Aisne: failure of Allied offensive as trench warfare develops
	28 Sep–1 Nov	Russian front-offensive by Austro-German forces, which withdrew after coming within 12 miles of Warsaw
	Sep–Oct	The 'Race for the Sea': series of unsuccessful outflanking attempts towards the Channel
	9 Oct	Antwerp falls to the Germans
	12 Oct–11 Nov	First battle of Ypres: failure of German attempts to break through to the Channel ports, and of the Allied counter-attack
	16 Oct	The battle of the Yser ends the 'Race for the Sea'

181

	2 Nov	Russian front-the Russians re-enter East Prussia
	5 Nov– 15 Dec	Balkan theatre-third Austrian invasion of Serbia repulsed
	11–24 Nov	Russian front-Germans almost succeed in enveloping the Russian Second Army in the battle of Lodz, and the Russians fall back
1915	8–15 Jan	Battle of Soissons: French attack repulsed
	7–21 Feb	Russian front-winter battle of Masuria: Germans encircle Russian Tenth Army, but Austrian attack in the Carpathians fails
	19 Feb– 18 Mar	The Dardanelles-failure of attempt by British navy to force the Straits
	10–13 Mar	Battle of Neuve-Chapelle: British advance halted by German counter-attack
	14–15 Mar	Battle of Saint-Eloi
	22 Apr– 25 May	Second battle of Ypres. First use of poison gas by Germans 22 Apr
	25 Apr	The Dardanelles-Allied troops land on Gallipoli Peninsula
	2– 4 May	Russian front-German-Austrian offensive breaks Russian line between Gorlice and Tarnow: Russians retreat 300 miles by 30 Sep
	9 May– 18 June	Second battle of Artois: French attack ends in stalemate
	15–25 May	Battle of Festubert: limited Allied successes
	23 May	Italy enters the war. The Italian army launches 11 major attacks against the Austrians on the Isonzo River 1915–17
	20 June– 14 July	Failure of German offensive in the Argonne
	16–18 July	Russian front-Russians defeated in battle of Krasnotav
	4–5 Aug	Russian front-Germans enter Warsaw
	6–21 Aug	The Dardanelles-failure of Allied attacks
	25 Sep– 6 Nov	The Allies mount offensives at Loos and in Champagne with limited success
	28 Sep	Middle East-British defeat Turks and enter Kut; but advance on Baghdad halted at Ctesiphon (22–5 Nov)
	7 Oct	Balkan theatre-beginning of combined German-Austrian-Bulgarian offensive against Serbia. Allied troops landed at Salonika from 3 Oct cannot prevent collapse of Serbian army, which is evacu-

		ated to Corfu (Jan–Feb 16), and then moved to the Salonika front
	7 Dec	Middle East-British besieged in Kut by the Turks
	20 Dec	The Dardanelles-Allied troops evacuated from Anzac and Suvla Bay
1916	9 Jan	The Dardanelles-last Allied troops evacuated
	21 Feb– 18 Dec	Battle of Verdun: German attempt to wear French down, which results in 550,000 French casualties and 450,000 German
	25 Feb	Verdun: Germans capture Fort Douamont
	29 Apr	Middle East-British garrison at Kut surrenders
	15 May– 17 June	Italian front-Austrians capture Asiago, but break off offensive to reinforce the Russian front
	31 May– 1 June	Naval operations-battle of Jutland
	4 June– 20 Sep	Russian front-massive Russian offensive south of the Pripet Marshes led by General Brusilov; heavy losses on both sides
	5 June	Middle East-beginning of Arab revolt against the Turks
	7 June	Verdun: Germans capture Fort de Vaux
	1 Jul– 18 Nov	Battle of the Somme: Allied offensive gains some ground, but no decisive breakthrough
	27 Aug	Balkan theatre-Romania enters war, and begins invasion of Transylvania
	10 Sep – 19 Nov	Balkan theatre-Allied Salonika offensive has limited success
	15 Sep	The Somme: use of tanks for the first time by the British
	24 Oct – 18 Dec	Verdun: successful French counter-attacks
	6 Dec	Balkan theatre-Bucharest falls: Russo-Romanian armies on the retreat
1917	31 Jan	Naval operations-Germans announce resumption of unrestricted submarine warfare
	23 Feb – 5 Apr	Germans withdraw to the Hindenburg Line in anticipation of an Allied offensive
	25 Feb	Middle East-British retake Kut
	11 Mar	Middle East-British enter Baghdad
	12 Mar	Russian front-Russian revolution begins; Tsar abdicates on 15 Mar; prelude to disintegration of Russian armies
	26–7 Mar	Middle East-first battle of Gaza: failure of British

		attempt to capture Gaza as initial step to invasion of Palestine
	9 Apr – 3 May	Battle of Arras. Canadians capture Vimy Ridge
	16 Apr– 9 May	Second battle of the Aisne: failure of Nivelle's offensive; mutinies in the French army
	17–19 Apr	Middle East-second battle of Gaza: British attack fails
	7–8 June	Battle of Messines: British capture Messines Ridge after large-scale mining operations
	25 June	First United States troops land in France
	31 July – 6 Nov	Third battle of Ypres: costly British offensive in the mud finally broken off when Passchendaele taken
	24 Oct – 12 Nov	Italian front-Italians routed by Austro-German attack in the battle of Caporetto; they retreat 70 miles to the Piave
	31 Oct – 7 Nov	Middle East-third battle of Gaza: Turks withdraw
	20 Nov – 3 Dec	Battle of Cambrai: massed tank attack breaks German line, but lack of reserves prevents exploitation of success
	2 Dec	Russian front-suspension of hostilities
	9 Dec	Balkan theatre-Romania signs armistice
	9 Dec	Middle East-British enter Jerusalem
1918	3 Mar	Russian front-Bolsheviks accept peace terms at Brest-Litovsk
	21 Mar – 4 Apr	First German offensive: on the Somme
	9–29 Apr	Second German offensive: on the Lys
	14 Apr	Foch appointed supreme commander of Allied armies in France
	27 May – 6 June	Third German offensive: on the Aisne
	9–13 June	Fourth German drive: Noyon-Montidier offensive
	15–24 June	Italian front-Austrian attack across the Piave beaten back
	15–17 July	Final German drive: Champagne-Marne offensive
	18 July– 6 Aug	Allies launch Aisne-Marne offensive and reduce Marne salient
	8 Aug – 3 Sep	Reduction of Amiens salient

3 Sep	Germans begin retreat to the Hindenburg Line
14 Sep	Balkan theatre-Allied offensive against the Bulgarians begins
19 Sep	Middle East-Turks defeated in battle of Megiddo
26 Sep	Foch begins final offensive: Hindenburg Line broken through (27 Sep)
29 Sep	Balkan theatre-Bulgarians sign armistice
1 Oct	Middle East-British enter Damascus
24 Oct – 4 Nov	Italian front-Austrians routed in battle of Vittorio Veneto
31 Oct	Middle East-armistice with Turks takes effect
3 Nov	Austrians accept truce terms
4 Nov	Armistice on Italian front
11 Nov	Armistice on western front
21 Nov	German High Seas Fleet surrenders to British

WORLD WAR I–NAVAL STRENGTHS (1914)
AND LOSSES

	Austria-Hungary	Britain	France	Germany	
NAVAL STRENGTHS 1914					
Dreadnoughts	3	24	14	13	
Pre-Dreadnoughts	12	38	9	30	
Battle-cruisers	0	10	0	6	
Cruisers	3	47	19	14	
Light cruisers	4	61	6	35	
Destroyers	18	228	81	152	
Submarines	14	76	67	30	
NAVAL LOSSES					
				Losses	*Surrendered*
Dreadnoughts	2	2	0	0	18
Pre-Dreadnoughts	1	11	4	1	0
Battle-cruisers	0	3	0	1	6
Cruisers	0	13	5	6	0
Light cruisers	3	12	0	17	23
Destroyers	6	67	12	66	92
Submarines	14	54	14	199	All

WORLD WAR I—NAVAL STRENGTHS (1914) AND LOSSES

Italy	Japan	Russia	Turkey	United States
1	4	4	1	10
17	2	7	3	26
0	2	1	0	0
5	9	8	0	21
6	15	5	2	11
33	54	106	8	50
20	15	36	0	39
1	1	2	0	0
3	0	2	1	0
0	1	0	0	0
1	0	2	0	1
2	2	0	1	0
8	1	20	3	2
8	0	20	0	0

MOBILIZATION OF MANPOWER AND CASUALTIES

	Standing armies and trained reserves	*Total mobilized*
Austria-Hungary	3,000,000	7,800,000
Belgium	117,000	267,000
British Empire	975,000[1]	8,904,000
Bulgaria	280,000	560,000
France	4,017,000[1]	8,410,000
Germany	4,500,000	11,000,000
Greece	230,000	230,000
Italy	1,251,000	5,615,000
Montenegro	50,000	50,000
Portugal	40,000	100,000
Romania	290,000	750,000
Russia	5,971,000	12,000,000
Serbia	200,000	707,000
Turkey	210,000	2,850,000

[1] Includes colonial troops.

WORLD WAR I–THE PEACE TREATIES

TREATY OF BREST-LITOVSK. *3 Mar 18*

The Soviet Union surrendered the Baltic Provinces and Russian Poland to the Central Powers, recognized the independence of Finland and the Ukraine, and ceded to Turkey the districts of Kars, Ardahan and Batum. The treaty was formally invalidated by the armistice in the West on 11 Nov 18.

TREATY OF VERSAILLES. *28 June 19*

The peace treaty between Germany and the Allied Powers. Germany surrendered territory to Belgium, Denmark, Poland and Czechoslovakia; Alsace-Lorraine was ceded to France. Germany also surrendered all her overseas territories. The Rhineland was declared a demilitarized zone, with Allied occupation for 15 years from when the treaty came into effect on 10 Jan 20. Severe restrictions were placed on the German armed forces; the army was limited to 100,000 men. The union of Germany and Austria was forbidden. The treaty declared Germany's responsibility for causing the war, and made Germany liable for the payment of reparations. The treaty also contained the Covenant of the League of Nations.

IN WORLD WAR I—EUROPEAN POWERS

Killed or died of wounds	Total military casualties	Civilian deaths (estimate)
1,200,000	7,020,000	300,000
14,000	93,061	30,000
908,000	3,190,235	30,000
87,000	266,919	275,000
1,363,000	6,160,800	40,000
1,774,000	7,142,558	760,000
5,000	27,000	132,000
460,000	2,197,000	..
3,000	20,000	..
7,222	33,291	..
336,000	535,706	275,000
1,700,000	9,150,000	2,000,000
125,000	331,106	650,000
325,000	975,000	2,150,000

TREATY OF ST GERMAIN. *10 Sep 19*

The peace treaty between the Austrian Republic and the Allied Powers. By the settlement Austria lost territory to Italy, Yugoslavia, Czechoslovakia, Poland and Romania. Hungary was recognized as an independent state, and the union of Austria and Germany was forbidden. The Austrian army was limited to 30,000 men and the republic was made liable for the payment of reparations.

TREATY OF NEUILLY. *27 Nov 19*

The peace treaty between Bulgaria and the Allied Powers. Bulgaria lost western Thrace to Greece, and territory to Yugoslavia. The Bulgarian army was limited to 20,000 men, and Bulgaria was made liable for reparations.

TREATY OF TRIANON. *4 June 20*

The peace treaty between Hungary and the Allied Powers. Hungary surrendered territory to Romania, Czechoslovakia, Yugoslavia, Poland, Italy and the Austrian Republic, to a total of about two-thirds of its pre-war lands. The Hungarian army was limited to 35,000 and Hungary was made liable for reparations.

TREATY OF SEVRES. *10 Aug 20*

The peace treaty made with Ottoman Turkey, but never ratified by the Turks.

TREATY OF LAUSANNE. *24 July 23*

Treaty made necessary by Turkey's refusal to accept the treaty of Sèvres. Turkey surrendered its claims to territories of the Ottoman Empire occupied by non-Turks, whilst retaining Constantinople and eastern Thrace in Europe. The Greeks surrendered Smyrna, but were confirmed in possession of all the Aegean Islands except Imbros and Tenedos, which were returned to Turkey. Turkey recognized the annexation of Cyprus by Britain and of the Dodecanese by Italy. The Bosphorus and the Dardanelles were declared to be demilitarized. (By the Montreux Convention of 20 July 36 Turkey was permitted to refortify the Straits.)

9 COLONIES AND DEPENDENCIES

The colonies and dependencies are arranged in alphabetical order of the European 'mother-country'–Belgium, Denmark, France, Germany, Great Britain, Italy, the Netherlands, Portugal, Russia, Spain and Sweden.

Details of Governors, Residents and Administrators of the colonies and dependencies are listed in:

Cook, C., and Keith, B., *British Historical Facts, 1830–1900*. Macmillan, 1975

The Statesman's Year-Book. Macmillan, from 1864

Henige, D. P., *Colonial Governors from the Fifteenth Century to Present*. University of Wisconsin Press, 1970

BELGIUM

The International African Association was formed by King Leopold II in 1876. The association's aim was to explore Africa and was non-political and multinational. By 1885 expeditions had claimed much of the river Congo basin and the Congress of Berlin recognized the King's authority over these territories. The Congo Free State was ruled, not by Belgium, but by the King. In 1908 Belgium assumed sovereignty and the colony was renamed Belgian Congo.

DENMARK

Danish Gold Coast. The prosperity of the trading centres of Danish Gold Coast depended on the traffic in slaves. Denmark abolished the slave trade by 1803. In 1850 Great Britain purchased all the fortifications and integrated them into the Gold Coast.

Danish West Indies. From 1756 to 1871 the seat of the governor-general was on Saint Croix and the other 2 islands retained a separate but subordinate administration. From 1801 to 1802 and again from 1807 to 1815 the Danish West Indies, like almost all overseas European colonies, were occupied by the British, but they were returned in 1815. By 1850 Denmark had disposed of its other colonies and was willing to dispose of the Danish West Indies as well. A treaty of sale was concluded with the United States in 1867 but never ratified by the US Senate. Denmark therefore retained the islands for another 50 years until the United States purchased them in 1917.

Tranquebar. Tranquebar was occupied by the British from 1808 to 1815. The 3 mainland posts were sold to Great Britain in 1845. The Nicobar Islands were gradually abandoned after 1848 and were ceded to Great Britain in 1869.

FRANCE

Algeria. Disputes over a debt owed by France to the Bey of Algiers led to a French invasion of Algeria in 1830. Dispensing with the form of a protectorate the French deposed the Bey and began from the first to rule the area directly. The coastal areas were easily conquered but it was not until 1847 that the near interior was controlled. Until 1879 Algeria was a military province, but after that date it had a civil government and a quasi-colonial relationship with the metropolis. After 1900 France began to extend her control over the vast desert interior.

Annam. In 1875 the Annamite ruler accepted, under duress, a French Resident at his court in Hué. In 1883 the powers of this Resident were expanded so that he became *de facto* ruler of the kingdom. The protectorate of Annam became a component of the Union of Indochina in 1887.

Cambodia. France proclaimed a protectorate over the kingdom of Cambodia in 1863. In 1887 Cambodia became a constituent member of the Union of Indochina.

Cameroun. During World War I France occupied the eastern and major part of the German colony of Kamerun. The remainder went to Great Britain.

Chad. The area of Chad came under French domination soon after 1890. but no administrative structure was established until 1900. From 1906 to 1920 Chad and Ubangi-Shari were administered as a unit. After 1920 Chad became a separate colony within French Equatorial Africa.

Cochin China. French interest in Cochin China culminated with the occupation of the area around the Mekong River delta beginning in 1858. In 1862 this conquest was recognized by Annam, which ceded the provinces to France. Until 1879 the governors of Cochin China were all admirals of the French navy: civil government was instituted in that year. Cochin China was the only part of Indochina officially ruled directly.

Dahomey. A protectorate was established over the small coastal state of Porto Novo in 1863 but withdrawn in 1867, only to be reasserted in 1883. In 1894 the interior kingdom of Dahomey was conquered and a temporary protectorate was established there. In 1900 the kingdom was abolished and the territory annexed. In 1899 Dahomey became part of French West Africa. Until 1886 the French settlements were under Gabon. From 1886 to 1894 under Rivières du Sud. In 1894 Dahomey became a separate colony.

Diégo-Suarez. After the French intervention in Madagascar in 1886, by which the Merina kingdom became a protectorate, the colony of Diégo-Suarez was established in the far north of the island. With the establishment of the colony of Madagascar and of French control over the whole island in 1896, Diégo-Suarez became a district of Madagascar.

French Equatorial Africa. French interest in French Equatorial Africa dates from 1838 when trade started along the coast of Gabon. In 1882 the French Congo was created and in 1886 de Brazza was appointed Commissioner-General.

French Guiana. In 1809 the colony was occupied by the Portuguese from Brazil, but it was returned to France in 1817. After 1852 the colony was the main penal colony for France.

French Guinea. After 1850 the French began to conclude treaties of cession with the local rulers and to construct forts. In 1882 the colony of Rivières du Sud was created. After 1886 this included the French establishments along the Gulf of Guinea as well. Until 1891 Rivières du Sud was subordinated to Senegal, but in 1893 the name of the colony was changed to French Guinea and it was given separate status. Between 1881 and 1897 the interior, known as Futa Jallon, was occupied and added to the colony. French Guinea was made a part of French West Africa in 1895.

French India. After 1816 French India, known as the Établissements français dans l'Inde, consisted of Pondichéry, Karikal, and Yanaon (Yanam) on the Coromandel coast, Mahé on the Malabar coast, and Chandernagore in Bengal.

French Polynesia. In 1841 the ruler of Tahiti sought and received French protection and later it was annexed. In 1847 the French government rescinded the annexation but retained the protectorate. In 1880 Tahiti was ceded to France. Other islands were acquired from 1842 onwards.

French Somaliland. Obock, at the southern end of the Red Sea, was acquired by France in 1862, but it was not occupied until 1884. Subsequently, protectorates were extended over neighbouring sultanates, particularly Tadjoura, and the colony was extended. In 1892 the capital was transferred to Djibouti, and in 1896 the colony was renamed Côte français des Somalis.

French Sudan. French interest in what was to become French Sudan began in the 1850s. In 1879 the desire to build a railroad connecting the Senegal and Niger rivers quickened this interest. Until 1892 and from 1899 to 1904 the colony was subordinate to Senegal. It was a part of French West Africa from 1895 to 1958. During its existence the colony was known under several different names: 1880–90 Upper River; 1890–9 French Sudan; 1899–1902 Upper Senegal/Middle Niger; 1902–4 Senegambia-Niger; 1904–20 Upper Senegal/Niger; 1920–58 French Sudan.

French West Africa. In 1895 French Guinea, French Sudan, Ivory Coast and Senegal were administratively united in a federation known as French West Africa. Dahomey joined in 1899, and Mauritania, Niger and Upper Volta joined as they became separate colonies.

Gabon. French settlements on the Gabon coast were subject to Senegal in 1843. In 1891 Gabon became subordinated to French Congo. After 1910 it was a component colony of French Equatorial Africa.

Gorée and Dependencies. From 1763 to 1778 Gorée was the only part of Senegal retained by the French. From 1854 it was detached from Senegal and together with the French posts in Gabon and along the Guinea coast became a separate colony. In 1859 Gorée was reincorporated with Senegal.

Guadeloupe. Guadeloupe was occupied by the British 1759–63, 1810–14, and 1815–16.

Indochina. Indochina was a federation formed in 1887 from the colony of Cochin China and the protectorates of Annam, Cambodia and Tonkin. To these, Laos was added in 1897, as a protectorate, and Kouang-Tchéou-Wan in 1900.

Ivory Coast. In 1843 'protectorates' were established at Grand-Bassam and

Assinie, and posts were established there and later at Dabou nearby. These establishments, like those in Gabon, were under the general authority of the commandant of the Naval Division of the West Coast of Africa. The French government abandoned its claims to the posts in 1871 and French influence was left to be carried on by agents of the trading firm of A. Verdier et Cie. In 1881, the commandant-supérieur at Gabon was granted responsibility for French interests in the Ivory Coast area. From 1886 to 1893 the area fell under the jurisdiction of the lieutenant-governor of Rivières du Sud. A Resident was appointed at Assinie in 1889. A separate colony called Côte d'Ivoire was created in 1893. In 1895 the Ivory Coast became a part of French West Africa.

Kouang-Tchéou-Wan. Kouang-Tchéou-Wan was occupied by France in 1898 for use as a naval station and coaling depot. In 1900 it was leased from China, and in the same year it was attached administratively to Indochina.

Laos. A French consulate was established in the kingdom of Luang Prabang in Laos in 1886. An agreement was reached between France, Siam and Great Britain, in which the area of Laos was left to the French, while the independence of Siam was guaranteed against foreign encroachment.

Madagascar. French interest in Madagascar dated from the early seventeenth century, and from 1643 to 1674 there was a French colony at Fort-Dauphin intended as a way-station on voyages to the East Indies and India. In 1750 France obtained Sainte Marie de Madagascar by cession, and in 1841 the island of Nosy Bé. In 1885 French forces invaded the Merina kingdom, which controlled most of the island's interior, and proclaimed a protectorate. At the same time the Merina ruler ceded Diégo-Suarez. In 1896 a second invasion resulted in the abolition of the Merina kingdom and the creation of Madagascar as a colony.

Martinique. Martinique was occupied and governed by the British 1762–3, 1794–1802 and 1809–14.

Mayotte. Mayotte, one of the Comoro Islands, was ceded to France by its ruler Andriantsuli in 1841. From 1886 the remaining islands of the Comoros, Great Comoro, Anjuan (Anjouan) and Mohilla (Mohéli) were proclaimed protectorates. In 1912 their protectorate status was abolished and they became direct dependencies of Mayotte. In 1914 all 4 islands were annexed to Madagascar and the colony ceased to exist.

Middle Congo. A separate administration for Middle Congo was established under French Congo in 1897. In 1911 a large part of the colony was ceded to Germany and attached to Kamerun in return for German non-interference with French interests in Morocco.

Morocco. France needed to secure control of Morocco in order to protect her North African possessions of Tunisia and Algeria but was unable to do so because of German opposition. In 1911 Germany agreed to increased interest in Morocco by France in return for an area of Middle Congo which was then attached to the colony of Kamerun. Morocco was then divided into the French and Spanish zones with Tangier becoming an international area.

New Caledonia. The island of New Caledonia was occupied by the French in 1853. Until 1884 the Governor of New Caledonia was also the commander of the French naval forces in the Pacific. From 1864 to 1894 the island served as a penal colony.

New Hebrides Condominium. An Anglo-French Naval Commission was established in 1887 and governed the islands until 1902. A formal condominium was established in 1906.

Niger. Niger was created as a colony in 1911 and remained under military rule until 1922.

Nosy Bé. Nosy Bé, an island off the northwest coast of Madagascar, was ceded to France by its Sakalava ruler in 1840. It was used as a naval station almost exclusively, although some settlement was attempted. Until 1843 it was under Réunion, then under Mayotte to 1878 when it was made a separate colony. In 1896 it became part of Madagascar.

Réunion. From 1810 to 1815 Réunion was occupied by the British, and afterwards, with the retention of Île de France and the Seychelles by the British, it became the only French colony in the Indian Ocean. Réunion was known by several names: 1649–1793 Bourbon; 1793–1806 Réunion; 1806–10 Bonaparte; 1810–48 Bourbon; 1848– Réunion.

Sainte Marie de Madagascar. Sainte Marie was ceded to the French by its Malagasy ruler in 1750, but it remained unoccupied until 1819. Until 1843 it was under Bourbon. From 1843 to 1853 it was subject to Mayotte, and from 1853 to 1877 it was a separate colony. In 1878 it was returned to Réunion's jurisdiction where it remained until 1896 when, like France's other small colonies on Madagascar, it became part of Madagascar.

Saint Pierre and Miquelon. St Pierre and Miquelon were taken by the British several times during the eighteenth and early nineteenth centuries but never separately administered. They have been in continuous French possession since the Treaty of Paris in 1814.

Senegal. The French retook the British possessions in 1778 but lost them all again in 1809, recovering them finally in 1817. In 1895 Senegal became the seat of French West Africa and lost its own individual administration until 1902.

Togo. The German colony of Togo was occupied by British and French forces in 1914.

Tonkin. Tonkin was the northern vice-royalty of the kingdom of Annam. In 1873–4 the French attempted to seize Tonkin but failed. In 1886 a Resident was appointed and in 1888 Tonkin became a full member of the Indochinese Union.

Tunis. In 1881 French forces occupied Tunis and proclaimed a protectorate.

Ubangi-Shari. The province of Ubangi-Shari was created in 1894 and was one of the 4 colonies comprising French Equatorial Africa.

Wallis and Futuna Islands. The Wallis Islands were governed as a protectorate under French Polynesia from 1842. In 1887 a protectorate was proclaimed over the Futuna Islands and the two groups were administered from New Caledonia. In 1917 they were made a colony.

GERMANY

German East Africa. In 1886 eastern Africa was officially divided into northern and southern spheres of influence between Germany and Great Britain. In 1890, under the terms of the Heligoland Treaty, Germany abandoned, in favour of Great Britain, its claims to Zanzibar, the Sultanate of Witu, in Kenya, and Nyasaland, in return for Heligoland, which had been governed by the British since 1807. The German East African Company relinquished its territorial rights to the German government in 1891 while retaining many of its economic privileges. The outbreak of World War I saw a German offensive from East Africa into neighbouring British territories, surrendering to British colonial forces after the armistice of Nov 1918.

German New Guinea. The New Guinea Company was formed in 1884 and within a year German sovereignty had been proclaimed over north-eastern New Guinea, the islands to the north, which were known as the Bismarck Archipelago, and the Marshall Islands. Nauru was annexed in 1888, and in

1899 Germany purchased the Mariana Islands (except Guam), the Caroline Islands and the Palau Islands from Spain.

German Samoa. An agreement was reached in 1879 by Great Britain, the United States and Germany, by which the Samoan Islands were to be under the joint supervision of the 3 countries represented by their respective consuls in Apia. Negotiations were concluded in the Tripartite Treaty of 1899: Germany and the United States divided the Samoan group between them with Great Britain receiving as compensation half of the Solomon Islands, as well as a free hand in the Tonga Islands and certain other colonial cessions from Germany. The western part of the Samoan group, known as the Territory of Western Samoa, was administered by Germany until 1914 when it was seized by New Zealand.

German Southwest Africa. In 1884 Germany declared the area a protectorate. The boundaries were defined by the Heligoland Treaty of 1890. Union of South African troops attacked and conquered the territory in 1915. Later a mandate was awarded to South Africa by the League of Nations.

Kamerun. German companies started trading on the Cameroon coast near Duala in 1884. In 1912 107,000 square miles of the French colony of the Middle Congo was added to Kamerun. Kamerun was conquered by the British and French in 1916 and during the remainder of the war was occupied by troops of both nations jointly.

Kiaochow. In 1898 China agreed to lease the peninsula to Germany for a period of 99 years. In Oct 1914 Japan occupied the German territory of Kiaochow.

Togo. German commercial interest on the Togo coast started in 1880. In 1884 German commercial agents began to sign 'treaties of protection' with the chiefs in the area. It was occupied by the British and French in 1914.

GREAT BRITAIN

Aden. The British established themselves in 1839 when they seized the town from the Sultan of Lahej.

Ajmer-Merwara. Ajmer and Merwara were ceded to the British by the Sindhia ruler of Gwalior in 1818, and between 1832 and 1871 were part of the North-West Frontier Provinces.

Andaman and Nicobar Islands. The Andaman Islands had been used as a penal colony by the British in India from 1789 to 1796 when the colony was abandoned. Soon after 1850 the penal colony was re-established.

Anglo-Egyptian Sudan. The Nilotic Sudan was occupied by Egyptian forces in a series of campaigns which ended in 1821, and it was administered by Egypt until 1881. In 1898 British and Egyptian forces reoccupied the Sudan.

Ashanti. The Ashanti kingdom was conquered in 1896.

Assam. The region of Assam was under Bengal until 1874. From 1905 to 1912 Assam was part of the short-lived government of East Bengal and Assam, but after 1912 it again had a separate government.

Assiniboia. Until 1836 Assiniboia was governed by Lord Selkirk and his heirs and thereafter, until 1870, directly by the Hudson's Bay Company. In 1870 Assiniboia was absorbed into the newly created province of Manitoba.

Australia. Until 1901 the Australian continent and its neighbouring islands were occupied by the separate British colonies of New South Wales, Northern Australia, Queensland, South Australia, Tasmania, Victoria and Western Australia. The Commonwealth of Australia was established in 1901.

Bahama Islands. The Bahamas became a Crown colony in 1783.

Bahrain. Bahrain, an island and sheikdom in the Gulf, was brought under British protection by a series of Treaties during the nineteenth century. In 1900 a British agent was appointed.

Baluchistan. A British Protectorate was established and a chief commissioner appointed 1877.

Barbados. Barbados was first settled 1627 and became a Crown colony in 1662. From 1833 to 1885 the governor of Barbados was also governor-in-chief of the Windward Islands.

Basutoland. The Sutu ruler Moshoeshoe requested the protection of Great Britain against the Boers, and in 1868 the area occupied by the Sutu was proclaimed a protectorate. In 1871 it was attached to Cape Colony but with special legislative provisions which ensured its autonomy. Under the Disannexation Act of 1883 Great Britain assumed direct responsibility.

Bay Islands. In 1841 the Bay Islands were claimed by the British Crown and in

199

1852 became a Crown colony. In 1860 Britain ceded the colony to Honduras.

Bechuanaland. Britain proclaimed a protectorate over Bechuanaland in 1885.

Bermuda. Bermuda has been a Crown colony since 1684.

British Columbia. Vancouver Island was granted to the Hudson's Bay Company in 1849. The mainland, known before 1858 as New Caledonia, was settled from Vancouver Island and made a separate colony in 1858 but with the same governor as Vancouver Island. From 1864 to 1866 the two colonies were divided, but in 1866 they were united and called British Columbia. In 1871 British Columbia became a province of the Confederation of Canada.

British Guiana. In 1803 Great Britain permanently occupied the Dutch Guianese settlements of Berbice, Demerara, and Essequibo. In 1831 these colonies were united to form British Guiana.

British Honduras. From 1862 to 1884 British Honduras was under Jamaica, but it became a separate Crown colony in 1884.

British Kaffraria. British Kaffraria became a Crown colony in 1847 and was annexed to the Cape Colony in 1866.

British New Guinea. In 1914, what was German New Guinea, was occupied by Australia.

British North Borneo. In 1877 and 1879 the territory later to comprise British North Borneo was ceded to a British syndicate. In 1882 the British North Borneo Company acquired the rights over the territory and in 1888 the British government assumed a protectorate.

British Solomon Islands Protectorate. In 1893 Great Britain assumed a protectorate over the southern islands, and in 1899 Germany ceded the northern islands to Britain in exchange for abandonment of British interests in Samoa.

British Somaliland. The part of the Somali coast opposite Aden had been occupied by Egyptian troops from about 1870 to 1884. Great Britain then established a protectorate over part of the coast.

British Virgin Islands. British Virgin Islands have been in British possession since 1666.

Brunei. In 1888 the sultan of Brunei surrendered the control of his external affairs to Great Britain and accepted a British protectorate.

Burma. Arakan and Tenasserim were annexed in 1824–6. Pegu was annexed in 1852–3. In 1862 the 3 provinces were united to form Lower Burma. In 1885 Upper Burma was annexed and the whole territory called Burma.

Canada. In 1841 Upper and Lower Canada were united. The eastern provinces were governed as separate colonies; these were Nova Scotia, Prince Edward Island, Cape Breton (until it was absorbed into Nova Scotia in 1921), New Brunswick and Newfoundland. In 1867 a confederation of Upper and Lower Canada with New Brunswick and Nova Scotia was established. In 1869 the Hudson's Bay Company sold its territorial rights to Canada, and in 1871 British Columbia joined the confederation. In 1873 Prince Edward Island acceded to the confederation (Newfoundland, although an original province, did not join until 1949). From the area acquired from the Hudson's Bay Company Manitoba was created in 1870 and Alberta and Saskatchewan in 1905. The Northwest Territory and Yukon Territory, although part of Canada since the Hudson's Bay Company cession of 1869, did not become provinces.

Cape Colony. The Cape Colony, settled by the Dutch in 1652, was seized by the British in 1795, but returned in 1803. In 1806 it was seized once again. The Dutch Boers founded the Orange Free State and Transvaal. In 1843 the British established Natal. In 1910 the Cape Colony joined with Natal and with the Orange River Colony and Transvaal, both annexed as a result of the Anglo-Boer War of 1899–1902, to form the Union of South Africa.

Cayman Islands. In 1670 the Cayman Islands were ceded by Spain to Britain but not settled until 1734. Until 1900 they were locally governed by justices of the peace. From 1900 to 1962 they were governed by Commissioners and Administrators subject to Jamaica.

Central Provinces and Berar. In 1853 the Maratha kingdom of Nagpur was annexed to British India.

Ceylon. This became a Crown colony in 1802. In 1815 the inland kingdom of Kandy was conquered and the entire island came under European control.

Cook Islands. A British protectorate was proclaimed in 1888 and Residents appointed by New Zealand.

Cyprus. The island of Cyprus in the eastern Mediterranean was, until 1878, a

201

part of the Ottoman Empire. In that year it was handed over to Great Britain for administrative purposes, although not formally ceded. However, on the outbreak of World War I in 1914 Cyprus was annexed to the British Empire.

Dominica. Dominica was ceded to Britain by France in 1763.

Egypt. In 1876 controllers were appointed by Britain and France and in 1882 Egypt was occupied by Britain. A protectorate was established in 1914.

Falkland Islands. After a brief Argentinian occupation the British reclaimed the islands in 1832 for the purpose of protecting whalers in the area. The Falkland Islands remained a Crown colony, although Argentina never abandoned its claims.

Federated Malay States. British control of the several states of the Malay peninsula spread after 1826 from their colony of the Straits Settlements. The states of Pahang, Perak, Selangor and Negri Sembilan became known as the Federated Malay States; the remaining states were called the Unfederated Malay States.

Fiji. Cakobau, ruler of Bau, offered the islands to Great Britain in 1858 and to Germany in 1872, but without success. A second tender was made to Great Britain in 1874. Eventually Great Britain accepted and Fiji was proclaimed a Crown colony.

The Gambia. A small fort was established in 1816. Five years later the Gambia became part of Sierra Leone. From 1843 to 1866 the Gambia was a separate colony, and from 1866 to 1888 it was part of the government called the West Africa Settlements, centred at Sierra Leone, which also included Lagos and the Gold Coast. From 1888 the Gambia was once again a separate colony.

Gibraltar. Gibraltar was ceded to Britain in 1713.

Gilbert and Ellice Islands. These became a British protectorate in 1892 and in 1915 were annexed as a Crown colony.

Gold Coast. In 1821 the Crown assumed direct control for the settlements along the Gold Coast, placing them under the control of Sierra Leone. In 1850 the nearby Danish settlements were purchased and the combined colony ceased to remain under Sierra Leone. From 1866 to 1874, however, the Gold Coast settlements were part of the West Africa Settlements, centred at Sierra Leone. In 1874 the colony of the Gold Coast was created, with Lagos subordinate to it until 1886. From 1874 to 1906 the colony expanded northwards, annexing Ashanti and the area known as the Northern Territories. In 1906 the limits of the colony were defined.

Grenada. Grenada was captured by the British in 1762 and ceded in 1763, retaken by the French in 1779 and restored to Britain in 1783.

Heligoland. Heligoland was seized from Denmark by Great Britain in 1807 and formally ceded 7 years later. The island remained a colony of Great Britain until 1890 when it was ceded to Germany.

Hong Kong. In 1841 the island of Hong Kong was seized by the British and subsequently ceded by China. In 1860 Kowloon Peninsula was also ceded to Great Britain.

Hudson's Bay Company. In 1869 the Hudson's Bay Company sold all its lands to the Dominion of Canada.

India. By 1818 all of India except the area of the Punjab was controlled by Great Britain. In 1846 and 1849 the Punjab was added. In 1858 the British Crown took over the administration of India. Between 1860 and 1900 the British possessions in India were increased by the addition of the Andaman and Nicobar Islands, Baluchistan, Burma and the area of the North-West Frontier Provinces. In 1867 the Straits Settlements was detached from India and created a separate colony.

Ionian Islands. The islands of Cephalonia, Cerigo, Corfu, Ithaca, Leucas, Paxos and Zante were occupied by Venice until 1797 when they were ceded to France. In 1799 Russia occupied the islands and created in 1800 the Septinsular Republic under its protection. Surrendered to France by the Treaty of Tilsit, they were occupied in 1809 by Great Britain. Britain established a protectorate over the islands. Finally, in 1864 they were ceded to Greece.

Iraq. The area of Mesopotamia came under British control as a result of World War I.

Jamaica. Jamaica was seized by the British in 1665 and ceded in 1670. Representative government was abrogated in 1866 and only partly restored in 1884.

Kenya. The Anglo-German agreement of 1886 designated the area later known as Kenya to be within the projected British sphere of influence under the terms of the Berlin Conference of 1884–5.

Kuwait. In 1904 the Sheikh recognized the protection of the British.

Labuan. In 1846 Labuan was ceded to Britain by the Sultan of Brunei.

Leeward Islands. In 1871 the Leeward Islands became a Federated colony.

Malta. Malta was ceded as a British colony in 1814.

Mauritius. Britain seized the island in 1810 and it was ceded as a British colony in 1814.

Montserrat. Montserrat became a British colony in 1632 and was captured by the French in 1644 and 1782 and restored to Britain in 1668 and 1783 respectively.

Natal. The colony of Natal was established in 1843 becoming part of the Union of South Africa in 1910.

New Brunswick. In 1784 New Brunswick was separated from Nova Scotia and created a separate colony. In 1867 it became part of the Confederation of Canada.

Newfoundland. In 1763 Labrador was included in the government of Newfoundland. Unlike the other Canadian colonies, Newfoundland did not confederate in 1867, and in 1918 it acquired dominion status.

New Hebrides Condominium. An Anglo-French Naval Commission was established in 1887 and governed the islands until 1902. A formal condominium was established in 1906.

New Munster/New Ulster. In 1848 New Zealand was divided administratively into New Munster, which included part of North Island, and New Ulster, which included the remainder of North Island and all of South Island. This experiment proved unsuccessful and in 1853 the two provinces were abolished.

New South Wales. Originally, New South Wales included the whole continent, except Western Australia, and New Zealand. Tasmania was detached in 1825, South Australia in 1836, New Zealand in 1841, Victoria in 1851, Queensland in 1859, and Northern Australia (which was placed under South Australia) in 1863. In 1901 New South Wales joined the Commonwealth of Australia. In 1911 the Australian National Capital Territory was created out of New South Wales.

New Zealand. Attempts at settlement in 1826 failed and in 1837 the New Zealand Association was formed. In 1841 New Zealand became a Crown colony. Beginning in 1843 a series of wars with the Maoris expanded the area of the colony until it included the entire area of both islands. From 1848 to 1853 New Zealand was briefly divided into New Munster and New Ulster. In 1907 New Zealand received dominion status. New Zealand began administering the Cook Islands in 1888 and Niue in 1901.

Nigeria. In 1849 a Consul was appointed for the Bight of Biafra. In 1851 a protectorate was established over the coastal state of Lagos. In 1862 Lagos was annexed as a Crown colony. From 1866 to 1874 Lagos was part of the West Africa Settlements, and from 1874 to 1886 it was subordinate to the Gold Coast. In 1886 the Royal Niger Company was granted a charter and rights to govern territory up the Niger River. In 1900 the company's charter was revoked. In 1906 the Colony and Protectorate of Southern Nigeria was established. The Protectorate of Northern Nigeria was established in 1900. In 1914 the two areas of Southern Nigeria and Northern Nigeria were amalgamated into the Colony and Protectorate of Nigeria.

Niue. Niue was discovered by James Cook in 1774. In 1900 a British Protectorate was proclaimed and in 1901 the island was annexed to New Zealand.

Norfolk Island. Norfolk Island was discovered by James Cook in 1774 and was used as a convict settlement by New South Wales, 1788–1844, and by Tasmania, 1844–56 (except 1853). In 1856 administration of the island reverted to New South Wales. In 1914 it became a national territory of Australia.

Northern Australia. The first settlement took place in 1824 but was abandoned in 1829. More permanent settlement occurred after 1838. A territorial government was created in 1863 and Northern Australia, which had hitherto been under New South Wales, was placed under South Australia, where it remained until 1910 when it became a national territory of the Commonwealth of Australia.

Northern Rhodesia. Until 1911 the area was divided into North-Eastern Rhodesia and North-Western Rhodesia, but in 1911 the 2 were combined to form Northern Rhodesia.

Nova Scotia. From 1820 Cape Breton was attached to Nova Scotia. In 1848 Nova Scotia achieved responsible government. In 1867 it became an original member of the Confederation of Canada.

Nyasaland. A protectorate was proclaimed over a limited area in 1889. In 1891 this protectorate was expanded to include the entire western shore of Lake Nyasa. The name of the colony was changed to the British Central African Protectorate in 1893, but reverted to its former name of Nyasaland in 1907.

Orange River Colony. In 1848 the area north of the Orange River occupied by the Boers was annexed by the governor of Cape Colony. This annexation proved abortive and British sovereignty was transferred, in 1854, to the Boers, who established the Orange Free State. This state was occupied and annexed as a result of the Anglo-Boer War of 1899–1902 and was renamed the Orange River Colony. In 1910 the Orange River Colony, together with the Cape Colony, Natal, and Transvaal, united to form the Union of South Africa.

Papua. Papua was annexed to the Australian colony of Queensland in 1883. In 1888 it was annexed to Great Britain under the name British New Guinea. In 1906 it was made a territory of Australia and renamed Papua.

Pitcairn Island. Pitcairn Island was discovered in 1767, and in 1790 it was settled by mutineers from the *Bounty*. In 1856 the inhabitants removed to Norfolk Island but 7 years later some returned to Pitcairn.

Prince Edward Island. Prince Edward Island was occupied by the French until its seizure by the British in 1758. Until 1769 it was part of Nova Scotia and then was created a separate colony. It joined the Confederation of Canada in 1873.

Punjab. As a result of the First Sikh War the eastern part of the Punjab was annexed to British India in 1846, and the remainder was annexed in 1849. Delhi was created a separate province in 1912.

Queensland. The first settlement in Queensland was a penal colony established from New South Wales in 1824 and free settlement was established in 1842. In 1859 it became a separate colony. New South Wales was granted responsible government, and in 1901 Queensland joined the Commonwealth of Australia.

Saint Helena. Saint Helena remained under the administration of the East India Company until 1834 except for the period of Napoleon's exile there from 1815 to 1821, when it was directly administered by the Crown.

Saint Kitts/Nevis/Anguilla. St Kitts (St Christopher) was settled by the British in 1624 and was partly occupied by the French until 1713 when the island was ceded to Britain. In 1871 St Kitts joined the Federation of the Leeward Islands.

Saint Lucia. St Lucia was finally ceded to Britain in 1814 and in 1848 it was attached to the Windward Islands.

Saint Vincent. St Vincent became a British colony in 1763.

Sarawak. Sarawak in northern Borneo was ceded to James Brooke by the Sultan of Brunei in 1841.

Seychelles Islands. In 1794 the Seychelles were captured by the British, but they were treated as a French colony until 1810 when they were formally annexed and attached to Mauritius. In 1903 they were made a Crown colony.

Sierra Leone. In 1808 Sierra Leone became a Crown colony. In 1896 the interior of Sierra Leone, called the Protectorate, was annexed.

Singapore. Singapore was purchased in 1819 from the Sultan of Johore. In 1826 it joined Penang and Malacca, acquired from the Dutch in 1825, to form the Straits Settlements.

South Australia. The area of South Australia was under New South Wales until 1836. From 1863 to 1910 Northern Australia, also known as the Northern Territory, was under the jurisdiction of South Australia. In 1901 South Australia joined the Commonwealth of Australia.

Southern Rhodesia. Until 1894 the colony was known as Mashonaland and was then renamed Southern Rhodesia.

Straits Settlements. Britain's control over the Malayan peninsula began with the establishment of Penang in 1786. In 1819 Singapore was acquired and in 1825 Malacca was ceded by the Dutch. They were united to form the Straits Settlements in 1826. Until 1867 the Straits Settlements colony was a part of British India and then became a Crown colony.

Swaziland. Swaziland was occupied by the Swazi about 1820. In 1820 it was placed under the administration of the South African Republic and it became a British protectorate in 1903.

Tanganyika. Tanganyika was the former colony of German East Africa and was conquered by British and Belgian forces, 1914–18.

Tasmania. Tasmania was discovered in 1642 by Tasman and named Van Diemen's Land. Great Britain annexed it to New South Wales in 1803 for use as an auxiliary penal colony. It was separated from New South Wales in 1825 and made a separate colony. In 1855 the island was renamed Tasmania. In 1901 Tasmania became a state in the Commonwealth of Australia.

Tobago. Tobago was ceded to Britain in 1814. In 1889 Tobago was separated from the Windward Islands and attached to Trinidad.

Tonga. Tonga became a British protectorate in 1900.

Transvaal. In 1877 British forces invaded and occupied the Boer Republic of Transvaal and it was annexed to the British Crown, but the British withdrew in 1881. In the Anglo-Boer War of 1899–1902 the territory was reoccupied by the British. In 1910 it was joined with the Cape Colony, Natal, and the Orange River Colony to form the Union of South Africa.

Trinidad and Tobago. In 1797 Trinidad was seized by Great Britain, and the occupation was confirmed under the Treaty of Amiens in 1802. In 1889 the neighbouring island of Tobago was added to Trinidad, and the Crown colony was then called Trinidad and Tobago.

Turks and Caicos Islands. The Turks Islands were annexed to the Bahamas in 1804 and the Caicos Islands were administered by the Bahamas from the 1790s. In 1848 the Turks and Caicos Islands were constituted a Presidency under the Governor of Jamaica and from 1873 became a dependency of Jamaica.

Uganda. The most powerful state in what was to become Uganda was Buganda. In 1894 Buganda was declared a protectorate, and similar proclamations followed for the other states of the area.

Union of South Africa. In 1910 the Cape Colony, Natal, the Orange River Colony and the Transvaal united to form the Union of South Africa.

Victoria. Victoria was colonized in 1834 by free settlers from Tasmania. In 1851 Victoria was separated from New South Wales. It joined the Commonwealth of Australia in 1901.

Weihaiwei. The port of Weihaiwei, in the province of Shantung, was leased by the British from China in 1898.

Western Australia. A penal colony was established in 1850 to supplement the population. Responsible government was granted to Western Australia in 1890. In 1901 Western Australia joined the Commonwealth of Australia.

Western Samoa. Western Samoa was the former German colony of Samoa. It was occupied by New Zealand troops in 1914.

Windward Islands. The Windward Islands government comprising Saint Lucia, Saint Vincent, Tobago, Grenada and the Grenadines, became a separate colony in 1885. In 1889 Tobago joined with Trinidad to form the colony of Trinidad and Tobago.

Zanzibar. Zanzibar became a British Protectorate in 1890.

Zululand. Zululand was a powerful Bantu kingdom established by Chaka in 1818 and dissolved after the war of 1879. It was annexed to Britain in 1888 and joined Natal in 1897.

ITALY

Eritrea. In 1870 the Italians established themselves at Assab, and at the withdrawal of the Egyptians in 1882 Italy proclaimed its sovereignty over Assab. Massawa was added in 1885. In 1890 the colony of Eritrea was established. By the Treaty of Uccialli in 1889 Ethiopia had, according to the Italian interpretation, accepted Italian rule in the Eritrean area. Conflicts over the validity of this interpretation led to an attempt by the Italians to expand into Ethiopia, but this effort was frustrated by the Ethiopians at Adowa in 1896.

Italian Somaliland. In the 1880s Great Britain and France established themselves in the northernmost Somali areas. In 1889 Italy proclaimed a protectorate over the Mijerstein sultanates of Alula and Obbia. After 1905 it was directly ruled as an Italian colony.

Libya. Libya was partially occupied by Italy during the Italo-Turkish war of 1911–12.

THE NETHERLANDS

Curaçao. From 1828 to 1845 Curaçao was subordinated to the Government-General of the Dutch West Indies with headquarters in Surinam. In 1845, with the addition of Saint Eustatius, Saint Martin and Saba, the colony became known as the Netherlands Antilles.

Gold Coast. In 1867 the eastern posts were sold to Britain and in 1872 the remaining posts were also sold for cash or for concessions in Sumatra.

Netherlands Antilles. In 1845 the colony of Curaçao with its dependencies of Aruba and Bonaire, and the colony of Saint Eustatius and its dependencies of Saint Martin and Saba, were united, with the seat of the government on Curaçao and were termed Netherlands Antilles.

Netherlands East Indies. From 1811 to 1816 Java and most of the rest of the East Indies were British-controlled but by an agreement of 1824 the Dutch were left with a free hand in the East Indies and during the rest of the nineteenth century gained control of Sumatra and various outlying islands.

Saint Eustatius. From 1828 to 1845 Saint Eustatius and its dependencies were part of the Government-General of the Dutch West Indies. Upon the dissolution of the Government-General in 1845 Saint Eustatius was attached to Curaçao and ceased to exist as a separate colony.

Surinam. Surinam was occupied by the British from 1804 to 1815 and was the only Dutch possession in Guiana which was returned after the Napoleonic Wars.

PORTUGAL

Angola. Angola was discovered by Diogo Cão in 1482 and came under Portuguese control from 1491 but remained nominally independent until 1883.

Cape Verde Islands. Settlement of the Cape Verde Islands began in 1462.

Macao. Macao was leased from China in 1557. In 1849 Portugal proclaimed its sovereignty over Macao and ceased paying an annual rent to China.

Mozambique. Vasco da Gama discovered Mozambique in 1498. Until the early nineteenth century prosperity depended on the slave trade.

Portuguese Guinea. This was probably discovered in 1446 and settled in the sixteenth century.

Portuguese India. Portuguese India consisted of 3 enclaves: Goa, seized in 1510, Diu, occupied in 1535 and Damão occupied in 1538.

São Tomé and Principe. Discovered in 1470.

Timor. Until 1844 Timor was under Portuguese India and from then to 1896 under Macao. In 1896 it became a separate colony.

RUSSIA

Russian America (Alaska). The coasts of Alaska were explored in 1741 by Bering. Various Russian trading companies were established from 1784. In 1867 Russia sold Alaska to the United States for $7·2m.

SPAIN

California. In 1822 California became part of the Republic of Mexico. Alta California fell into the hands of the United States in 1846, while Baja California continued to be a state of Mexico.

Ceuta and Melilla. Governed separately until 1847. With the formation of the Spanish zone of Morocco in 1913 they lost their administrative identity.

Cuba. In 1898 Cuba was occupied by the USA.

Guam. Ceded to the USA in 1898.

Philippine Islands. Ceded to the USA, 1898.

Puerto Rico. Ceded to the USA, 1898.

Spanish Guinea. Ceded to Spain by Portugal in 1777. The islands were leased to Britain in 1827, and in 1855 Spain started to administer the area.

Spanish West Africa. In 1860 Spain secured rights in the area from Morocco and in 1884 proclaimed a protectorate over the coast.

SWEDEN

Saint Bathélemy. This was a neutral port during the French Revolution and became prosperous. After the revolution it became an economic liability to Sweden, which had bought it from France in 1784, and the Swedish government attempted to sell it to the USA in 1845, 1868 and 1870. France repurchased the island in 1878 and incorporated it as a dependency of Guadeloupe.

10 POPULATION AND URBANIZATION

In the period 1848–1918 there were considerable major and minor boundary changes, and the notes in this chapter and the details of boundary changes on pp. 12–15 should be taken into consideration.

ALBANIA

1914	800–850,000
1924	831,877

AUSTRIAN EMPIRE[1,2]

1840	16,575,118
1851	17,534,950
1857	18,224,500
1869	20,217,531
1880	21,981,821
1890	23,707,906
1900	25,921,671
1910	28,571,934

URBANIZATION (towns greater than 10,000)

		% of pop.
1846	1,128,137	6·4
1857	1,551,494	8·5
1869	1,898,000	9·3
1880	2,836,457	12·8
1890	3,789,365	15·8

[1] All figures are exclusive of Bosnia and Herzegovina.
[2] Although censuses were taken before 1857, Weber considers these very unsatisfactory, and it is therefore best to treat these as estimates.

Vienna

1840	356,869
1850	431,147
1857	476,222
1869	607,514
1880	705,402
1890	798,719
1890	1,341,897[3]
1909	2,085,888

[3] In late 1890 Vienna incorporated numerous suburbs.

BELGIUM

1846	4,337,196
1856	4,529,461
1860	4,732,000
1866	4,827,833
1870	5,088,000
1876	5,336,185
1880	5,520,009
1890	6,069,321
1900	6,693,548
1910	7,423,784
1920	7,465,782

URBANIZATION (towns greater than 10,000)

1846	900,819
1890	2,105,436

Brussels[1]

1846	312,332
1866	287,241
1876	376,965
1889	469,317
1898	561,130
1908	637,807

[1] Inclusive of suburbs.

BULGARIA

1881	2,008,000
1888	3,154,375[1]
1905	4,035,623
1910	4,337,516
1917	5,517,000[2]

Sofia

1850	30,000
1893	47,000
1905	100,000

[1] All population figures from 1888 include E. Rumelia.
[2] Includes net gain of approximately 364,000 persons by the Treaty of Bucharest 1913.

CYPRUS

1871	150,000
1881	186,173
1891	209,286
1908	258,997

Nicosia

1891	12,515
1908	16,079

DENMARK[1]

1840	1,289,075
1850	1,408,000
1860	1,608,362
1870	1,794,723
1880	1,980,259
1886	2,097,000
1890	2,185,335
1906	2,605,268
1916	2,921,362

[1] All population figures include Faroes.

URBANIZATION

		%
1840	251,502	20·7
1860	360,919	22·5
1880	515,758	26·1
1890	663,121	34·0
1916	1,209,975	41·4

Copenhagen[2]

1840	123,740
1860	155,143
1880	234,850
1890	375,251
1906	514,134
1916	605,772

[2] After 1890 figures include suburbs.

FINLAND

1830	1,372,077
1870	1,768,769
1880	2,060,782
1890	2,380,140
1897	2,592,864
1905	2,892,088
1915	3,300,650

URBANIZATION

1830	76,489
1870	131,603
1890	235,227
1897	291,584
1905	398,797
1915	788,424

Helsinki

1887	55,740
1897	81,119
1907	130,844

FRANCE

1841	34,230,178
1851	35,783,170
1861[1]	37,386,313
1866	38,067,000
1872[2]	36,102,921
1881	37,672,048
1886	38,219,000
1891	38,342,948
1901	38,961,945
1911	39,601,509

URBANIZATION[3]

		%
1851	9,135,459	25·5
1861	10,789,766	28·94
1872	11,234,899	31·1[5]
1881	13,096,542	34·8
1891	14,311,292	37·4
1901	15,957,190	40·9
1911	17,508,940	44·0

Paris

1841	935,261
1851	1,053,262
1861	1,696,741[6]
1872	1,851,792
1881	2,269,023
1886	2,345,000
1891	2,447,957
1901	2,714,068
1911	2,888,110

[1] Includes 669,000 persons gained by the annexation of Nice and Savoy (1859).

[2] Includes loss of Alsace-Lorraine (1870).

[3] Since 1846 the French census reports have grouped together, as urban communes, all the communes which contain a population of more than 2000, living in contiguous houses. They do not have to all live in one community of over 2000, but they must all live in 'groups not entirely scattered'.

[4] Includes annexations of suburbs made by Paris (1859), Lyons (1852), Lille (1858), and Le Havre.

[5] Reflects loss of Alsace-Lorraine.

[6] Includes annexation of suburbs—approximately 500,000 people.

Note: French census statistics are generally regarded as being among the best in the nineteenth century.

217

GERMANY[1, 2]

1837	31,589,547 (est.)
1849	35,128,398 (est.)
1858	36,960,742 (est.)
1871	41,058,792
1880	45,234,061[3]
1885	46,856,000
1890	49,428,470
1900	56,367,178
1910	63,051,979

URBANIZATION[4]

		%
1871	14,790,798	36·1
1880	18,720,530	41·4
1890	23,243,229	47·0

Berlin

1840	328,692
1852	433,000
1858	458,637
1861	548,000
1867	702,437
1871	826,000
1875	966,872
1885	1,315,287
1895	1,677,304
1905	2,040,148
1910	2,071,257

[1] The statistics before 1871 are best treated as estimates.
[2] The population statistics for Germany are for all lands, except Heligoland, included in the German Empire in 1910.
[3] After 1871, includes Alsace-Lorraine.
[4] Urbanization figures are for *Gemeinder* containing more than 2000 persons.

218

PRUSSIA

1840	14,928,503 (est.)
1849	16,331,187 (est.)
1858	17,739,913 (est.)
1861	18,497,000
1867	23,971,337
1875	25,693,634
1880	27,251,000
1885	28,318,470
1895	31,849,795

GIBRALTAR

1862	15,462
1871	14,764
1889	24,089
1898	24,093
1911	25,367

Note: The population figures must be treated cautiously. Thus, the 1911 total includes 5781 military and naval personnel, the 1898 census contains 4965 and the 1889 census contains 5708 such personnel. It is *probable* that the 1871 and 1862 statistics are exclusive of the military, although the decline in population during 1862–75 is difficult to explain.

GREECE

1835	690,000
1852	1,002,112
1861	1,332,508
1870	1,457,894
1879	1,973,768[1]
1889	2,188,008
1896	2,433,806
1907	2,631,952
1913	4,821,300[2]

Athens

1852	31,125
1861	45,000
1870	46,000
1879	63,379
1889	107,251
1896	111,486
1907	167,479

[1] From and including 1879 all estimates include Thessaly, which was annexed in 1881. Without Thessaly, the 1879 population estimate was 1,679,775.

[2] The 1913 estimates include the annexations made from Turkey and Bulgaria.

219

HUNGARY [1]

1831	11,450,000
1850	13,191,553
1857	13,768,513
1869	15,417,327
1880	15,642,102
1890	17,349,398
1900	19,254,559
1910	20,886,487

URBANIZATION [2]

		%
1850	1,609,400	12·2
1857	1,858,800	13·5
1869	2,158,400	14·0
1880	2,408,900	15·4
1890	2,793,200	16·1

Budapest

1831	104,600
1850	156,506
1857	186,945
1869	254,476
1875	270,474
1886	422,557
1888	443,000
1890	505,763
1900	732,322
1910	880,371

[1] The statistics are for the Hungarian monarchy, not for Hungary proper. They therefore include Croatia, Slavonica, Slovakia and Transylvania.

[2] The Hungarian statistics regard as urban the population of 131 towns and cities possessing special political privileges. The relationship of the cities to size is this: 25 of the cities are known as 'towns with municipal charters' and contain, in each case, more than 10,000 inhabitants, their average population being, in 1880, 44,513, and in 1890, 53,243. The other cities are towns with magistrates appointed by the crown; they numbered 106 in 1880 (average population 8793) and 118 in 1890 (average population 10,550).

ICELAND

Sovereign state only since 1918, so these figures relate to the period when it was under Denmark's control.

1870	69,703
1880	72,445
1890	70,972
1901	78,470
1910	85,183

URBANIZATION

1910   27,464 lived in towns and villages greater than 300.

ITALY[1] [2]

1848	23,618,000
1861	21,777,334[3]
1871	27,577,640
1881	29,277,927
1888	30,565,000
1901	33,370,138
1911	35,694,582

URBANIZATION[4]

		%
1861	5,482,000	25·17
1871	6,875,600	24·93
1881	7,911,400	27·02

Rome

1860	184,049
1871	244,484
1881	273,268
1898	500,610
1909	575,000
1915	590,960

[1] It is difficult to obtain statistics prior to 1861; therefore all such statistics given should be treated as estimates.

[2] All figures for population before 1861 are for the territories included in the Kingdom of Italy in 1910.

[3] The 1861 figure excludes the annexed areas of Venezia, Rome and Mantua.

[4] In Italy, agricultural communities tend to be very large. Therefore, the figure of greater than 6000 inhabitants is taken as the definition of urban.

LUXEMBOURG

1895	217,583
1900	236,543
1916	263,824

MALTA[1]

1862	147,683
1871	149,084
1888	162,423
1898	180,320
1909	212,888
1911	228,534

[1] Inclusive of military.

MONTENEGRO[1]

1879	220,000
1900	228,000
1910	250,000
1917	436,789[2]

Cetinje

1890	1,500
1900	2,920
1910	4,500

[1] All statistics for Montenegro are estimates.
[2] The figures for 1917 include annexations made in the Treaty of Belgrade 1913.

THE NETHERLANDS

1849	3,056,879
1859	3,309,128
1869	3,579,529
1879	4,012,693
1886	4,391,000

(continued

THE NETHERLANDS

1889	4,511,415
1899	5,104,137
1909	5,858,175
1914	6,339,705

URBANIZATION[1]

		%
1849	884,938	29·0
1889	1,939,483	43·0

Amsterdam

1861	268,355
1877	296,200
1889	399,424
1898	512,953
1908	565,589
1918	644,070

[1] The urbanization figures are for towns greater than 10,000 persons. These figures present problems, because the township (*gemeerte*) includes a considerable rural population owing to its territorial extent.

NORWAY

1845	1,328,471
1855	1,490,047
1865	1,701,756
1875	1,818,853
1885	1,947,000
1891	2,000,917
1900	2,240,032
1910	2,391,782

URBANIZATION[1]

		%
1845	163,726	12·34
1855	203,265	13·62
1865	266,292	15·62
1875	332,398	18·25
1891	474,129	23·68
1900	627,650	27·99

[1] The urban definition is a medieval one. Its relation to population size is given by the following figures:
1890, of urban population of 474,129, all but 30,570 lived in towns greater than 2000.

223

Christiania

1845	33,177
1855	41,715
1865	57,382
1879	112,977
1886	130,027
1891	151,239
1900	227,626
1918	259,445

PORTUGAL

1850	3,471,000
1857	3,908,861
1860	3,608,000
1868	3,995,152
1878	4,550,699
1890	5,049,729
1900	5,423,132
1911	5,957,985

URBANIZATION (towns greater than 10,000)

		%
1857	465,000	11·89
1878	500,000	10·98
1890	648,935	11·96

Lisbon

1868	275,286
1878	246,343
1890	307,661
1900	356,009
1911	435,359

ROMANIA[1]

1859	4,424,961
1878	5,073,000
1887	5,500,000
1894	5,800,000
1912	7,508,009

URBANIZATION (towns greater than 10,000)

1889	710,500

Bucharest

1859	100,000
1876	221,805
1894	232,000
1914	345,628

[1] All statistics should be treated with some reserve.

RUSSIA[1]

1835	60,000,000
1846	65,900,000
1851	68,000,000
1859	74,000,000
1870	85,685,945
	78,281,447[2]
1887	113,354,649[3]
	98,870,810[2]
1897	129,209,297
	106,154,607[2]
1908	155,433,300
1915	182,182,600
	131,796,800[2]

[1] The first modern census was taken in 1897.
[2] European Russia includes Finland and Poland.
[3] Includes Bessarabia (from Romania) and Ardahan, Kars and **Batum** (from Turkey)—as result of 1878 treaty. Approximately 740,000 persons.

URBAN POPULATION

		%
1838	4,745,632	–
1856	5,684,000	–
1870	9,064,039	10·57
1885	13,947,825	–
1897	16,280,978	12·59
1908	19,832,800	12·75

Moscow

1863	351,627
1871	611,970
1884	753,469
1897	988,614
1907	1,359,254
1915	1,817,100

St Petersburg

1869	667,926
1888	978,309
1897	1,267,023
1905	1,678,000
1915	2,318,645

SERBIA

1874	1,352,522
1878	1,719,522[1]
1888	2,013,691
1895	2,312,484
1905	2,492,882
1910	2,911,701
1914	4,393,315[2]

URBANIZATION[3]

		%
1888	249,730	12·4
1895	307,490	13·3
1900	351,015	–

[1] Includes annexation of 367,000 inhabitants, by the Treaty of Berlin 1878.
[2] Includes gains of 1,481,614 persons, by the Treaty of Bucharest 1913.
[3] 'Actual agglomerated population' rather than communes.

Belgrade

1874	27,605
1888	38,313
1895	59,494
1905	77,890
1911	90,890

SPAIN[1]

1846	12,168,774
1857	15,464,340
1860	15,673,481 (est.)
1870	16,799,000
1877	16,634,345
1887	17,634,345
1897	18,132,475
1910	19,950,817

URBANIZATION (towns greater than 10,000)

		%
1857	2,570,000	16·2
1887	5,200,000	29·6

Madrid

1857	281,178
1877	384,636
1887	470,283
1900	539,835
1918	652,157

[1] The first reliable census is 1887.

SWEDEN

1840	3,138,887
1850	3,482,521
1860	3,859,728
1870	4,168,525
1880	4,565,668
1890	4,784,981
1900	5,136,441
1910	5,522,403
1918	5,813,850

URBANIZATION

		%
1840	303,683	9·67
1850	351,078	10·09
1860	434,519	11·26
1870	539,649	12·95
1880	690,431	15·12
1890	899,698	18·80
1900	1,103,951	21·49
1908	1,322,097	—
1918	1,657,864	28·52

Stockholm

		%
1840	113,310	2·68
1850	131,110	2·67
1860	149,830	2·90
1870	165,030	3·27
1880	186,800	3·70
1890	214,350	5·15
1908	339,582	—
1918	408,456	7·01

SWITZERLAND

1850	2,393,000
1860	2,507,170
1870	2,669,138
1880	2,846,102
1888	2,933,339
1900	3,315,443
1910	3,741,971

URBANIZATION

	Greater than 10,000	Greater than 5,000
1850	176,128	301,538
1888	480,388	726,060

228

Berne

1870	36,001
1904	68,958
1918	105,000

TURKEY[1]

About 1846	Population (sq. miles)	Area (sq. miles)
Turkey in Europe	15,500,000	207,438
in Asia	16,050,000	660,870
in Africa	3,800,000	943,740
	35,350,000	1,812,048
About 1879[2][3]		
Turkey in Europe	4,275,000	62,028
in Asia	15,715,000	710,320
in Africa	1,010,000	344,500
	21,000,000	1,116,848
About 1890		
Immediate possessions		
Europe	4,790,000	63,850
Asia	16,133,900	729,170
Africa	1,000,000	398,873
	21,923,900	1,191,893
Nominally subject states		
Bulgaria	3,154,375	37,860
Bosnia, Herzegovina and Novibazar	1,504,091	23,570
Samos	41,156	210
Egypt	6,817,265	400,000
	11,516,887	461,640
TOTAL	33,440,787	1,652,533

[1] Treat all the statistics for Turkey as estimates.

[2] These figures are exclusive of any nominally independent states.

[3] The figures are for Turkey after the Treaty of Berlin 1878, before this Turkey in Europe was 138,264 sq. miles and 8,315,000 persons.

About 1900

Immediate possessions	Population	Area (sq. miles)
Europe	5,711,000	62,744
Asia	16,823,500	650,097
Africa	1,300,000	398,900
	23,834,500	1,111,741
Nominally subject states		
Bulgaria	3,309,816	37,860
Bosnia, Herzegovina and Novibazar	1,568,092	23,570
Crete	294,190	3,326
Samos	49,733	180
Egypt	9,734,405	400,000
	14,956,236	464,936
TOTAL	38,790,736	1,576,677

About 1910[4]

Immediate possessions		
Europe	6,130,200	65,350
Asia	17,683,500	693,610
Africa	1,000,000	398,900
	24,813,700	1,157,860
Nominally subject states		
Crete	310,200	3,400
Cyprus	237,000	3,580
Samos	53,400	180
Egypt	10,000,000	400,000
	10,600,600	407,160
TOTAL	35,414,300	1,565,020

Constantinople

1885	equivalent to	873,565
1900	equivalent to	880,000
1910	equivalent to	1,000,000

---

[4] Does not include Bulgaria or Bosnia and Herzegovina. The former became independent, and the latter were annexed by Austria-Hungary in 1908.

230

UNITED KINGDOM [1]

1841	26,730,929
1851	27,396,629
1861	28,927,485
1871	31,484,661
1881	34,884,848
1891	37,732,922
1901	41,458,721
1911	45,367,344
1921	42,767,739 [2]

[1] Exclusive of the Isle of Man and Channel Islands.
[2] Excluding Northern Ireland, where no census was taken.

ENGLAND AND WALES

1841	15,914,148
1851	17,927,609
1861	20,066,224
1871	22,712,266
1881	25,974,439
1891	29,002,525
1901	32,527,843
1911	36,070,492
1921	37,886,699

SCOTLAND

1841	2,620,184
1851	2,888,742
1861	3,062,294
1871	3,360,018
1881	3,735,573
1891	4,025,647
1901	4,472,103
1911	4,760,904
1921	4,882,497

IRELAND

1841	8,196,597
1851	6,574,278
1861	5,798,967
1871	5,412,377
1881	5,174,836

1891	4,704,750
1901	4,458,775
1911	1,250,531[1]
1923	1,278,000[2]

[1] Northern Ireland only.
[2] Estimate.

LONDON[1]

1850/1	2,685,000
1860/1	3,227,000
1870/1	3,890,000
1880/1	4,770,000
1890/1	5,638,000
1900/1	6,586,000
1910/11	7,256,000
1920/1	7,488,000

[1] Greater London.

GLASGOW

1850/1	357,000
1860/1	420,000
1870/1	522,000
1880/1	587,000
1890/1	658,000
1900/1	776,000
1910/11	1,000,000
1920/1	1,052,000

11 ECONOMIC DEVELOPMENT

CHRONOLOGY OF ECONOMIC EVENTS

Feb 1848	Marx and Engels: *Communist Manifesto*.
25 Feb 48	National workshops erected in Paris; abolished, 21 June. Louis Blanc: *Droit au travail*.
1 May 48	Ten-hour day in English textile industry for women and youths.
7 Sep 48	Serfdom in Austria abolished. J. S. Mill: *Principles of Political Economy*. Public Health Act (Britain), first sanitary measure on statute book. Slavery abolished in French colonies.
9 Feb 49	Prussia again obliges tradesmen to join a guild. Schultze-Delitzsch founds first credit associations for working classes. Raiffeisen institutes co-operative loan banks in Germany. Prussia prohibits truck system.
7 May 49	Navigation Laws of 1651, 1661, 1662 and 1823 repealed (Britain).
22 Aug 49	Universal Peace Congress meets in Paris.
18 Mar 50	Insurance for the aged introduced in France. R. W. von Bunsen invents Bunsen burner.
1 May–15 Oct 51	Great Exhibition in London.
24 July 51	Window tax repealed (Britain).
7 Sep 51	Commercial treaty between Prussia and Hanover.
13 Nov 51	First submarine cable from Dover to Calais.
26–7 July 52	First congress of Co-operative Societies in London. Industrial and Provident Societies Act. Crédit Foncier, first great bank, founded in Paris. First airship flight, by Giffard.
–53	Hanover and Oldenburg join German *Zollverein*. Prussia prohibits child labour up to age of 12.
1 Jan 54	Commercial treaty between German *Zollverein* and Austria (–31 Dec 65). End of Chartist movement. Semmering

	railway, first railway across Alps. Heinrich Goebel invents electric bulbs.
−55	Paris World Exhibition. Hughes invents printing-telegraph. Austrian Creditanstalt, first bank for estate credits, founded.
15 June 55	Stamp on newspapers abolished (Britain).
−56	Bessemer invents process of converting iron into steel. Production of aniline dyes begins.
14 June 57	Monetary convention of Vienna introduces silver standard in Austria and *Zollverein* countries.
15 Jan 58	Alexander II begins emancipation of serfs in Russia. A. W. Hoffman discovers rosaniline. First European oil well drilled at Wietze, Hanover.
−59	De Lesseps begins Suez Canal.
24 Dec 59	First iron-clad launched at Toulon. Kirchhoff and Bunsen discover spectrum analysis.
23 Jan 60	Anglo-French commercial treaty ('Cobden Treaty'), with most-favoured-nation clause, abolishes English protective duties.
11 Mar 61	German Commercial Law Code.
16 Sep 61	Post Office Savings Banks opened (Britain).
29 Mar 62	Commercial treaty between Prussia and France, based on free-trade principles.
−62	Companies Act, introduces limited liability company (Britain).
16 July 63	Scheldt duties abolished. First international postal congress in Paris. *Crédit Lyonnais* founded as deposit bank. First underground railway (Metropolitan Line, London).
−64	Right of combination granted to workers in France.
30 May 65	Commercial treaty between Britain and *Zollverein*.
31 Dec 65	Commercial treaty between Prussia and Italy.
−66	W. Siemens invents dynamo. First condensed milk factory in Switzerland. The (later Royal) Aeronautical Society founded in London.
8 July 67	Customs treaties between North German Confederation and South Germany. Nobel invents dynamite. Typewriter and collotype process invented.
−70	Austro-Hungarian Chamber of Commerce in Constantinople, first Chamber of Commerce abroad.
29 June 71	Trade Unions legalized (Britain).
20 July 71	Purchase system in British army abolished.
4 Dec 71	Germany adopts gold standard.
Nov 72	Anglo-French commercial treaty. National Union of Agri-

cultural Workers founded (Britain). Union of Social Politics (*Kathedersozialisten*) founded in Germany.

−73 Severe economic crisis in Europe, America and Australia. Germany adopts mark coinage. Drainage of Het Y, Amsterdam, begun (−77).

30 Aug 74 Factory Act, institutes working week of 56½ hours (Britain).

9 Oct 74 *Union générale des postes* formed at Berne. France introduces factory inspectors and prohibits women working underground and child labour.

1 July 75 Universal Postal Union founded.

13 Aug 75 German Reichsbank founded. National bankruptcy in Turkey.

−76 First International dissolved. Industrial and Provident Societies Act. Graham Bell invents telephone. Enclosure of Commons Act (Britain).

23 Mar 77 Switzerland introduces factory inspection. Edison invents phonograph.

−78 Germany introduces factory inspection. Mannlicher invents repeating rifle. Factory and Workshop Act, regulating hours and conditions of employment.

12 July 79 British Chamber of Commerce established in Paris. Edison constructs electric bulb. Henry George: *Progress and Poverty*, agrarian reform, single tax on land (Britain).

7 Sep 80 Employers' Liability Bill (Britain). 'Boycotting' in Ireland.

22 Aug 81 Irish Land Law Act.

25 Jan 82 First meeting of London Chamber of Commerce.

18 Aug 82 Married Women's Property Act.

−83 Benz and Daimler factories established (Germany).

Jan 84 Russia abolishes poll tax, last relic of serfdom. French trade unions recognized by legislation. St Gotthard Tunnel opened. Fabian Society founded. First practical airship, by Renard and Krebs.

26 Apr 86 Prussian law expropriating Polish landowners in Western Prussia and Posen.

−Oct 88 France floats Russian loan.

14−15 Oct 88 Hamburg and Bremen join German Customs Union.

−88 Pasteur Institute, Paris, established. Hertz detects electromagnetic waves.

19 Aug−14 Sep 89 London dockers' strike. Belgium introduces factory inspection. Gustave Eiffel builds Eiffel Tower, Paris.

15−28 Mar 90 First international congress for protection of workers, in Berlin.

31 May 90	Siberian Railway begun (completed 1904).
25 May 91	Papal encyclical on Labour.
–92	Income tax adopted in Netherlands.
1 Feb 92	Gold standard adopted in Austria-Hungary.
14 June 92	National bankruptcy in Portugal. Commercial treaty between Austria-Hungary and Serbia (–1905).
6 Aug 93	Corinth Canal opened (Greece).
–95	French Trade Unions form Confédération Générale du Travail. Röntgen discovers X-rays. Lumière brothers invent cinematograph. Marconi invents wireless telegraphy.
1 Mar 97	Marconi founds Wireless Telegraph Company.
5 Aug 97	Workmen's Compensation Act (Britain). Ramsay discovers helium.
26 Nov 98	Gold standard in Russia. Zeppelin invents airship. M. and Mme Curie discover radium. Diesel motor first used.
26 June 99	Pupin invents inductance coils for telephone.
1 June 1900	Private postal services abolished in Germany.
2 July 00	First trial flight of Zeppelin.
26 Oct 00	Belgium adopts old age pensions. Browning revolver invented.
13 Dec 01	First wireless communication between America and Europe.
10 May 02	National bankruptcy in Portugal.
14 Aug 03	Krupp Company founded.
–04	Ten-hour day in France.
–05	Sunday labour further reduced in England.
–06	Night work by women internationally forbidden. *Confederazione Generale del Lavoro* founded in Italy. Norway adopts unemployment insurance.
19 May 06	Simplon tunnel opened. Zuider Zee drainage begun.
–07	Shell Oil Trust founded. Lumière invents colour photography.
–08	Old Age Pensions Bills in Britain and Australia.
Aug–Dec 08	Wilbur Wright flies in France, revolutionizes European aviation.
25 July 09	Blériot makes first crossing of English Channel by aeroplane.
–10	International Motor-Car Convention. Swiss railways nationalized. Old Age Pensions in France.
–11	British National Insurance Act.
–12	French *Code du Travail* issued. Russia adopts Workmen's Insurance.

−13   Netherlands and Switzerland adopt old age and sickness insurance.

−14   Belgium adopts old age, sickness, and disablement insurance. Switzerland extends measures against female and child labour.

INTERNATIONAL TRADE

	IMPORTS			EXPORTS		
	1861−70 *£m.*	*1871−80* *£m.*	*1881−90* *£m.*	*1861−70* *£m.*	*1871−80* *£m.*	*1881−90* *£m.*
United Kingdom	2,701	3,714	2,746	2,129	2,778	1,986
France	1,090	1,560	1,157	1,100	1,390	945
Germany	950	1,740	1,095	680	1,270	1,083
Russia	270	490	346	280	480	401
Austria	302	570	350	350	505	422
Italy	361	472	376	263	444	301
Spain and Portugal	222	253	273	164	242	235
Belgium	305	562	416	246	441	360
The Netherlands	319	630	618	258	432	487
Scandinavia	169	348	278	151	262	200
Total Europe	6,872	10,513	8,175	5,846	8,403	6,790

INTEREST RATES

	1851−60 %	*1861−70* %	*1871−80* %	*1881−5* %	*Average 35 years* %	*1889* %
Great Britain	4·17	4·23	3·28	3·30	3·81	3·55
France	4·30	3·55	3·94	3·34	3·84	3·18
Germany	4·05	4·56	4·30	4·20	4·28	3·70
Austria	5·26	4·77	4·79	4·71	4·91	4·12
Italy	5·35	5·69	4·85	4·74	5·22	
The Netherlands	3·60	3·98	3·40	3·56	3·64	2·50
Belgium	3·62	3·59	3·60	3·66	3·62	3·62
Europe	4·27	4·30	3·71	3·93	4·12	3·44

237

BANKING (1870)

	Capital employed £m.	Deposits £m.
United Kingdom	284	626
France	140	168
Germany	85	146
Russia	42	64
Austria	45	102
Italy	25	83
Spain	31	16
Portugal	6	4
Sweden	9	15
Norway	5	1
Denmark	2	21
Belgium	11	19
The Netherlands	14	6
Switzerland	5	12
Europe	704	1,243

MINERAL PRODUCTION

AUSTRIA[1]

	Coal[2] (tons '000)	Petroleum (tons)	Iron Ore (tons '000)	Steel[3] (tons '000)
1845	689			
1850	877			
1855	1,820		599	
1860	3,189		—	
1865	4,450	300	—	
1870	7,217	400	835	22
1875	11,401	600	705	89
1880	14,311	1,000	697	124
1885	17,893	2,200	931	289
1890	24,260	99,000	1,362	516
1895	28,112	195,000	1,385	753
1900	32,533	349,000	1,894	1,170
1905	35,278	797,000	1,914	1,459
1910	38,907	1,768,000	2,628	2,174
1915	38,354	578,000	2,547	—

[1] Figures from 1845 apply to the Kingdom of Austria.
[2] Figures are for hard coal and lignite.
[3] Statistics are for the whole Austro-Hungarian Empire

BELGIUM

	Coal (tons '000)	Steel (tons '000)
1831	2,305	
1835	2,639	
1840	3,930	
1845	4,919	
1850	5,821	
1855	8,409	
1860	9,611	
1865	11,841	
1870	13,697	
1875	15,011	54
1880	16,867	132
1885	17,438	155
1890	20,366	221
1895	20,458	408
1900	23,463	655
1905	23,348	1,227
1910	25,523	1,892
1915	14,178	99
1918	13,891	11

BULGARIA

	Coal (tons '000)
1880	1
1885	6
1890	25
1895	62
1900	123
1905	173
1910	227
1915	533
1918	673

FRANCE

	Coal (tons '000)	Iron ore (tons '000)	Steel (tons '000)
1845	4,202	2,460	
1850	4,434	1,821	
1855	7,453	3,876	
1860	8,304	3,033	
1865	11,600	3,011	
1870[1]	13,330	2,614	84
1875	16,957	2,506	239
1880	19,362	2,874	389
1885	19,511	2,318	554
1890	26,083	3,472	683
1895	28,020	3,680	876
1900	33,404	5,448	1,565
1905	35,928	7,395	2,255
1910	38,350	14,606	3,413
1915	19,533	620	1,111
1918	26,259	1,672	1,800

[1] From 1871 to 1918 parts of Alsace and Lorraine ceded to Germany are excluded.

GERMANY

	Coal (tons '000)	Petroleum (tons '000)	Iron Ore (tons '000)	Steel (tons '000)
1845	5,600		429	
1850	6,900		830	
1855	12,800		1,345	
1860	16,731		1,259	
1865	28,553		2,546	
1870[1]	34,003		2,918	126
1875	47,804	1	3,690	318
1880	59,119	1	5,065	690
1885	73,675	6	6,509	1,203
1890	89,251	15	8,047	2,135
1895	103,877	17	8,437	3,891
1900	149,569	50	12,793	6,461
1905	173,797	79	16,848	9,669
1910	222,302	140	22,446	13,100
1915	234,816	99	17,710	12,278
1918	258,854		18,392	14,092

[1] From 1871 to 1918 parts of Alsace-Lorraine are included.

240

GREECE

	Coal (tons '000)
1910	1·5
1915	40
1918	213

HUNGARY

	Coal (tons '000)	Petroleum (tons '000)
1845	21	
1851	159	
1855[1]	147	
1860	475	
1865	620	
1870	1,140	
1875	1,452	
1880	1,818	
1885	2,543	
1890	3,247	1·0
1895	4,543	2·1
1900	6,497	2·2
1905	7,177	4·7
1910	9,036	2·5
1916	9,084	5·9

[1] From 1855 total includes hard coal and lignite.

ITALY

	Coal	Petroleum	Sulphur (tons '000)	Iron Ore	Steel
1861	34		166	83	
1865	37	0·3	172	142	
1870	59	—	204	89	
1875	117	0·1	207	228	
1880	139	0·3	360	289	3
1885	190	0·3	426	201	3
1890	376	0·4	369	221	108
1895	305	3·6	371	183	50
1900	480	1·7	554	247	116

241

ITALY

	Coal	Petroleum	Sulphur (tons '000)	Iron Ore	Steel
1905[1]	413	6·1	569	367	270
1910	562	7·1	430	551	732
1915	953	6·1	358	680	1,009
1918	2,171	4·9	234	694	933

[1] Hard coal and lignite from 1905.

LUXEMBOURG

	Iron Ore	Steel
	(tons '000)	
1868	722	
1870	912	
1875	1,091	
1880	2,173	
1885	2,648	
1890	3,359	97
1895	3,913	135
1900	6,171	185
1905	6,596	398
1910	6,263	598
1915	6,140	980[1]
1918	3,131	888

1 Including castings from 1915.

THE NETHERLANDS

	Coal[1]
	(tons '000)
1870	32
1875	43
1880	39
1885	46
1890	109
1895	127
1900	320
1905	468
1910	1,293
1915	2,333
1918	5,032

[1] Figures to 1885 relate to state-owned mines only, and from 1890 to 1918 they relate to Limburg province only

NORWAY

	Coal[1]	Iron Ore
	(tons '000)	
1861		24
1865		50
1870		21
1875		29
1880		7
1885		−
1890		1
1895		1
1900		18
1905		63
1910	5	102
1915	18	715
1918	55	96

[1] The entire output came from Spitzbergen.

PORTUGAL

	Coal
	(tons '000)
1902	1
1908	5
1915	60
1918	185

ROMANIA

	Coal	Petroleum
	(tons '000)	
1857		0·3
1860		1·2
1865		5·4
1870		12
1875		15
1880		16
1885		27
1890		54
1895		80
1900	86	247
1905	130	681
1910	−	1,326
1915	254	1,588
1918	−	969

243

RUSSIA

	Coal	Petroleum	Iron Ore	Steel
		(tons '000)		
1860	300	4		1·6
1865	380	9		4
1870	690	33		9
1875	1,700	153		13
1880	3,290	382		307
1885	4,270	1,966		193
1890	6,010	3,864	1,736	378
1895	9,100	6,935	2,851	879
1900	16,160	10,684	6,001	2,216
1905	18,670	8,310	4,976	2,266
1910	25,430	11,283	5,742	3,314
1915[1]	31,440	9,442	5,940	4,120
1918	13,100	4,146	590	402

[1] From 1915 statistics apply to the 1923 boundaries of the Soviet states.

SERBIA

	Coal
	(tons '000)
1893	118
1895	62
1900	156
1905	185
1910	277

SPAIN

	Coal	Iron Ore	Steel
		(tons '000)	
1860	340	173	
1865	495	192	
1870	–	436	
1875	610	520	
1880	847	3,565	
1885	946	3,933	20
1890	1,210	6,055	80
1895	1,784	5,514	100
1900	2,675	8,676	122

SPAIN

	Coal	Iron Ore (tons '000)	Steel
1905	3,372	9,077	265
1910	4,058	8,667	316
1915	4,687	5,618	387
1918	7,238	4,693	303

SWEDEN

	Coal	Iron Ore (tons '000)	Steel
1845		234	
1850		281	
1855		359	
1860	26	395	
1865	34	497	
1870	37	616	12
1875	64	822	19
1880	101	775	37
1885	174	873	77
1890	188	941	168
1895	224	1,904	197
1900	252	2,610	300
1905	322	4,366	368
1910	303	5,549	472
1915	412	6,883	600
1918	404	6,624	545

UNITED KINGDOM

	Coal	Iron Ore (tons '000)	Steel
1845	46,600		
1850	50,200		
1855	65,487	9,707	
1860	81,327	8,153	
1865	99,726	10,069	
1870	112,203	14,602	
1875	135,445	16,075	719
1880	149,327	18,315	1,316
1885	161,908	15,665	1,917

245

UNITED KINGDOM

	Coal	Iron Ore	Steel
		(tons '000)	
1890	184,528	14,002	3,636
1895	192,704	12,817	3,312
1900	228,794	14,253	4,980
1905	239,918	14,825	5,905
1910	268,676	15,470	6,476
1915	257,269	14,463	8,687
1918	231,404	14,847	9,692

AGRICULTURAL PRODUCTION

AUSTRIA

	Wheat	Rye and Spelt	Barley	Oats	Potatoes
			(hectolitres '000)		
1842	9,399	23,521	15,996	28,850	41,992
1851	9,630	23,519	15,501	29,433	40,765
1859	11,598	29,762	16,030	32,002	43,840
1870	12,835	27,401	16,226	28,530	83,008
1880	14,302	22,753	17,809	32,680	85,770
			(metric tons '000)		
1890	15,528	28,538	19,188	36,731	8,234
1900	1,114	1,394	1,339	1,714	11,702
			(metric tons '000)		
1910	1,567	2,771	1,472	2,063	13,366
1918	140	270	92	188	585

BELGIUM

	Wheat	Rye	Barley	Oats	Potatoes
			(hectolitres '000)		
1846	3,584	2,055	1,143	4,770	15,292
			(metric tons '000)		
1871–80[1]	432	417	78	389	2,487
1900	375	504	104	569	2,393
1910	381	583	92	631	2,912

[1] Averages.

BULGARIA

	Wheat	Rye	Barley	Oats	Potatoes
			(tons '000)		
1900	706	171	237	92	—
1910	1,150	230	307	156	12
1918	631	110	148	52	15

DENMARK

	Wheat	Rye	Barley	Oats	Potatoes
			(hectolitres '000)		
1875	1,759	5,956	8,154	10,798	4,183
1880	1,797	6,591	8,857	12,131	4,798
1890	1,330	5,993	8,265	13,148	4,390
1900	1,270	7,032	8,045	14,212	8,222
1910	1,925	6,352	7,832	14,816	832[1]

[1] In metric tons. (metric tons '000)

	Wheat	Rye	Barley	Oats	Potatoes
1918	172	323	467	603	1,105

FINLAND

	Wheat	Rye	Barley	Oats	Potatoes
			(hectolitres '000)		
1878	36	3,103	1,639	2,683	3,307
1890	51	4,518	2,312	5,518	6,068
1900	56	4,044	1,634	6,239	5,415
1910	44	3,632	1,736	7,106	6,127
1917	80	3,141	1,587	6,625	6,737

FRANCE

	Wheat	Rye	Barley	Oats	Potatoes
			(tons '000)		
1840	6,070	1,970	1,080	2,290	6,920
1850	6,600	1,790[1]	1,110[1]	2,940[1]	4,170
1860	7,620	1,770[2]	1,330[2]	3,330[2]	10,270
1871	5,200	1,940	1,650	4,040	8,470
1880	7,550	1,870	1,220	3,990	10,470
1890	8,970	1,730	1,080	4,420	11,040
1900	8,860	1,510	910	4,140	12,250
1910	6,880	1,110	970	4,820	8,520
1918	6,140	730	600	2,560	6,520

[1] 1852.   [2] 1862.

247

GERMANY

	Wheat	Rye	Barley	Oats	Potatoes
			(tons '000)		
1846	1,416	2,927	1,533	2,383	7,055
1850	1,846	4,499	1,872	3,098	10,942
1860	2,491	6,561	2,261	4,623	11,925
1870	2,409	6,247	2,101	3,973	20,366
1880[1]	3,236	5,862	2,550	5,128	22,795
1890	3,743	6,926	2,712	5,934	27,316
1900	4,307	8,551	3,002	7,092	40,585
1910	4,249	10,511	2,903	7,900	43,468
1918	2,528	6,676	1,850	4,381	24,744

[1] Alsace-Lorraine included from 1880.

HUNGARY

	Wheat	Mixed Corn and Rye	Barley	Oats	Potatoes
			(hectolitres '000)		
1851	20,134	19,520	18,653	29,103	16,980
1859	27,922	28,927	19,300	35,842	17,694
1870	22,260	17,728	11,132	12,777	12,159
1880	27,954	14,465	17,943	21,729	31,024
			(metric tons '000)		
1890	52,165	20,235[1]	18,647	18,777	29,755
1900	3,843	1,113	1,173	1,025	4,497
1910	4,619	1,329	1,168	1,026	4,816
1918	2,588	824	879	667	3,122

[1] Rye only from 1890.

IRELAND

	Wheat	Barley	Oats	Potatoes
			(tons '000)	
1847	624	297	1,639	2,081
1850	331	287	1,471	4,009
1860	271	140	1,258	2,785
1870	161	191	1,073	4,286
1880	113	175	994	3,034
1890	72	156	904	1,839
1900	46	141	890	1,872
1910	47	149	955	2,917
1918	154	182	1,472	3,925

ITALY

	Wheat	Rye	Barley (tons '000)	Oats	Potatoes
1861	3,290	168	182	231	864
1870	4,039	162	197	337	1,248
1880	4,702	176	327	347	1,151
1890	3,613	112	255	335	1,202
1900	3,903	127	204	333	1,521
1910	4,064	156	212	370	2,545
1918	4,856	149	216	587	2,331

THE NETHERLANDS

	Wheat	Rye	Barley (hectolitres '000)	Oats	Potatoes
1842	1,051	2,642	1,101	2,296	–
1850	1,531	3,368	1,280	2,504	9,651
1860	1,774	3,758	1,485	3,261	12,472
1870	2,056	3,892	1,849	4,093	16,446
1880	2,080	3,301	1,751	4,767	13,923
1890	1,912	3,916	1,464	4,666	18,941
1900	1,646	4,808	1,615	6,095	28,338
1910	1,565	5,412	1,093	6,357	31,144
1918	1,914	4,589	922	6,561	45,913

NORWAY

	Wheat	Rye	Barley (tons '000)	Oats	Potatoes
1835	1·1	7·6	44	86	261
1900	9	23	68	159	554
1910	8	23	70	186	570
1918	30	27	128	274	780

PORTUGAL

	Wheat	Rye	Barley (hectolitres '000)	Oats	Potatoes
1882	2,054	1,718	773	294	–
			(metric tons '000)		
1911	322	–	–	–	–
1916	206	81	28	57	171
1918	261	123	32	66	152

ROMANIA

	Wheat	Rye	Barley	Oats	Potatoes
			(hectolitres '000)		
1867	10,230	1,039	2,947	740	—
1870	9,864	1,345	2,840	740	—
1876	7,558	1,182	6,364	1,413	—
1890	18,267	1,671	5,699	2,678	—
1900	19,875	2,119	5,122	3,064	—
			(metric tons '000)		
1910	3,016	201	644	446	132
1918	584	43	109	85	72

RUSSIA

	Wheat	Rye	Barley	Oats	Potatoes
			(hectolitres '000)		
1870	99,000	278,000	58,000	265,000	146,000
1879	60,000	202,000	44,000	179,000	122,000
1890	94,000	197,000	72,000	238,000	146,000
			(metric tons '000)		
1900	9,200	22,700	4,500	11,500	25,300
1910	22,800	22,200	10,600	15,500	36,600
1913	28,000	25,700	13,100	18,200	35,900

SERBIA

	Wheat	Rye	Barley	Oats	Potatoes
			(tons '000)		
1893	238	33	55	47	22
1900	221	17	49	39	29
1910	348	35	88	63	44

SPAIN

	Wheat	Rye	Barley	Oats	Potatoes
			(tons '000)		
1901	3,726	721	1,738	331	—
1910	3,741	701	1,661	421	3,617
1918	3,693	773	1,970	442	2,601

SWEDEN

	Wheat	Rye	Barley (tons '000)	Oats	Potatoes
1839-40	36	308	244	167	596
1849-50	48	366	282	209	624
1860	69	436	286	536	–
1870	89	551	365	760	1,511
1880	105	568	382	917	1,501
1890	108	562	356	1,205	813
1900	150	669	333	1,193	1,587
1910	209	622	330	1,290	1,604
1918	242	490	252	814	1,833

SWITZERLAND

	Wheat	Rye	Barley (tons '000)	Oats	Potatoes
1910	75	41	9	63	650
1918	142	47	15	75	935

UNITED KINGDOM

	Wheat	Barley (hectolitres '000)	Oats	Potatoes (metric tons '000)
1884	26,169	26,877	39,780	3,803
1890	26,674	26,885	43,704	2,857
1900	19,142	22,660	41,763	2,779
		(metric tons '000)		
1910	1,526	1,360	2,200	3,533
1918	2,467	1,320	3,013	5,446

12 THE CHURCH

AUSTRIA

1855   18 Aug. Concordat with Papacy, *volte-face* achievement of Franz Joseph's mother, Sophie, and Archbishop Rauscher of Vienna, who was made a cardinal as a reward. State control of the church abolished. Clergy given control of education, censorship and marriage. Church acquired right to ask for help from the state to apply ecclesiastical penalties. The state promised that it would not alter confessional laws without the consent of the church.

1861   Clericals attacked constitution as being too liberal.

1868   Attack on church privileges, Prince Auersperg fighting Cardinal Rauscher

Civil marriage restored and the state regained the supervision of schools. Church entitled only to open new ones. Protestant churches given the same rights as those enjoyed by Catholics.

The Pope denounced the new laws as 'truly unholy . . . destructive, abominable and damnable'. Some bishops urged people to disobey the laws. Bishop Riegler of Linz jailed. Jews granted full civil liberties. Immigration, mostly from Galicia and particularly into Vienna, followed. Jews in Vienna: 1870, 40,000; 1880, 70,000; 1910, 145,000.

1870   Government forbade the promulgation of the papal dogma of infallibility from the pulpit. Concordat cancelled 30 July. Branches of Old Catholics formed in Austria.

1874   May Acts limited the powers of the church regarding support of clergy, appointments to spiritual office and new religious orders. Denominational schools restored. The bishops said they would obey the laws only in so far as they were in agreement with the concordat. In practice the laws were not enforced.

1894   Civil marriage made obligatory and sufficient. Fine imposed on any priest blessing spouses before civil registration of marriage. Pope Leo XIII made a show of interest in the racial elements of the empire, pro-Slav, pro-Hungarian.

1897   *Los von Rom* (freedom from Rome) movement grows.

Pope Pius X would not condemn anti-Jewish campaigns of the

Social Christians, claiming that the Jews inspired the secularizing laws.

1909   Archduke Franz Ferdinand, energetic head of the Central Commission for the Care of Monuments, did much to preserve the little churches particularly of Upper Austria. 'Every priest seems to have got it into his head that he is in duty bound to have his church redecorated from top to bottom, regardless of the ruin of the ancient and beautiful objects in his charge.'

1918   Population said to be:

%
93·68   Roman Catholics
3·11   Protestants
2·93   Jews—chiefly in Upper Carinthia, the upper valleys of Traum, Enns and Drava, and in Vorarlberg

Austria maintained toleration in Bosnia-Herzegovina, annexed 1908. The population was estimated at 800,000 Orthodox, 400,000 Catholics, 600,000 Moslems, 8000 Jews. Moslem recruits in the Austrian army had to perform their religious duties strictly. One Catholic archbishopric formed, Sarajevo 1881.

In the territories represented in the Imperial (Austrian) Diet there were seven archiepiscopal provinces of the Latin rite and one each of Latin and Armenian.

Vienna (Primus), Salzburg, Prague, Olmutz, Gorz, Zara, Lemberg. The Prince Bishopric of Cracow was directly subject to the Holy See.

Lemberg-Armenian rite.

Lemberg-Greek-Ruthenian (1808).

Religious estimates were:

Latin Rite	20,661,000
Greeks	3,134,000
Armenians	2,000
Jews	1,225,000
Greeks, Eastern	607,000
Evangelicals	491,000
Old Catholics	13,000

BELGIUM

1850   Pope Pius IX protested against law making secondary education subject to state control. Bishops proclaimed Antwerp Rule, requiring only Catholic chaplains in state establishments.

Church conflict between the rigid traditionalists Cardinal Sterckx and Henri de Mérode, and the more liberal Barthelemy Dumertier and Adolphe Deschamps, allied with Journal de Bruxelles.

1865   Death of Leopold I, Protestant King who supported Catholic Church as force for order.

Great Belgian support for missionary school of Father Alberic de Foresta, Jesuit of Avignon.

1871   Christian-Democrat movement founded by Gustave de Jaer. Belgium dedicated to Sacred Heart by Mgr Dechamps. Social Catholicism strong and Congrès des Oeuvres Sociales led by Mgr Doutreloux, bishop of Liège.

July 79   Frère-Orban, liberal and freemason Prime Minister, secured law creating free 'neutral schools'. Catholic faith to be taught only outside class hours. Belgian bishops protested and resulting quarrel ended in diplomatic relations with the papacy being ended. Private Catholic schools organized.

1884   Catholics, united in Fédération des cercles and led by Comité central catholique, won election (70 in Chamber against 52 liberals). Catholics in power for 30 years, obtained new education law making many public schools Catholic and restored relations with papacy.

20 Sep 84   Worker priests among miners.

1895   Religious instruction obligatory in all public schools.

1911   Tendency among Belgian Catholic Party to make common cause with non-Catholics, which alarmed conservatives.

Dioceses: Bruges, Ghent, Liège, Malines, Namur, Tournai, under archbishop of Malines, the primate.

Schools: Private schools founded to provide Catholic teaching

1880   580,380 private primary pupils against 333,500 in state schools.

1909   16,538 private secondary pupils against 6,000 in state schools.

Religious schools

1829   4,791

1846   11,968

1910   38,140

BULGARIA

1856   Porte promised church reform with Bulgarian bishops and recognition of Bulgarian language in church and school. Promises not implemented.

1860   Bulgaria refused to recognize any longer patriarchate of Constantinople. Russia opposed move to bring the church in Bulgaria under Rome.

1870   Turks promised to make Bulgarian church free and national. Bulgarian Exarchate established at Constantinople (1872).

1876   In reply to civil disorders the Turks massacred at least 12,000 Bulgarian Christians. Outburst of anger in England. Gladstone, in pamphlet *The Bulgarian Horrors and the Question of the East*, which sold 40,000 copies in four days, demanded that the Turks should go 'bag and baggage . . . from the province they have desolated and profaned'.

1894   Turkey agreed to two bishops of the Bulgarian (exarchist) church working in Macedonia. This lessened the power of the Greek patriarchate at Constantinople and also favoured the Bulgarian claim to Macedonia, disputed by Greeks and Serbs.

1908   Bulgaria independent.

In 1918 the Orthodox Greek Church, the state religion in Bulgaria, was estimated to have 4 million members in Bulgaria. In addition there were 690,000 Moslems and 35,000 Roman Catholics in the diocese of Nicopolis and vicariate of Sofia.

DENMARK

1849   By the constitution all citizens could worship God as they pleased. Only the King had to be a member of the national church. Article three of the constitution said 'The Evangelical Lutheran Church is the Danish Folk-Church and as such is supported by the State.' No constitution was agreed for the church, parliament acting as legislative and money-voting authority with a politically elected Minister of State as top administrative authority.

1855   Members of Folk-Church allowed to transfer allegiance from one parish to another.

1868   Group within a parish allowed to form its own congregation with right to select priest, use parish church and have Folk-Church's organization for oversight.

1870   Home Mission Movement (Indre Misjon) introduced Sunday schools under English influence.

Social Democrat Party, anti-clerical, demanded disestablishment.

Søren Kierkegaard (1813–55), philosopher who discussed the basic principles of Christianity and held that life must be lived individually with Christ, bitterly attacked the principles of the Danish church.

N. F. S. Grundtvig (1783–1872), pastor who campaigned for freedom in education, laid emphasis on baptism and eucharist, and collective life in church and state. His followers set up folk high schools.

1890   Church fund for building churches in residential areas.

1903   Congregational councils set up, one to each parish, consisting of clergy and an elected membership of 6–15, according to size of parish. Members elected for 4 years. Duties primarily to manage fabric and funds but members took part in election of clergy and bishops.

The King appointed to all permanent posts after submission of names by the Ministry of Churches, which received selection from congregational council.

FRANCE

1850   Falloux's law permitted secondary education outside the state system, which resulted in almost as many pupils in Catholic secondary schools as in state schools. Napoleon III, welcomed by Te Deum sung in Notre Dame, helped the clergy while they served him. Church budget increased from 39·5m. francs to 48m. Generals and prefects at Mass in full uniform. *Tartuffe* banned in some cities. Children in Roman Catholic elementary schools:

	1850	*1866*
	%	%
Boys	15·7	20·9
Girls	44·6	55·4

Napoleon III dealt lightly with anti-religious forces to counter-balance Catholic critics of his policy, which had reduced the temporal power of the Papacy. Anti-clericalism grew.

1863   *Life of Jesus* by philosopher Ernest Renan (1823–92) caused great controversy. Treated Christ simply as an historical figure.

Empress Eugénie accused of fomenting war with Protestant Prussia.

1870   Commune hated the monarchy and the church which had supported it. It enacted (i) the separation of church and state; (ii) the abolition of the religious affairs budget. Of 67 Paris Catholic churches 30 were used by Communards as clubs. 120 priests were imprisoned, 24 were killed including the Archbishop of Paris, Mgr Darboy. The National Assembly was friendly towards the Roman

Catholic Church. It approved preliminary consultation with the Pope about the choice of bishops.

Sacre-Coeur in Paris, started 1875, was a symbol of the church and state alliance. The Crédit Foncier was founded to put the savings of Catholics to productive use. Opposition to the church grew as the Third Republic became more firmly established. *Le cléricalisme, voilà l'ennemi* – Leon Gambetta. Catholics, by their tactlessness, fomented anti-clericalism, e.g. Cardinal Pie, bishop of Poitiers, was aggressively monarchical: 'France awaits a leader, France calls for a master.' Priests rebuked teachers for singing the Marseillaise; republican shopkeepers were named from the pulpit and a boycott urged of their goods. The Ligue d'Enseignement, to which teachers belonged, was anti-clerical.

1877   The Masonic Assembly of Grand Orient, to which French lodges belonged, struck from its rules the obligation of freemasons to accept a belief in God and the immortality of the soul.

Jules Ferry (1832–93), minister of public instruction, an atheist freemason.

Bishops removed from superior council of public instruction, seminaries conscripted for military service, subsidies for public worship reduced.

1880   State primary education made free and compulsory. Religious teaching in schools abolished.

1882   Collapse of Union Générale, founded by Catholics to break Jewish and Protestant grip on finance. Bitter attack on Jews in Catholic *La Croix*, controlled by the Assumptionist order.

The Pope tried to curb anti-republic attitude of Catholics.

1884   Encyclical *Nobilissima Gallorum gens* bade clergy obey their 'legitimate superiors'.

1885   Encyclical *Immortale Dei* encouraged understanding with Republicans.

1886   Teachers belonging to religious orders removed from state schools.

Boulanger crisis. Many Catholics, seeking the overthrow of the republic, supported him and were compromised when he fled (1889).

1890   Pope Leo XIII's Ralliement to encourage Catholics to accept the republic and so lessen anti-clerical attacks. Encyclical *Sapientiae christianae*: 'To draw the Church towards one party, or to seek her as an ally against one's political foes, is an abuse of religion.' The Pope used Cardinal Lavigerie, founder of the White Fathers (1868), Archbishop of Algiers and Carthage, a former monarchist, as his mouthpiece.

Assumptionist order dissolved.

1891 Five French cardinals produced an indictment of the government in recording the anti-religious legislation of the previous ten years.

1892 Encyclical *Au milieu des solicitudes*, declaring 'acceptance of the new régime is not only permitted but demanded . . .'

1894 Most Catholics assumed Dreyfus was guilty and lay themselves wide open to attack when his innocence was proved.

Anti-clerical campaign led by René Waldeck-Rousseau (1846–1904) and Emile Combes (1835–1921), a former seminarist.

1901 Law allowed associations to be formed freely but congregations had to be licensed.

1904 Law suppressing teaching congregations resulted in disorders in Finistère.

Quarrels on the choice of bishops, Pius X's protest at President Loubet visiting Rome, French government's refusal to allow the bishops of Dijon and of Laval to be judged by a papal tribunal, resulted in:

1905 Separation of church and state.

Napoleon's concordat and 77 Organic Articles repealed. Republic would neither recognize nor subsidize any religious creed. Churches remained the property of the state but were at the disposal of ministers and congregations. Roman Catholic bishops henceforth to be appointed by Rome.

1906 Encyclical *Vehementer nos* condemned principle of separation.

1914 Pope Benedict XV attacked as favouring the Central Powers, e.g. Clemenceau called him, 'the Bosche Pope'.

1920 Steps towards reconciliation with Papacy. Canonization of Joan of Arc. Government represented.

Church population

Roman Catholic ordinations:

1814	715
1821	1,400
1829	2,350
1841	1,100
1847	1,309
1869	1,753
1878	1,582

Roman Catholic regulars:

		females
1789	70,000	
1830	3,000	
1851	3,100	34,200
1861	17,700	89,200
1877	30,200	127,700
1909	55,000	

In 1909, of population of 39m., 38m. Roman Catholics (estimate), 600,000 Protestants (Lutherans and Calvinists) and 77,000 Jews.

Roman Catholic hierarchy in 1909 numbered 17 archbishops, (Aix, Albi, Auch, Avignon, Besançon, Bordeaux, Bourges, Cambrai, Chambèry, Lyons, Paris, Rheims, Rennes, Rouen, Sens, Toulouse, Tours) and 67 bishops with sees generally coinciding with departments.

Roman Catholic pilgrimages

Lourdes: Vision of Bernadette Soubirous (1858) recognized by Bishop of Tarbes 1862. In 1872 119,000 pilgrims.

La Salette, Dauphiné: vision of two children (1849) recognized. By 1855 total of 500,000 pilgrims. Ars, Dombes: Jean-Baptiste Vianney (1786–1859) made curé, 1818. 80,000 pilgrims a year for 30 years. Declared venerable 1872, beatified 1905, canonized 1925 and declared patron of Parish priests 1929.

GERMANY

North and east Germany were mostly Protestant, south and west mostly Catholic. In the Protestant states church land was secularized at the Reformation. State churches were governed by consistory. Territorial rulers normally became *summus episcopus* but as they grew more secular so the church became a branch of the state administration, e.g. the Prussian law code of 1794 made canon law part of administrative law.

Napoleonic action and influence encouraged the secularization of church property in Catholic states. The secularization of the archbishoprics of Cologne, Trèves and Mainz brought 3,161,766 people under civil rulers, mostly Protestant. In the post-1815 reaction even Catholic rulers were not expected to restore church land. No church confederation was attempted. Catholics now became ultramontane to protect themselves against state interference.

BADEN

Protestant in the north, Catholic in the south, with approximately two-thirds of the population Catholic.

1854   Archbishop of Freiburg, Mgr von Vicari, told that he could publish no pastoral letter without leave of government and that state would appoint 60 of the 80 parish priests in his diocese. Imprisoned for disobedience.

1861   Census showed:

Roman Catholics	896,683
Protestants	445,539
Jews	24,099

June. Synod of Carlsruhe provided for self-government for Protestants. Church councils and clergy popularly elected.

Education secularized.

Heidelberg University had faculty for Lutheran theological students, Freiburg University for Roman Catholic.

1870   In the *Kulturkampf* the government supported separatist Catholic communities. It recognized Dr Reinkens, leader of the Old Catholics, and paid stipends of Old Catholic clergy.

One Roman Catholic bishop removed.

1874   Law defining appointment to parishes and rules for the examination of theological students, Catholic and Protestant.

Compulsory civil marriage and undenominational schools.

Grand Duke a Protestant and head of the Protestant church, was governed by synod and administered by board.

Roman Catholic archbishop of Freiburg had 4 suffragans outside grand duchy.

1910   By census:

Roman Catholics	1,271,015
Protestants	826,364
Jews	25,896

(By 1919 the Catholic total was falling slightly, the Protestant rising.)

State grant to Roman Catholics, Protestants, Old Catholics and Jews. The Jews had 15 rabbinates.

1919   United Evangelical Protestant National Church reorganized.

BAVARIA

1848   Jesuit college in Altöting closed.

Bishops met at Wurzburg to oppose tendency for a national church.

1852   Census returns showed:

Roman Catholics	3,176,333
Protestants	1,233,894
Jews	56,033

1866   The Roman Catholic Church reported to own lands valued at £8,500,000. It had 2 archbishops, 6 bishops, 171 deaneries and 2,756 parishes.

Protestants had a general consistory and 4 provincial consistories. The state paid clergy £130,000 a year.

Two Roman Catholic universities, Munich and Wurzburg; one Protestant university, Erlangen.

Catholics objected to the rise of the Protestant Hohenzollerns at the expense of the Catholic Habsburgs.

1869   Prince Hohenlohe, a devout Catholic, Minister President of Bavaria, invited the powers to confer on 'coming papal contingencies', i.e. suspected intention of the Papacy to proclaim the dogma of infallibility. No response to invitation.

1870   Bavaria refused *placet* to Papal Bull on dogma of infallibility. The government disputed papal claims but the Diet was under ultramontane influence. The clergy accepted the dogma and promulgated it in defiance of the government, coercing or excommunicating their opponents. Bishops claimed that officials and soldiers were absolved of their duty of obedience and loyalty to the state.

The government temporized but followed Prussia in laws against Roman Catholic clergy (see Prussia—*Kulturkampf* p. 266.). Three Roman Catholic bishops removed.

Impetus for Old Catholics, who would not accept the dogma, came from Munich. The government allowed their leader, Dr Reinkens, to hold confirmations.

1910   Census returns:

Roman Catholics	4,862,233
Protestants	1.942,385
Jews	55,065
Old Catholics	5,816

1918   The 2 Roman Catholic archbishops each had 3 suffragans. 3101 Roman Catholic parishes. Protestants had general consistory, 3 provincial consistories, 1,049 parishes.

BREMEN

1849	Jews granted equal rights but no Jew to become Bremen citizen without special permission of Senate.	
1866	Lutherans	63,000
	Calvinists	30,000
	Roman Catholics	4,000
1910	Protestants	257,930
	Roman Catholics	21,074
	Other Christians	1,217
	Jews	1,251

BRUNSWICK

Lutheran majority.

1861   Census showed population was Lutheran except for 1107 Calvinists, 2458 Roman Catholics, 83 other Christian sects and 1078 Jews. Jews had complete equality.
Two members of the single chamber elected by Protestant clergy.

1910   Of population of 494,339 only 25,888 were Catholics.

HAMBURG

1866   Lutheran, except for 2000 Calvinists, 4000 Roman Catholics and 7000 Jews.

1910	Protestants	930,071
	Roman Catholics	51,036
	Other Christians	3,942
	Jews	19,472

HANOVER

1861	Census showed:	
	Lutherans	1,555,448
	Reformed Church	97,018
	Roman Catholics	221,576
	Jews	12,085

1870   Ultramontanes led in *Kulturkampf* against Bismarck by Dr Ludwig Windthorst (1812–91), former Hanoverian Minister of State.

HESSE-CASSEL

1866		
	Calvinists	373,595
	Lutherans	133,800
	United Evangelicals	102,490
	Roman Catholics	107,695
	Jews	16,358

Reformed Church was under three consistories; Cassel, Marburg and Hanau. Lutherans were under a general superintendent appointed by the Minister of the Interior. United Evangelicals were under a central committee and occasional synod, and Roman Catholics under a bishop at Fulda.
There were early signs of anti-Semitism in the state.
1873   Roman Catholic bishops met at Fulda and declared their determination not to obey May Laws of the *Kulturkampf*.

HESSE-DARMSTADT

1866		
	Lutherans	398,807
	Calvinists	29,200
	United Evangelicals	167,534
	Roman Catholics	217,405
	Jews	28,759

Three Protestant superintendents and a Roman Catholic bishop at Mayence.

LIPPE

1866   All Protestant except 5925 Roman Catholics, 780 Jews.

1910   Of population of 46,652, 715 Roman Catholic, 230 Jews.

LUBECK

1866   All Lutheran except 400 Calvinists, 200 Roman Catholics and 500 Jews.

1910		
	Protestants	111,543
	Roman Catholics	3,802
	Other Christians	276
	Jews	623

MECKLENBURG-SCHWERIN

1860	Census figures:	
	Lutherans	537,986
	Calvinists	168

	Roman Catholics	882
	Jews	3,112

In 1860 1 birth in every 3·8 was illegitimate. Jews were not allowed to settle in many parts of the grand duchy.

1910	Protestants	615,512
	Roman Catholics	21,043
	Other Christians	1,288
	Jews	1,413

MECKLENBURG-STRELITZ

1910   Of population of 106,347 only 2,627 were Roman Catholics, 253 Jews.

NASSAU

The Evangelical bishop of Wiesbaden and the Roman Catholic bishop of Limburg were in the upper chamber.

1866	United Evangelicals	237,953
	Roman Catholics	208,842
	Jews	7,112

OLDENBURG

1861	Census showed:	
	Lutherans	191,877
	Calvinists	1,369
	United Evangelicals	25,916 (mostly in Birkenfeld)
	Roman Catholics	72,939
	Jews	1,497
1910	Protestant	371,650
	Roman Catholics	107,508
	Other Christians	2,359
	Jews	1,525

PRUSSIA

1847   Edict of Toleration. Prussian government recognized right of secession from state church of all who refused to accept official creed and liturgy. Church purged of dissident leaders, their followers neutralized by threats.

Mar 48   Clergy of all denominations joined funeral of March Heroes, killed on Berlin barricades. Separation of church and state formally decreed by Frankfurt Parliament.

Sep 48   Wittenberg Kirchentag, organized by Neo-Pietists and allies. Five hundred clergy celebrated success against Revolution, which was described by Hengstenberg faction as 'blasphemous violation of temporal and divine authority'. 5 Nov kept as Day of Repentance.

1850   Articles 15–19 of the constitution provided that the Evangelical, Roman Catholic and all other religious associations could administer their affairs independently and remain in possession of their establishments, foundations and funds destined for religious, educational and charitable purposes. Intercourse between religious associations and their superiors was unimpeded. Publication of ecclesiastical ordinances was subject only to such restrictions as affected all other publications. But all nominations to, and proposals for, elections and confirmations of, and possessions of ecclesiastical functions, independent of the State, and not arising from special patronage or legal titles, were abolished. Civil marriage introduced by special law appended to constitution.

Catholic bishops met to fight tendency for a national church. Beginning of Catholic Action and Zentrum party, exclusively Roman Catholic. Its opponents were those who wished to keep the church subordinate to the state and radicals who believed in religious freedom.

1851   Mgr von Ketteler appointed Archbishop of Mainz.

1852   All *Landeskirchen* participated in conference at Eisenach, its decisions advisory on matters common to German Evangelical Churches.

1861   Population of Prussia estimated as:

Protestants	11,273,730
Roman Catholics	6,867,574
Mennonites	13,718
Other Christians	14,166
Jews	252,592

Clergy of the kingdom of Prussia reported to be:

Protestant   5,740 ordained, with 140 assistant ministers.

Roman Catholic   3,510 priests and 2,033 vicars, chaplains and curates.

The higher Catholic clergy paid by the state. Archbishop of Breslau receiving £1700 a year, other bishops about £1135 (1862 conversion). Parochial clergy, Protestant and Catholic, normally paid from endowments.

Proselytism, or attempting to induce a person to change religion, forbidden by law.

1869   9 Apr. Prince Hohenlohe, Minister President of Bavaria, a devoted Catholic, invited powers to 'confer' on 'coming papal contingencies', i.e. likelihood of the dogma of infallibility being proclaimed. Prussia procrastinated, though anxious; France and Austria declined.

German Roman Catholic bishops were expected to oppose the Papacy if it attempted to invade the sphere of public and political action. They met at Fulda, producing a pastoral to allay fears of a new dogma.

Jan 70   German Roman Catholic bishops produced a memorial against a new dogma.

18 July 70 Declaration of the dogma of papal infallibility. German bishops capitulated to orders of Rome within one month.

Nov 70   Elections to Prussian Diet gave Zentrum 54 seats.

Kulturkampf–name given by Professor Rudolf Virchow, Radical deputy of Prussian Diet, distinguished pathologist.

There were now two separate struggles:

(i) Some German Catholics, now known as Old Catholics, preferred to secede from Rome rather than accept papal infallibility and omnipotence of Rome in administration. Led by Dr Ignaz Dollinger (1799–1890), eminent Catholic liberal, former friend of the Oxford Tractarians Manning and Pusey.

(*ii*) Struggle by Bismarck against ultramontanism, involving control of education and civil disobedience of Roman Catholic clergy. Ultramontanes led by Dr Ludwig Windthorst (1812–91), former Hanoverian Minister of State; party organ *Germania* founded Jan 1871.

Dec 70   Archbishop of Cologne ordered theological professors of Bonn University to accept the dogma on pain of being forbidden to lecture to Roman Catholic students or exercise priestly function. Minister of Public Worship supported the professors and also teachers at a Roman Catholic higher school at Breslau, similarly threatened.

1871   Elections for Imperial Diet gave Zentrum 63 seats, chiefly in Bavaria, West Prussia and Polish provinces. Emperor made it clear that Prussia would not assist in restoring the Pope to temporal power.

Apr 71   Bishop of Ermeland threatened to excommunicate all teachers refusing to accept dogma.

8 July 71 Roman Catholic Department for Spiritual Affairs abolished. Government said that those excommunicated remained Catholics and did not forfeit their civil rights.

10 Dec 71 Imperial law made politics in the pulpit (*Katheder*) an offence punishable by imprisonment for maximum of 2 years.

1872   30 Jan. Dr Paul Ludwig Adalbert Falk (1827–1900) appointed Minister of Cults.

Chaplain General's office abolished after he had disobeyed the Minister for War.

Apr. Cardinal Hohenlohe, brother of Bavarian statesman, chosen German representative at the Vatican. Refused by Papacy as inexpedient in May.

14 May. Bismarck's secret instruction to German ambassadors to organize joint action to influence the future election of a pope. Bismarck: 'Have no fear–to Canossa we shall not go, either in body or spirit' (cf. Emperor Henry IV who was humbled by Pope Gregory at Canossa 1077).

24 June. The Pope warns Bismarck that a triumph against truth and the Church is the greatest of follies.

4 July. Bill expelling Jesuits from the empire. Prussia claimed there were 800 foreign Jesuits in empire, Catholics said 200.

School Inspection Bill, to remove schools from clerical control.

Salary of the Bishop of Ermeland suspended when he forbade Catholics to have intercourse with excommunicated, contrary to Prussian common law.

1873   15 May. Dr Falk's May laws:

(1) Took much disciplinary power from bishops and made it an offence for any servant of the church to threaten or impose penalties in matters not strictly religious.

(2) Education of clergy placed under state supervision. Clerical office to be filled only by Germans after liberal training. Government had right to veto clerical appointments. Law also applied to Protestants.

(3) To secede from a church only a declaration before local judge needed.

(4) Ecclesiastical discipline of Catholic clergy brought under state control, with appeal to ordinary courts of law.

Catholic bishops met at Fulda and declared their determination not to obey the May laws.

9 June. Bismarck said that the imperial government would not interfere in the election of a pope.

Nov. Zentrum became second strongest party in the lower house in elections to Prussian Diet. Dr. Joseph Hubert Reinkens, former professor of church history at Breslau University, chosen first bishop of the Old Catholics, with headquarters at Bonn. His salary voted by the Prussian Diet. But hopes of forming a national Catholic Church were disappointed. By 1875 the Old Catholics had only 47,737 communicants in Germany, 100 congregations,

54 priests.

The Cardinal Archbishop of Posen, Count Ledochowski, was deprived of his salary and told to vacate his seat. He refused and facing an impossible fine was imprisoned. The Archbishop of Cologne just escaped arrest but the Archbishops of Paderborn and Münster were jailed. Six out of 12 bishops were deposed, 400 parishes were deprived of their priests.

Jan 74   Zentrum increased their seats. Law to provide for vacated offices.

Mar 74   Prussian bill to make civil marriage obligatory.

May 74   Imperial Diet passed law by which contumelious clerics could be told where to live, be deprived of citizenship and expelled.

5 Feb 75   Papal letter to Prussian bishops declared null and void all Prussian laws which denied divine sanction and authority of the Roman Catholic Church. Letter was banned by Prussia but read in the lower house and so published.

6 Feb 75   Principle of civil marriage applied to the whole empire.

22 Apr 75 Prussia's Bread-basket Law, suspending state grants to disobedient Roman Catholic sees. The Protestant and Roman Catholic churches were to be regulated by state laws and the control of Roman Catholic church estates and funds changed.

31 May 75 Prussian law dissolving all religious orders and congregations except those nursing the sick. It was claimed that the numbers in orders had increased from 913 to 7992 since 1855.

1876   Coalition of ultramontanes and conservatives.

1877   Eight Roman Catholic archbishops and bishops now removed, leaving only 4 bishops.

1878   1400 clergy now sequestered, all Catholic seminaries closed.

7 Feb 78   Death of Pius IX. Leo XIII succeeded. Leo XIII and Bismarck sought reconciliation.

July 79   Dr Falk resigned. Bismarck lessened persecution of Roman Catholics without conditions—'a compromise'.

May 80   Reinstatement of clergy. Thousand parishes (2m. population) supplied with priests. But Jesuits still banned, and the pulpit paragraph, school laws and civil marriage retained. The *Kulturkampf* had increased the mistrust between the two great confessions.

Oct 80   Cologne Cathedral (Roman Catholic) completed and consecrated in presence of Emperor William II.

1883   Crown Prince Frederick visited the Pope.

1886   State examination of priests and control of seminaries given up.

1892   Revision of Luther's Bible completed.

1910   Tercentenary of St Charles Borromeo. Papal encyclical attacking Protestant reformers provoked strong reaction.

1914   Manifesto of 76 leading Roman Catholics exalted the war as 'the new springtime of religion'.

Mgr Gerlach, German bishop and member of the Pope's household, convicted of belonging to spy network which blew up Italian cruiser *Leonardo da Vinci.*

The United Evangelical Church of Prussia, 20m., was the largest Protestant church in the world. All persons registered as Protestant had to pay a church tax unless they made a declaration of renunciation before a magistrate. At the 1918 revolution there was a marked increase in 'contracting out'.

Before 1918 the state appointed 56 per cent of German Protestant clergy; 34 per cent of benefices belonged to private patrons and municipalities. In the remaining 10 per cent of parishes parishioners elected their pastor.

Until the Weimar Republic a declaration before a magistrate was necessary in some states to change 'confession'.

In 1918 the *Landeskirchen* secured state support with minimum control. Civil authorities still paid some subsidies (interest on church property secularized in the Napoleonic wars), parochial endowments, schools and charitable foundations.

At the 1918 revolution Roman Catholics, with funds from abroad, were able to buy up monasteries and convents which had been secularized for centuries.

SAXE-ALTENBURG

1866	Protestant except for 300 Roman Catholics. No Jews.	
1910	Protestants	207,825
	Roman Catholics	7,246

SAXE-COBURG-GOTHA

1866	Protestant except for 851 Roman Catholics, 1,578 Jews.	
1910	Protestants	250,454
	Roman Catholics	4,951
	Jews	783

SAXE-MEININGEN

1866	Protestant except for 872 Roman Catholics, 72 Mennonites and 1530 Jews.	
1910	Protestants	271,433
	Roman Catholics	5,233
	Jews	1,137

SAXE-WEIMAR

1852   All *Landeskirchen* in conference at Eisenach on matters common to German Evangelical Churches.
Census figures:

Protestants	262,272
Roman Catholics	9,824
Jews	1,088

SAXONY

1861   Census figures:

Lutherans	2,175,392
Calvinists	4,515
Roman Catholics	41,363
Jews	1,555

Clergy paid by local rates and endowments and state contribution of £12,830. Protestants under a national consistory, Roman Catholics under papal delegate.

1918   Saxony objected to *Landeskirchen* receiving state support with a minimum of control but was condemned to conform by supreme court of the Reich.

SAXONY (grand duchy)

1910   Census figures:

Protestants	393,774
Roman Catholics	19,980
Jews	1,323

SCHWARZBURG-RUDOLFSTADT

1866   Lutheran except for 73 Roman Catholics, 169 Jews.

1910

Protestants	99,210
Roman Catholics	1,288
Other Christians	88
Jews	78

WURTTEMBERG

1861   Census showed:

Evangelical Protestants	1,179,818
Roman Catholics	527,057
Jews	11,388

Administration of Evangelical Church was in hands of a consistorium of 1 president, 9 councillors, 6 general superintendents. Representative body of Evangelical communes the Landes-Synode, consisting of 25 clerical and 25 lay representatives of the diocese and one of the theological faculty of the university, with 3 clerical and 3 lay members appointed by Evangelical princes.

1870 *Kulturkampf* caused little upheaval as Roman Catholics were in a minority and Swabians showed their customary accommodation.

1910 Census showed:

Protestants	1,671,183
Roman Catholics	739,995
Jews	11,982

GREECE

1850 Patriarch of Constantinople finally recognized Greek Orthodox Church as autocephalous. Metropolitan of Attica *ex-officio* President of the Holy Synod, composed of 5 bishops, 2 laymen. Higher Orthodox clergy salaried by state (e.g. in 1884 Metropolitan of Athens 6000 dr., archbishops 5000 dr., bishops 4000 dr. a year, plus revenue from church lands). Lower clergy dependent on contributions and fees so forced to have other occupations. Fixed number of state-paid preachers, distinct from local clergy, assigned to each province. Deacons allowed to marry, parish priests must be married. Bishops must be unmarried, widowers or renounce wife and children.

Orthodox monks all of the order of St Basil the Great. Monasteries either coenobitic, where all live in common under an abbot, or idiorhythmic, where each monk owns a share in conventual property, including piece of land. 15,000 monks (1884), and monasteries reduced to a total of 80 by law; 250 nuns. In 1926 government recognized Mt Athos, with its 20 monasteries, as self-governing community.

Roman Catholics: final break between the Roman Catholic Church and the Orthodox Church of the East came in 1054. Points of difference: papal supremacy, doctrine of purgatory, use of *filioque* in Nicene Creed. Orthodox regard statues or figures in relief as heretical.

In 1840 the Roman Catholic Brothers of the Christian Schools made themselves responsible for elementary education in Greek islands. By late nineteenth century estimated to be 25,000–30,000 Roman Catholics, chiefly in the Cyclades, descendants of Venetian settlers.

271

Three archbishops (Athens, Naxos, Corfu) and 5 bishops Tenedos, Santorini, Syra, Zante, Kephallenia).
Protestants: English church, Athens, gothic, built 1840–3.

HUNGARY

Tithe abolished. Equality for received religions. Anti-Jewish rioting.
Roman Catholic archdioceses: Esztergom (Primate, *legatus natus*), Kalocsa, Eger, Zagreb.
Greek Rite: (1854) Fogaras.
343,000 Jews.
Concordat.
The Compromise – independence. Jews granted full civil liberties and freedom of religion guaranteed.
Compromise (revised 1873, 1881) with Croats, who were Catholic and used the Latin alphabet.
Party of the Serbs, who were Orthodox and used the cyrillic letters.
House of Magnates, reformed by Act of this year, included 38 archbishops, bishops and other dignitaries of Roman Catholic and Greek churches; 12 ecclesiastical and lay representatives of Protestant confessions.
Theological colleges:

Roman Catholic	27
Greek Catholic	4
Greek Orthodox	3
Protestant	8
Unitarian	1
Jewish	1

Civil marriage.
Catholic party formed, achieved little despite approval of the Archduke Franz Ferdinand.
Estimated to be 850,000 Jews or 8·49 per cent of population. Nearly half the population of Budapest was Jewish.
Official figures for adherents:

Catholics Latin	10,299,190
Greek	1,907,936
Evangelicals	3,823,061
Greek Orthodox	2,882,695
Jews	886,466
Unitarians	70,000

1918   Religions recognized: Roman and Greek Catholic, Evangelical
        (Augsburg and Helvetian), Unitarian, Greek – Oriental,
        Gregorian – Armenian, Baptist (since 1905), Jewish and Moham-
        medan (since 1916). Each had independent administration.
        Secular priests (not including bishops, canons, vicars, provosts):

Roman Catholic	6,665
Greek Catholic	2,424
Greek – Oriental	2,861

Orders:

Roman Catholic	2,534 males; 6,807 females
Greek Catholic	47
Greek – Oriental	157
Protestant clergy	3,883
Jewish	1,823

Adherents:

Roman Catholics	10,888,138
Greek Catholics	2,025,508
Evangelicals (Hel.)	2,621,329
Evangelicals (Aug.)	1,340,143
Unitarians	74,296
Jews	932,458
Others	17,452

ITALY

1860   Most Roman Catholics boycotted politics because the Pope would
        not recognize a government which had seized Papal States.
        Nationalism stood for secularization but even the religious
        Bettino Ricasoli wanted church reform.
        Piedmontese secularist laws introduced into newly acquired areas.
        Unrest in Naples. Papacy encouraged brigands with money and
        recruitment. Neopolitan bishops transmitted orders.
        Neopolitan concordat denounced. Sixty-six bishops arrested.
        Other ecclesiastics were refused the royal *exequatur* allowing them
        to enter office, and the revenues of their sees thus became forfeit.
        Giovanni Bosco, 1815–88, founder of Salesian order and later
        beatified, was held by police. Five cardinals prosecuted.
        Cardinal of Pisa refused Ricasoli's order to celebrate Inde-
        pendence Day with a Te Deum. His cathedral was stormed and the
        service sung without him. The cardinal was taken under arrest to
        Turin.

Cavour tried to solve the Roman problem secretly through his personal agent, the Jesuit Passaglia, who opened negotiations with Cardinal Antonelli, Secretary of State. But the Pope insisted on retaining his temporal power.

1864 Papal encyclical *Quanta cura*, with its accompanying syllabus of errors, caused great indignation among liberals.

1866 Law dissolved houses of almost all religious orders and congregations and confiscated their goods. 13,000 already suppressed, now 25,000 followed. Land held in mortmain sold by state in buyer's market. The sale was meant to help peasants but the land was chiefly bought by speculators, and existing landowners paid rent to rapacious landlords instead of church. By 1880 more than 1m. acres alienated but the number of people owning land dropped between 1860 and 1901. Cathedral chapters and bishops were compelled to surrender their capital to state, receiving 5 % in return after 30 % of capital had been deducted for educational and charitable purposes.

Seminarists made liable for military service. New civil code said a civil ceremony was necessary to make a marriage legal.

Papacy officially prohibited Catholics taking part in politics. Sacred Penitentiary later said a Roman Catholic might sit in parliament if he added to his oath 'as far as divine and ecclesiastical law allow'. Count Crotti, who tried the expedient in 1867, was overheard and expelled after uproar.

1867 Religious-minded liberals and many anti-clericals were agreed on disliking the idea of Rome as the capital. Rome itself remained loyal to Pius IX. There was no rising to support Garibaldi's attack.

1870 Rome falls. Dogma of papal infallibility produced no schism in Italy.

Law of Guarantees passed to regularize the Pope's position. He was granted the honours due to a king, free communication with Roman Catholics throughout the world and diplomatic immunity for ministers attached to the Vatican. He was granted an income of over 3m. lira a year in perpetuity. The state abandoned most of its restrictive control over church action and renounced the hereditary apostolic legateship which the King claimed in Sicily. State and church were to be separate. Church property was to be secularized and ecclesiastical salaries paid out of nationalized *fondo per il culto*. The Papacy repudiated the Law of Guarantees but a *modus vivendi* was found. Even religious orders held property again and became richer. Cardinals joined in land speculation for building on the Quirinal and Esquiline hills.

1873 Protestant church built in Rome.

1874	In general election church declared it inexpedient to vote, and the veto lasted into twentieth century. Many Roman Catholics disobeyed.
1875	Masonic temple built in Rome.
1876	*Opera dei Congressi* approved by Pius IX to unite all Catholic associations of Italy in 'common and concerted action in defence of the Holy See's rights and of the religious and social interests of all Italians . . .' Francesco Crispi was anti-clerical but tried to solve the Vatican impasse. It was rare for any leading minister to be devout after 1870.
1878	Pius IX gave special permision of King Vittorio Emanuele to receive the last sacraments.
1881	Anti-papal riots when the remains of Pius IX were transferred to San Lorenzo fuori le Muri. Heretical ex-canon of Mantua, Roberto Ardigo (1828-1920) appointed a professor at Padua University.
1882	Martinucci case decided that every inhabitant of the Vatican might be held subject to the Italian courts, only the Pope excepted. Theological faculties suppressed and religious seminaries threatened with closure if they refused government inspection.
1888	Parents had to ask for religious education for their children, not ask to opt out.
	Pope Leo XIII's encyclical *De libertate humana* almost seemed to demolish the anti-liberal syllabus of Pius IX.
1889	Zanardelli's penal code increased penalties for clergy who condemned from the pulpit institutions or acts of government.
1890	Compulsory payment of tithe abolished and most remaining church charities, which gave priests great power, taken over by the state.
	Crispi claimed that only one-tenth of the 9m. lire annual revenue of 9464 pious fraternities was spent on public assistance.
	Growing fear of revolution improved *modus vivendi* between church and state. Monasteries had been quietly re-endowed since dissolution.

	1881		*1901*	
Monks and friars	7,191	Monks and friars	7,792
Nuns	28,172	Nuns	40,251

1891	Encyclical *Rerum Novarum* urging charity and fair division of property.
1895	20 Sep made a public holiday to celebrate day in 1870 when army turned guns against walls of Rome.
1898	Violence in Milan, with 80 killed in May, resulted in Socialists being arrested. Three thousand Catholic organizations dissolved,

	Milanese *Osservatore Cattolico* suppressed.
1904	World congress of freethinkers in Rome.
	Roman Catholics began to think that policy of non-cooperation achieved nothing. Giolitti made overtures to Catholics in election.
1905	Bishops allowed to decide if Catholics of diocese might participate in political life.
1911	Catholics supported Giolitti's wide extension of the franchise, thinking that they could control how the peasants voted.
	Anti-clericals angry that the *Banco di Roma*, bank of the Holy See, should be saved from its rash investments in Libya by state action, i.e. war. Catholics supported a crusade of Cross v. Crescent.
1914–18	Clerical pacifism strong.

LOMBARDY – VENEZIA

Jan 48	*I Lutti di Lombardia*, powerful pamphlet by Massimo d'Azeglio on the attack on unarmed Milanese by Austrian soldiers. Clergy said to be leading national movement. Austrian army forbade other ranks to confess to Italian chaplains because they were among 'our most open and dangerous enemies'.
11 Nov 59	By treaty of Zurich religious corporations of Lombardy were given privileged position: their lands and houses were left to the disposal of individual members.

THE PAPACY

Pius IX (254) 1846–78

	As Cardinal Mastai Ferretti, bishop of Imola, Pius IX won reputation as liberal. Openly attacked Austrian police repression.
1846	Proclaimed amnesty, reforms and constitution in Papal States. 'We had foreseen everything except a liberal Pope'– Metternich.
1848	Revolution spread to Rome. Pius fled to Gaeta. Giacomo Antonelli (1806–76) Secretary of State for remainder of pontificate.
1850	French restored order in Rome. Pius IX returned to concentrate on dogma and discipline.
1854	Bull *Ineffacibilis Deus*, declaring Immaculate Conception of the Virgin Mary. Curia overhauled, Sacred College de-Italianized, Church centralized and absolute power of the Pope greatly increased. Renewal of church in old countries, missions in new lands.

| 1859 | Pope refused to renounce temporal power so unity of Italy became associated with anti-clericalism. Patriots of National Society took the four legations for Piedmont. |

1859   Pope refused to renounce temporal power so unity of Italy became associated with anti-clericalism. Patriots of National Society took the four legations for Piedmont.

1860   Encyclical *Nullis certe* threatened with excommunication all who attacked domains of the church. Papacy raised 20,000 international volunteers who were defeated at Castelfidardo near Loreto. Piedmont occupied Umbria and the Marches. Only presence of French troops saved Rome. Peter's Pence introduced. Spiritual authority of Pius IX grew as temporal dangers increased, e.g. 200 bishops at proclamation of Immaculate Conception (1854); 275 at canonization of Japanese martyrs (1862); 500 at eighteenth centenary of martyrdom of St Peter and St Paul.

1864   Catholics split and others enraged by Encyclical *Quanta cura* and the syllabus (catalogue of ideas) 8 Dec 64 which seemed to condemn all liberty, liberalism and progress. It asserted that freedom of discussion corrupted the soul (79) and clergy had natural right to avoid military service (32). Religious toleration, freedom of conscience and press, and validity of secularist legislation, were challenged.

1869   Vatican Council, first since 1537.

1870   Papal infallibility *ex cathedra* proclaimed in bull *Pastor Aeternus*. French troops withdrawn from Rome which fell to Piedmontese.

1871   Encyclical *Ubi nos* rejected Law of Guarantees by which Italian government sought to regularize position of the Pope (*see* Italy). Pius IX shut himself in the Vatican where the Pope remained a 'prisoner' until the treaty of reconciliation, 11 Feb 1929, between Pius XI and Mussolini.

Leo XIII (255) 1878–1903

Reorganization, particularly of curia, after stagnation since 1870. Leo XIII accepted *de facto* situation, teaching that Catholics must obey Caesar provided Caesar did not overstep his rights. Relations with European powers improved, Leo XIII even being used as international arbiter. But he was unyielding on Roman question and forbade Catholics in Italy to take part in political activities.

1884   Encyclical *Humanum genus* against Freemasonry.

1891   Encyclical *Rerum Novarum* was accused of being socialist. It condemned condition of workers, said class hatred was not solution, and advocated just wage, right of association and right of peasant over land. Worker priests proposed. Missions encouraged and Vatican archives opened to historians. But firm efforts made to check 'Americanism', modernism and rationalism. Cardinal Mariano Rampalla (1843–1913) Secretary of State.

Pius X (256) 1903–14

First Pope since French Revolution not from nobility or professional classes; father a postman. Secretary of State a Spanish grandee, Cardinal Merry del Val (1865–1930). Pius X wished to subject all things to law of Christ and authority of Church—*omnia instaurare in Christo*. Reorganized central administration of church, revised Vulgate and Breviary, promoted Gregorian chant, reformed canon law. Stern condemnation of modernism. The Pope (1906) refused to recognize the separation of church and state in France.

Benedict XV (257) 1914–22

Lawyer – diplomat. Strict neutrality during the Great War pleased neither side. 'The Pope is not neutral, he is impartial' – Benedict XV. He called for a 'white peace' without annexations. But states seeking representation at Vatican rose from 15 to 27 – Britain 1914; Holland 1916; Japan 1917; Portugal 1918; Brazil, Finland, Poland, Peru, Estonia, the Ukraine, Yugoslavia and Czechoslovakia 1919.

Secretary of State Cardinal Gasparri (1852–1934).

PAPAL STATES

1846   Marquis Massimo d'Azeglio (1798–1866) published *Degli ultimi casi di Romagna* after touring Papal States. It pilloried government of Pope Gregory XVI. This was banned.

17 June. Election of Mastai Ferretti as Pope Pius IX (1846–78). His Provisional Council: Cardinals Macchi, Lambruschini, Mattei, Amat, Gizzi and Bernetti, with Mgr Corboli-Bussi as secretary. Only Amat, Gizzi (Secretary of State) and Corboli-Bussi were liberals, which made reform difficult. 'Your Holiness should clear out the Secretary of State's office even down to the cats'–attributed to Cardinal Micara.

2 July. Pius IX walked to the Church of the Umiltà almost unaccompanied instead of riding in a heavily guarded carriage. This sign that he trusted the Romans delighted them.

17 July. Pius declared amnesty for approximately 1000 prisoners and exiles promising to fulfil faithfully every duty of a good subject. Demonstrations by great crowds shouting 'Viva Pio Nono'. Enthusiasm for Pius spread through Papal States and rest of Italy. Liberals made use of these demonstrations and huge banquets to influence the Pope to speed reform. Some reform of courts, some laymen introduced into legal organization, return to

be made of prison visitations and suspects, etc.

Three conservative cardinals retired—Vannucelli, legate at Bologna; Ugolino, delegate at Ferrara; Della Genga, delegate at Pesaro; and Mgr Marini, governor of Rome. Replaced by Amat, Ciacchi, Ferretti and Mgr Grassellini.

11 Nov. Encyclical declaring Pius to be on the conservative side in all matters of dogma and faith.

1847   15 Mar. Freedom granted to press, with almost lay censorship. Among censorable writing was any in contempt of religion or the church or its ministers; anything that brought the acts and reforms of papal government into hatred.

17 June. Anniversary of Pius celebrated with immense enthusiasm, even by Bologna.

22 June. *Notificazione* (produced by Gizzi) in which Pius gave warning that he could only introduce reforms which were in accordance with the sovereignty and temporal government of the church.

17 July. Austrians chose Amnesty Day to display troops on papal territory in Ferrara. Pius personally involved in protests. Moderates became extremists against Austrians. International sympathy for the Pope. Palmerston spoke of the 'brutal and insulting way' of treating him; Garibaldi from Montevideo offered to fight for the Holy See.

23 Dec. Austrian troops withdrawn from Ferrara but incident made war of 1848 inevitable.

12 Jan 48   Padre Gavazzi, preaching before Consulta in church of San Carlo in Rome, used as his text 'Fuori i Barbari'—out with the barbarians.

8 Feb 48   Tumult in Rome, crowds demanding lay ministers.

10 Feb 48   Pius published *A Motu Proprio* in which he used the phrase 'Benedite Gran Dio l'Italia' (O Lord God, bless Italy) which was taken as a secret blessing of war against Austria.

Feb 48   Pius sought to obtain a defensive league of Italian states, following Gioberti's idea. But Piedmont wanted troops, not words.

3 Mar 48   General Giovanni Durando (1804–69) commanding papal troops, told to march to frontier, not to cross it.

5 Apr 48   Durando issued proclamation, written by Massimo d'Azeglio, which claimed to speak in the name of the Pope as spiritual head of the church. It hinted at excommunication of the Austrians and seemingly turned the war into a Christian crusade against them. Pius was furious when he heard of the proclamation.

22 Apr 48   Durando crossed the Po into Austrian Italy.

29 Apr 48   Pius addressed a famous allocution to the cardinals in consistory

279

in which he stated that he did not intend to declare war because as Pope he could not do so. It was a crushing blow to the millions who had regarded him as their champion against Austria. Pius also defended himself from the charge of instigating revolution. Pius was alarmed that the Germans were already speaking of schism from the Papacy which seemed to preach a holy war against them. The allocution led to (i) the failure of the war of 1848 and (ii) eventual loss of the Papal States, but (iii) it ended risks of schism and saved international character of the Roman Catholic Church.

3 May 48   Pius appealed to Emperor to withdraw from Lombardy and Venezia.

10 June 48 Papal troops defeated at Vicenza. By terms of surrender they had to retire behind the Po and not serve against Austria for three months.

14 July 48 Austrians crossed Po and forced papal troops back to Ferrara.

Sep 48   Pelegrino Rossi provided for a subsidy from the clergy assessed on all ecclesiastical property. Thus, with the Pope's consent, he raised 2m. scudi from Church property which had already been mortgaged for 2m. scudi. The conservatives mistrusted Rossi because of his early Carbonarism, Protestant wife and the taxation of Church lands.

15 Nov 48 Murder of Rossi and plot to overthrow papal government.

16 Nov 48 The Pope, facing the arrival of a giant mob at the Quirinal, refused to flee when reminded that so many families depended on his presence in Rome. Only 2 cardinals remained with Pius, Soglia and Antonelli. Ambassadors and ministers of Catholic powers gathered at Quirinal to support him.

24 Nov 48 Pius fled to Gaeta, in the territory of the hated Neopolitan Ferdinand II (1830–59).

1849   Jan. Father Ugo Bassi, hero of Palermo cholera outbreak, joined the Garibaldini at Rieti. Constitution guaranteed the Pope's spiritual authority. Edict to transform the church's wealth into small holdings for the poor.

3 May. 'Priests, by the way, walk about in great comfort – arm in arm with a soldier, perhaps' – Arthur Clough in Rome.

Rome recaptured by the French for the Pope. Revenge and repression.

7 Aug. Ugo Bassi captured at Comacchio and executed at Bologna.

Father Gavazzi, who escaped, toured England.

Jan 59   Pius told Odo Russell, the British resident, 'It is not understood that those very reforms, which would consist in giving the country a government of laymen, would make it cease to exist. It is called the "States of the Church" and that is what it must remain.'

7 Sep 59   Piedmont sent ultimatum to Pius.

11 Sep 59   Invasion of Marches and Umbria. Crusaders appealed to Napoleon.

18 Sep 59   Papal crusaders under Lamorciere defeated at Loreto in sight of shrine.

27 Oct 59   Lord John Russell's despatch that the Italians were the best judges of their own interests. 'It is difficult to believe, after the astonishing events that we have seen, that the Pope and the King of the Two Sicilies possessed the love of their people.' Britain rejected the censures of Austria, France, Prussia and Russia on Piedmont for attacking papal territory.

Dec 59   Napoleon III inspired publication of *Le Pape et le Congrès* which proposed to confine papal territory to Rome and Patrimony of St Peter. Pius appointed Mgr de Mérode War Minister.

1866   7 July. Law continued the suppression of religious corporations in territory taken from the Pope. Law extended to city and province of Rome 19 June 73. Legal status of religious corporations was abolished so that they could not hold property. The administration of the revenue from the proceeds of land destined for charity given to communes; that from property of foreign religious orders in Rome (400,000 lire) to the Holy See; remainder administered by two institutions which paid for pensions and other dues and provided for beneficent work and for worship in Rome, and for worship in the rest of Italy.

Of the 58 cardinals 1 was a native of the Netherlands, 3 of Germany, 1 of Hungary, 4 of France, 3 of Spain, 1 of Portugal. Rest Italian. Average age 65.

Ecclesiastical population of Rome:
     1894 seculars or priests
     2569 regulars
     2031 nuns

Six seminaries, 19 colleges, 16 charitable institutions, 16 conservatories, 43 schools directed by nuns, 56 religious orders.

1870   French troops withdrawn. Fall of Rome.

SARDINIA (PIEDMONT, SAVOY, SARDINIA)

1846   Marquis Massimo d'Azeglio (1798–1866) published *Degli ultimi casi di Romagna* after touring papal states. It pilloried government of Pope Gregory XVI.

One in every 214 Piedmont inhabitants was an ecclesiastic, including members of religious orders. The Archbishop of Turin refused to give up any privileges or endowments of the church.

8 Feb 48   Petition to Charles Albert from 20,000 Genoese asking for the expulsion of the Jesuits and for a civic guard.

25 Aug 48 Jesuits and the Sacred Heart expelled.

4 Oct 48   Anti-clerical law on teaching.

1849   Conflict with the Archbishop of Turin, the Bishop of Asti and the Pope.

1850   . Siccardi laws suppressed ecclesiastical immunities. Archbishops of Turin and of Sassari (Sardinia) imprisoned.

1851   Civil power to regulate church teaching.

1852   Civil marriage.

Church property secularized.

1854   Laws on convents.

1855   Church academy of Superga suppressed.

Confiscated by royal decree in the Kingdom of Sardinia:

      66 monasteries on mainland with 772 monks

      46 monasteries on mainland with 1085 nuns

      40 monasteries in Sardinia with 489 monks and nuns

   182 alms-seeking convents with 3145 monks

      65 chapters with 680 priests

  1700 benefices with 1700 clergy

Total of 2099 establishments, with 7871 persons and income of £145,640.

Suppression of religious corporations was continued for the whole country by law of 7 July 1866 and completed by law of 19 June 1873 which extended measure to the city and province of Rome. Legal status of religious corporations was abolished so that they could not hold property.

11 Nov 59 Corporations of Lombardy were privileged by the Treaty of Zurich. Their lands and houses were left to the disposal of individual members.

1873   By this year a total of 3037 houses for men and 1027 for women had been closed. Pensions were paid to 54,000 religious.

The administration of the revenue from the proceeds of land destined for charity or instruction was given to the communes.

THE TWO SICILIES (NAPLES, SICILY)

21 Jan 48 Two priests in Piazza Vigliena (later Quattrocenti), Naples, raised their crucifixes and called people to arms in the name of God.

9 Mar 48 Demonstration against Jesuits in Naples.

14 Mar 48 Disorders in Naples because the poor feared the liberals would expel the Carmelites.

Ferdinand II, extremely superstitious, increased privileges of church. Troops driven to confession and services but allowed to terrorize civil population.

1850   Gladstone, visiting Naples, saw with disgust the trial of some prisoners from 1848 rising. Told that clergy used confessional to aid government. He later wrote: 'This is the negation of God erected into a system of government.'

1860   Sicilian priests and religious bodies were nationalist and on the side of the revolution. Peasants believed that Garibaldi must be related to Santa Rosalia, patroness of Palermo. Neopolitan troops robbed and sacked churches in Palermo.

Priests and monks helped to dismantle the Castellamare, the Bourbon fortress at Palermo, and the Archbishop blessed Garibaldi's troops.

In Naples the lower clergy often took the popular side in contrast to the bishops. The rich Bishop of Mileto and other bishops fled.

Feb 61   Monastic orders partially suppressed. There were 1020 houses containing 13,611 men, of whom 8899 lived entirely on alms and 4712 were monks. The 272 nunneries had 8001 inmates.

THE NETHERLANDS

1848   Constitution guaranteed freedom of education. This opened the way for churches to start denominational schools.

Dutch Reformed Church (Presbyterian) disestablished.

1853   Protestant outcry when Pope Pius XI recreated 5 dioceses, headed by Mgr Zwijssen as Archbishop of Utrecht.

Calvinists seek separate schools.

1862   Slaves in Dutch West Indies freed.

1870   Political parties largely formed according to religion: Catholic People's Party (the Catholics claimed to be 36·5 per cent of population); Anti-Revolutionary Party (Orthodox Calvinist); Christian Historical Party (Dutch Reformed Church).

1899   First Peace Conference at The Hague. The Queen asked Pope Leo XIII for his 'moral support'. Palace of Peace 1913.

1906   Catholic Social Weeks started.

NORWAY

1845	Storting voted Dissenter Law which gave all Christian bodies the right to exercise their religion publicly and make propaganda. Norwegian citizens, except civil servants, allowed to leave national church. Parents could have children exempted from religious instruction in elementary and secondary schools.
1880	Civil servants allowed to leave national church. Bishops and ordinary clergy paid by state from funds which originated from church property. Seven bishoprics: Oslo, Hamar, Kristiansund, Bergen, Trondheim, Tromsö, Stavanger. The King must be crowned in Trondheim Cathedral.

PORTUGAL

1886	Concordat with the Vatican. Bishops to be nominated by the government, appointed by the Pope and paid by the state. Parish priests to be appointed by the Minister of State. Schism of Goa ended—King Louis I renounced his privilege of patronage over all churches of India and East Indies.
1896	Existence of religious orders allowed under certain conditions.
1908–	King Carlos I assassinated; republic set up. The church was the prime target of the provisional government. Alfonso Costa (1871–1937) believed that religion was destined to disappear and set out to remove all vestiges of Catholicism. Religious congregations were expelled, parish administration was to be run by lay committees, and revenues were to be restricted to the offerings of the faithful. The chair of ecclesiastical law at Coimbra was abolished, as was religious teaching in schools, saints' days as holidays, religious oaths in universities and theology courses. The army was forbidden to appear at religious ceremonies.
24 Dec 10	Prelates published a pastoral censuring the government. The Minister of Justice ordered its suspension. The Bishop of Oporto ordered the priests of his diocese to read the document in church and was deposed.
1911	Law of Separation. Church disestablished. Decree containing 196 articles. Ministers of Religion forbidden to criticize the government or laws

of the republic. Churches, chapels, land, chattels belonging to the church became the property of the state. Boards of laymen were to take charge of Catholic worship. Only Portuguese who had studied in Portugal were to officiate. Ministers permitted to marry. Moderate republicans were shocked by these attacks on the church and the party started to split. At this time the church had 3 metropolitans, 12 dioceses (9 suffragan).

Sidonio Pais (1872–1918) led a successful coup against Alfonso Costa, made overtures to the church, revoked anti-clerical measures and reopened diplomatic relations with the Vatican in an attempt to reunite the country. Three children claimed to have seen the Virgin on a hillside in Estremadura, now the shrine of Our Lady of Fatima. The disestablishment of the church, combined with the spiritual revival which followed the visions, brought new life to the church.

ROMANIA

Romania is possibly the only country with no history of feuds between religious creeds in the period. The Greek Orthodox clergy were foreigners (Greeks from Constantinople) up to the nineteenth century and did not seek to influence the Romanians spiritually. Religious observance was largely in external practices.

1861   Independence. Monasteries, which had acquired a fifth of country's land, were secularized (1863) and transferred to the state. For 30 years no provision made for clergy.

1864   Romanian church, which had been under the patriarchate of Constantinople, proclaimed national and autocephalous. The patriarchate recognized this independence in 1885.

1878   Congress of Berlin demanded abolition of Article 7 of constitution, aimed against Jews, by which non-Christians could not become Romanian citizens.

Romania retained individual naturalization, achieved only by special act of parliament.

1893   Priests incorporated as government officials. Maintenance of church and clergy included in general budget.

Holy Synod of Bucharest, composed of the Metropolitans of Bucharest and Jassy and the 8 bishops, settled questions of dogma. Administration of church supervised by Minister of Education.

1914 Minorities estimated to be:
    Jews   800,000
    Moslems 45,000
    Gipsies 200,000, mostly converts to Orthodox Church

RUSSIA

Nicholas I (1825–55)
The reign of Nicholas saw the rise of the Slavophils, intellectuals who were strongly religious and believed in a utopian, Christian peasant kingdom. Russian Orthodoxy to them represented Christianity uncorrupted by Western influence, as against the Westerners who believed in the superiority of Western civilization and that Russia should westernize as quickly as possible.

1853 Dispute over Holy Places. The Tsar intervened to 'protect' Christians in Turkey and to confirm Russian rights over the Holy Places. Due to British intervention Russia failed to obtain a treaty with Turkey giving Russia a protectorate over Christians in the Ottoman Empire. Nicholas refused to compromise where the cause of Orthodox religion was concerned. The Western European powers saw Russian imperialism at work behind a religious pretext and allied themselves with Turkey.

1 Nov 53 Russia declared war on Turkey.

Alexander II (1855–81)
Panslavism. During this period the Slavophil movement was gradually transformed into Panslavism. The Slavs that the Russians wished to liberate were not all Orthodox; some opposed the Russian Orthodox Church and simply wanted independence, considering Russia to be backward culturally and politically. The Panslav movement was less religious than the Slavophil and more concerned with power politics and with Slavs as an ethnic group.

During the 1860s the clergy ceased to be a hereditary caste and the number of clergy per head of the population declined. They were responsible for keeping the civil registers.

1858 Opposition to the proposed emancipation of serfs. The church still owned about 3m. serfs attached to its monastic estates. Most of the bishops were against reform but Bishop Gregory of Kaluga preached that Christianity and slavery were incompatible.

Metropolitan Philaret of St Petersburg believed that the serfs belonged to God and to free them would mean giving them to a Satan-dominated world. Reform would alienate the nation from God. The metropolitan represented his views strongly both to

Count A. P. Tolstoy, the Procurator and to the Tsar, and succeeded in making the final draft of the liberation manifesto more ambiguous.

1861   Metropolitan Philaret suggested that Admiral Count Poutiatin should be made Minister of Education in order to deal with student unrest. Poutiatin was devout and reactionary. Student riots broke out in St Petersburg and Moscow. St Petersburg University closed. Poutiatin dismissed.

1863   Catholic rising in Poland. Priests executed, Catholics deported, churches and religious houses sacked. Bismarck handed back to the Tsar Polish refugees who had escaped to Prussia. Pope Pius IX denounced the persecution. The concordat between Russia and the Holy See repudiated by the Tsar.

1866   Diplomatic relations between Russia and the Holy See broken off.

1867   Panslav Congress in Moscow.

1874   Panslav committee paid for the construction of an Orthodox church in Prague.

1875   Last Apostolic See of the Roman Catholic Church in Russia suppressed.

1877   Holy War against Turkey to 'liberate Balkan Christians', to make the church of Santa Sofia Orthodox again and to re-establish Constantinople as a great Christian centre. In Europe these aims were seen as a cloak to hide Russian ambitions; by Queen Victoria as a straight contest between Russia and Britain. Russia won the war against Turkey but she was not allowed by Britain to occupy Constantinople and thus control the Straits.

1880   Constantine Petrovich Pobedonostsev (1827–1907) appointed Procurator of the Holy Synod in April. A brilliant scholar, he became professor of civil law at Moscow University, advocated legal reforms and helped in the reorganization of the Russian judicial system 1864. He was tutor to the future Alexander III in 1861. Radical in his youth, he became an extreme conservative, isolationist and devout believer in Orthodox Christianity.

Pobedonostsev was very much influenced by the failure of the Panslav movement (*see* 1855). While tutor to Alexander III he introduced him to Panslav writings. In 1877 he wrote to him, 'To surrender the Orthodox Slavs to Austria means to surrender them and ourselves to a cunning, selfish and jesuitical enemy.' He was an enthusiastic Panslav until the effects of the Turkish war became clear. Then, deeply shocked, he recoiled from the movement.

Panslavism he now believed to be a danger to autocracy. It could lead to internal revolution and European hostility. Pobedonostsev turned to Pan-Russianism in which Russian Orthodoxy was paramount. Russia must be a community of believers.

In his 25 years as procurator Pobedonostsev was very influential as adviser to the Tsar, though his influence declined considerably towards the end of his life. He was described as the 'Apostle of Absolutism and Orthodoxy' but popularly known as the 'Black Tsar'. He saw the Orthodox Church as the cement unifying the social structure and persecuted other churches or beliefs as disintegrating forces. In particular he persecuted the Jews, who were unlikely to be converted to Christianity. 'The Church, and the Church alone, has allowed us to remain Russian and to unite our scattered strength.'

Pobedonostsev petitioned the Tsar in October to raise the office of Procurator to ministerial status, and was appointed to the Council of Ministers. Though in a minority he successfully opposed the programme of constitutional reform of Count Loris-Melikov (1825–88). Lord Radstock, a Plymouth Brother, was expelled from Russia and his Russian followers exiled.

Alexander III (1881–94)

Alexander III was brought up on Panslav ideals under the influence of Pobedonostsev but after the failure of Panslavism in the 1870s the idea of Russia for the Russians took its place. The test of being a true Russian became orthodox belief which enshrined the idea of the Tsar as head of the church. This was a reversion to the cult of Orthodoxy, Autocracy and Nationality which was started in the reign of Nicholas I. He was convinced that his father's assassination was part of an international Jewish plot to do away with monarchy and terrible pogroms followed his accession, thousands of Jews being murdered especially in Kirov and Kiev. These pogroms continued at intervals throughout the reign. The Holy Band was formed to protect the life of the Tsar but was amateurish. Members of the Holy Band, given power to arrest suspects, arrested half the police force, so the Minister of the Interior persuaded the Tsar to disband it.

Throughout the 1880s Pobedonostsev worked with Count Dmitri Tolstoy, former Procurator now Minister of Interior, in setting up laws to Russify Estland and Livland. Pobedonostsev's view was that 'Russia and Orthodoxy are synonymous—the whole so-called Baltic problem lies clearly in the question of unity of the local population to Orthodoxy.' Improvements were made to the seminary at Riga, new churches and schools built, and there was a missionary effort, reinforced by police and courts.

Mar 81 Alexander II assassinated. Anti-Jewish pogrom.

May 81 Pobedonostsev produced a manifesto calling for the Tsar to reassert autocratic rule. On his advice Loris-Melikov was replaced by Nikolai Pavlovitch Ignatiev (1832–1906). Pope Leo XIII tried to improve the position of Catholics in Russia. Pobedonostsev opposed this but talks began. The Tsar insisted that Catholics must remain out of politics.

1882 Orthodox Palestine Society founded.

Diplomatic relations between Russia and the Holy See resumed.

May Laws. Decrees to restrict Jews to the south-west of Russia. No Jew could hold an administrative post, become a lawyer, appeal against a court sentence, own land, or marry a Christian unless converted to Christianity. Jewish schools were closed and books in Hebrew banned. An estimated 225,000 Jewish families left Russia for Western Europe because of these decrees.

Ignatiev was dismissed on Pobedonostsev's advice when he proposed a territorial assembly.

1883 Pobedonostsev launched a drive to establish parish schools throughout European Russia.

Pobedonostsev wrote and published the Moscow Collection, papers putting forward the view that religion was the foundation of civilized life, but that modern civilization especially parliamentary democracy posed a direct threat to correct values.

Pobedonostsev tried to censor Leo Tolstoy's work. When Tolstoy supported student disorders he accepted a suggestion that Tolstoy should be officially removed from membership of the Russian Orthodox Church.

May 83 Act allowing schismatics to hold religious services at home, to work, and to hold internal passports, but not to build new places of worship, not to worship publicly, nor to proselytize.

1884 Lord Radstock and Russian supporters exiled again for circulating Bunyan's *Pilgrim's Progress* without permission.

Decree establishing many more parish schools, with emphasis on Christian doctrine, literacy and singing.

  1880 4348 church schools with 108,990 students.

  1905 43,407 church schools with 1.9m. students.

Half the primary schools in Russia were under the Synod.

1885 Synod forbade mixed marriages in Estonia and Latvia unless the children were raised in the Orthodox faith. Protests by Lutheran clergy and gentry and by the Evangelical Alliance who complained to the Tsar. Pobedonostsev denied that there was a persecution of religion, only of proselytizing, and that the survival of Russia depended on religious unity.

Pobedonostsev embarrassed the Tsar by giving official support to the disastrous Abyssinian colony project.

1889 A clergyman named Dalton published an open letter to Pobedonostsev in Russian, German and English, accusing him of fabricating charges against the Lutheran clergy and asserting that there was no basis in law for his policies. The Tsar was extremely angry at the revelations in Dalton's pamphlet.

Russian Ecclesiastical Mission merged with the Palestine Commission, bringing it under government control and making it suspect to Greek and Middle East interests. Worked closely with Russian consuls, produced scholarly publications, arranged tours for pilgrims, protecting them from harassment, built schools in Palestine and Syria. Friction with Greek Orthodox Church, Ottomans and Catholics.

1738	106 churches for every 100,000 Orthodox of population.
1890	56 churches for every 100,000 Orthodox of population.

1891	Pobedonostsev published history of the Orthodox Church.
1892	Pobedonostsev persuaded Alexander III to grant 250,000 roubles towards raising the salaries of the clergy. Number of clergy increased by reducing training and increasing salaries.

Antoni Vadkovsky made archbishop and member of the Holy Synod. His desire for church reform was hindered by conservatives inside and outside the church. He admired Slavophil philosophers. Vadkovsky was a moderate politically and appealed on behalf of political prisoners. Mediator and reconciler. Ecumenical links with the Anglican Church.

Anti-Jewish pogroms in Moscow. Thousands sent to the Pale in south-west Russia. Alexander III wrote in the margin of a report: 'We must never forget that it was the Jews who crucified the Lord and spilled his precious blood.'

Nicholas II (1894–1917)

Nicholas II pledged himself to uphold his father's reactionary policy and resisted demands for reform. But the tide of unrest, in the country and the church, proved overwhelming. Within the church there was a demand for structural reforms. Since the time of Peter the Great the church had played a mainly passive role, whatever political influence it had being on the side of reaction. Now social and intellectual problems drew it into the centre of the political storm. Even Metropolitan Antoni, who declared that he was not a politician and never would be and that it was the task of the church to talk only of heaven, found himself involved.

1894	Papal encyclical said that Polish Catholic clergy would no longer oppose Russia.

Izvolski appointed minister to the Vatican. Pobedonostsev successfully opposed appointment of papal nuncio to St Petersburg and rejected Church of England efforts to establish relationship with the Orthodox Church. Persecution of Evangelical sects. Stundists declared dangerous and their schools and chapels closed.

1897   99 % of funds for Pobedonostsev's Synod staff came from state. The Synod itself discussed trivia. Bishops were moved every few years to prevent them becoming too powerful.

1898   Antoni Vadkovsky made Metropolitan (senior bishop) of St Petersburg.

1900   Revolts in seminaries. Church weighed down by bureaucracy. Rift between Orthodox and Russian intelligentsia.

1901   Founding of the Religious Philosophical Society. Meetings in St Petersburg 1901−3. Attempt to work with intelligentsia on problems.

1904   Official membership of Russian Orthodox Church put at 88 m., 66 dioceses, 40,000 parishes, 106,620 clergy (47,743 priests, 14,701 deacons, 44,176 cantors).
27,000 parish churches received 11.5m. roubles from state funds. Committee set up to review church matters and recommend legislation.

1905   5 Jan.   Bloody Sunday. St Petersburg Union of Factory Workers led by the priest George Gapon (1870−1906) demonstrated, carrying ikons and church banners. Demonstrators petitioned the Tsar for freedom of the press, constitutional parliament, 8-hour day and distribution of land to peasants. They were met by armed resistance by the Palace Guard and an unknown number (estimates 2−4000) killed or wounded. Group of Thirty-two (St Petersburg priests) founded. Petitioned for church reform. Spokesman of group, Father Gregori Petrov, elected as Constitutional Democrat deputy, to second Duma. Sentenced by Synod to 3 months confinement in a monastery and later unfrocked.
Mar − Apr.   Declaration by 32 clergy, approved by Metropolitan Antoni, calling for freedom of church from state control so that it could be involved in social problems. Asked for restoration of the patriarchate, abolished 1700, and local councils. The group saw riots as 'just judgement of God'. They did not question Tsarist rule or social structure.
17 Apr.   Religious Tolerance Law. It now became legal to leave the state church and join another denomination. This law brought relief in particular to the Evangelical sects who became active. They founded the League of Freedom, whose platform included

schooling, equal rights for denominations, constitutional monarchy and equal suffrage.

The political programme of the Old Believers, who split from Orthodox Church in seventeenth century, embraced constitutional monarchy, suspension of class privileges, distribution of land to the peasants. This led to persecution by the Minister of the Interior.

Persecution of the Old Believers and Evangelicals lost the Romanovs their support at the Revolution.

By May 09 301,450 people had left the Orthodox Church mainly to become Roman Catholic, but some Muslims and Lutherans. Pope Pius X protested at the persecution, especially in Poland.

Conference of Ministers wished to consider new regulations of church – state relations as well as reform but this was stopped by Pobedonostsev who appealed to the Tsar. Metropolitan Antoni officially proposed 'over-control by the secular authority to be removed or relieved'. Witte said that the church had been paralysed since the time of Peter the Great. The Tsar refused to permit the discussion of these problems by the Committee of Ministers but referred them to the Synod. The Synod asked the Tsar for permission to elect a Patriarch and carry out reforms. The Tsar refused to discuss the matter 'in the present time of unrest'. A committee was set up to prepare for a council but this was suspended by the Tsar a year later.

17 Oct. Constitutional monarchy established. Pobedonostsev replaced as Procurator by Lukyanov. During 1905, state grants towards clergy salaries amounted to 25m. roubles.

1906	Metropolitan Antoni refused to have anything to do with the right-wing League of Russian People, but other dioceses and clergy supported the League actively. George Gapon assassinated.
1907	Synod declared that it was incompatible with priestly office to belong to parties which strove to overthrow the state, the social order or the authority of the Tsar. A new electoral law prevented left-wing clergy being members of the Duma.

Archimandite Mikhail published 'How I became a People's Socialist'. He lost his position and priesthood and joined the Old Believers. At some time during the period 1905–8 the *staretz* (holy man) Grigory Rasputin (*c*. 1870–1916) was introduced to the royal family and credited with having helped the Tsarevich back to health.

1908   Reaction instead of reform from the Synod. Seminaries were not allowed independence but were told to make the rebellious students 'submissive to the throne and fatherland'. Parish reform was blocked by the hierarchy of the church, which became increasingly identified with political reaction. The Synod told the bishops to permit and bless participation of the Orthodox clergy in the work of the League of the Russian People and other monarchist patriotic societies. Other clergy joined socialist parties. Fourth Missionary Conference in Kiev concerned with socialism. Courses at seminaries and academies on the 'true nature of socialism'. Church apologists attacked German, French and English socialist thinkers and defended the existing social order. Poverty was rooted in the sinful nature of man. The hard life of the poor and secure well-being of the rich were the will of God. Socialism appealed for class struggle and enmity, Christianity for unity and love. Therefore Christian socialism was impossible.

Russian Evangelical League founded, calling for moral regeneration to replace class struggle.

Suppression of public meetings of Old Believers.

Rasputin claimed that he averted a war with Austria over Bosnia and Herzegovina by telling the Tsar that a war with Austria would be the end of Russia and that the Balkans were not worth the life of a single Russian.

1909	*Signposts* published an attempt to reconcile Christian convictions with political and social involvement. Bulgakov and Berdyaev, former Marxists, led the movement. Bulgakov founded League of Christian Politics.
1910	Synod calculated that a yearly grant of 75m. roubles was necessary for the renunciation of church land and congregational gifts.

Every Baptist and Evangelical conference had to be vetted by the Minister of the Interior. Police agent to be present. No instruction for children allowed. The Prime Minister Stolypin became alarmed at Rasputin's influence with the Tsar. The Procurator Lukyanov was convinced that the discrepancy between Rasputin's claim to be a holy man and his promiscuous sexual behaviour was due to his membership of the Khlysty sect whose rites included sexual orgies. |
Mar 11	As the result of growing hostility in St Petersburg Rasputin made a pilgrimage to the Holy Land.
Aug 11	Stolypin assassinated. Rasputin returned to St Petersburg. Metropolitan Antoni and Procurator Lukyanov failed to remove Rasputin from the court. The new president of the Duma, Rodzianko, persuaded Rasputin to leave St Petersburg.
1912	Tsarevich ill again, recovered after Rasputin had prayed for him. Rasputin back in favour with the royal family although police reported him to be living a life of promiscuity and drunkenness.

Rasputin told the Tsar 'While I live your throne is secure. If I die you will lose your throne and your life.' Lukyanov replaced as Procurator by Sabler who was under the influence of the Rasputin group. Sabler prevented modernization and gave Rasputin power over the Synod.

State church put forward clergy as conservative candidates for the fourth Duma. 46 entered, 2 of them Progressives, 2 Octobrists and 40 right-wingers. All attacked Sabler.

Article in *Golos Moskvy* denounced Rasputin as a member of the Khlysty sect. Political factions united in hatred of him. People believed that the Tsarina was his mistress. The Rasputin scandal damaged the authority of the church and completely alienated it from the monarchy.

Nov 12	Metropolitan Antoni died, succeeded by Metropolitan Vladimir.
1914	Attempted assassination of Rasputin at the same time as the Archduke Ferdinand was murdered at Sarajevo. Protestants suspected of German affiliations, persecuted. As a result the Old Believers and Evangelicals ceased to support the monarchy, welcomed the fall of the Romanovs and supported the Provisional Government.
1915	Second Law of Tolerance. Procurator Sabler opposed canonical self-government.
	Sabler succeeded by A. D. Samarin who tried to resist Rasputin and was dismissed.
1916	22 Feb. Prime Minister Goremykin dismissed and Stürmer, incompetent hanger-on of Rasputin, given the post. Rasputin now so hated that even the Metropolitan of Petrograd pretended not to know him.
	Dec. Stürmer dismissed. Rasputin denounced in Duma.
	30 Dec. Rasputin assassinated.
	During 1916 31,000 parish churches received 18·8m. roubles from State funds.
1917	27 Feb. Synod refused to condemn the Revolution.
	20 June Provisional Government withdrew church schools from church administration and put them under the Ministry of Education.
	V. N. Lvov appointed Procurator. Reforms led to the formation of an All Russian Council of the Church which had not been convened for 200 years. It included bishops, clergy and laymen. The council rejected the separation of church and state. The Patriarch was restored.
	Oct. Bolshevik Revolution. Provisional Government overthrown.

5 Nov. Metropolitan Tikhon elected Patriarch of the Orthodox Church. The Patriarch and Council were anti-Soviet. The remainder of the Group of Thirty-two formed a league of democratic Orthodox clergy and laity. It supported the socialist revolution.

By 1917 there were 200,000 Evangelicals in Russia, mostly in the Ukraine and Siberia.

1918   Jan.   Separation of church and state formally proclaimed. Abolition of religious teaching, censorship of sermons, ban on religious youth groups, confiscation and ban on the sale of religious objects. Council of People's Commissars laid down that 'Church and religious societies do not have a right to property. They do not have the legal rights of a person.'

Sep.   The All Russian Council of the Church dissolved. The new society was to be based on the negation of God and of all religion. According to Marx the extinction of religion would be accomplished by the forward march of society. Meanwhile, because religion was an ally of capitalism, it was to be annihilated.

SPAIN

1851   Government signed concordat with the Papacy by which Catholicism was declared religion of the state 'to the exclusion of all others'. The government recognized the right of the clergy to supervise education and books and settle marriage disputes without civil intervention. The Papacy guaranteed the right of the Crown to appoint bishops and recognized the loss of church lands already secularized.

1868   Abdication of Isabella. Cortes proclaimed universal suffrage, freedom of worship and teaching for the first time, and introduced civil marriage. Religious houses suppressed and clergy, most of whom were Carlist, deprived of their salaries.

1876   Alfonso XII enthroned. Church property restored. Catholic schools reopened, diplomatic relations with Papacy revived. The constitution proclaimed Catholicism the official religion although it recognized 'the existence of non-Catholic cults'. The state accepted responsibility to maintain the church and raised the religious budget from 3m. to 91m. pesetas. It abolished civil marriage and closed Protestant chapels.

Growing hostility between the church and liberals and secularists, who curbed clerical power after turn of the century. In the Great War the anti-clerical left was pro-Ally, the reactionary clerical party pro-German. In 1918 Alfonso XIII dedicated Spain to the Sacred Heart.

SWEDEN

1853	Roman Catholic diocese of Stockholm replaced Vicariate Apostolic.
1855	Obligatory Communion for all who held public office ended. *Swedish Church Times (Kyrko Tidning)* founded. Had great influence.
1856	Evangelical National Institute founded for lay work at home. It started foreign missions 1861 in Abyssinia and India, and a seaman's mission with stations at Lübeck, Hamburg, Bremerhaven, Grimsby, Liverpool, Marseilles, Boston (USA) and Melbourne.
1858	International protests when 6 women were exiled for conversion to Roman Catholicism.
1859	Members of non-Lutheran faiths allowed to organize their own congregations and enjoy religious freedom. Jews emancipated but still barred from some positions.
1865	Riksdag reorganized, 2 chambers replacing 4 estates. In return the clergy were granted the right of meeting every fifth year in a special conclave (*Kyrkomôte*) to legislate in eccelesiastical affairs. Members of *Kyrkomôte* half clergy (direct election), half laymen (indirect election).
1873	By decree of toleration Swedes obtained the legal right to leave the Lutheran church and join another Christian community. But until 1951 they could not join a non-Christian body.
1874	Followers of P. P. Waldenström (1838–1917), who succeeded Rosénius as editor of the *Pietist*, became a separate church group over atonement and were known as Mission Friends or Waldenströmians. The group soon had 300,000 members. Missionaries of the *Svenska Kyrkans missionstyrelse* sent to South India, South Africa and Palestine.
1900	Swedish school in Jerusalem and medical mission in Bethlehem. But for many Swedes Communion at confirmation the only Communion of their lives.
1919	Religious instruction in schools made non-denominational and

less time given to it. Catechism not to be taught and the Bible only as an historical book. The King is the highest earthly ruler of the Swedish church professing the pure doctrine of the Augsburg Confession. He must take counsel of the Minister for Church Affairs and Council of State. According to Swedish fundamental law, 'the Riksdag, in conjunction with the King, has the right to pass church laws, to alter them or to repeal them; but for this matter the consent of a general *Kyrkomôte* is requisite.'

Purely ecclesiastical matters, e.g. changes in the prayer book or a new translation of the Bible, lie within the administrative competence of the Crown.

SWITZERLAND

1845	Ultramontane leader Siegwart-Muller, having vainly appealed to Metternich and Roman Catholic states, formed (1845) secret armed separatist union of Roman Catholic cantons, the Sonderbund. The confederation Diet voted (1847) for dissolution of the Sonderbund, expulsion of Jesuits and revision of constitution. Sonderbund's 79,000 men defeated in brief war by Diet's 100,000.
1870	Pope Pius IX's *Syllabus errorum* (1864) and dogma of infallibility quickened quarrels over mixed marriages, education and freedom of press. Roman Catholic Bishop of Basle, Mgr Lachat, who had deprived priests refusing to obey Vatican decrees, ejected by civil authority. Canton of Berne, following Roman Catholic disturbances in Oberland, asserted right of communities to elect own priests. Pope Pius IX sent Mgr Mermillod to Geneva as auxiliary bishop 'to convert the city which fears not to call itself the Protestant Rome'. Geneva would not recognize him. Federal government broke off diplomatic relations with Papacy. Accommodation reached in 1883 when Mgr Lachat was moved and Mgr Mermillod (cardinal 1890) became Bishop of Fribourg-Lausanne-Geneva.
1872	Roman Catholics who could not accept papal dogma of infallibility formed separate Christian Catholic ('Old Catholic') congregations in Lucerne, Valais and Ticino. Elected and supported own priests. Congregations reject transubstantiation, immaculate conception, obligatory auricular confession and celibacy, etc.
1874	Constitution made civil marriage obligatory, forbade foundation of new monasteries or congregations, and gave wider guarantees

of religious freedom. Switzerland has no federal church, each canton having its own ecclesiastical constitution.

Religion and language of cantons:

Aargau	Protestant	German
Appenzell		
Ausser-Rhoden	Protestant	German
Inner-Rhoden	Roman Catholic	German
Basle		
City	Protestant	German
District	Protestant	German
Berne	Protestant	German
Fribourg	Roman Catholic	French, German
Geneva	Protestant	French
Glarus	Protestant	German
Grisons	Protestant	German, Romance
Lucerne	Roman Catholic	German
Neuchâtel	Protestant	French
St Gallen	Roman Catholic	German
Schaffhausen	Protestant	German
Schwyz	Roman Catholic	German
Solothurn	Roman Catholic	German
Thurgau	Protestant	German
Ticino	Roman Catholic	Italian
Unterwalden		
Nidwalden	Roman Catholic	German
Obwalden	Roman Catholic	German
Uri	Roman Catholic	German
Valais	Roman Catholic	French, German
Vaud	Protestant	French
Zug	Roman Catholic	German
Zurich	Protestant	German

TURKEY

1849   To forestall Russian claims Christians admitted to office and guaranteed the free exercise of religion. This offended Moslems and resulted in Druze massacre of Maronite Christians in the Lebanon and Damascus (1860). Christians preferred to pay tax rather than do military service and recruiting was restricted to Mohammedans (1869).

1854   One aim of Britain and France in Crimean War was to make

Russia renounce her exclusive patronage of Balkan Christians, held to mask territorial ambitions. At Peace of Paris Christians were put under aegis of great powers.

1876   Massacres in Bulgaria, Bosnia. Russian claim to be protector of Christians renewed.

1895   More than 200,000 Gregorian Armenians massacred: Orthodox protected by Russia, Roman Catholics by France.

1915   Armenians massacred in attempt at extermination to stifle bid for autonomy.

Turkey, a secular republic since 1923, abolished the Caliphate, old-style religious education and religious courts (1924); ended Islam as official state religion (1928) and prohibited clerical garb (1934).

Freedom of religion guaranteed by the constitution in 1924.

UNITED KINGDOM

ENGLAND

Church of England

1841   Tract no. 90, claiming 39 Articles do not disavow Catholicism, condemned by college heads at Oxford.

1845   Newman and others became Roman Catholics. (Newman made cardinal 1879.) But Keble and Pusey remained in Church of England and the movement's influence spread.

1848   Gorham controversy over baptism represented further conflict between evangelicals and High Church school.

1850   No-Popery riots at Exeter, etc.

1851   Archdeacon Henry Edward Manning (1808–92) joined Church of Rome (cardinal 1875).

1864   Newman's *Apologia pro Vita Sua*.

Low churchmen feared that popery would be introduced by ceremonial. From 1850 ritual and 'No Popery' disorders in churches resulted. Extremists formed Church Association (1865) to prosecute clergymen on points of ritual, the most famous defendant being Edward King, Bishop of Lincoln (1885–1910).

The English Church Union (founded 1860) agreed (1875) that ritualists should fight for vestments, eastward position, altar lights, wafer bread, incense, addition of water to wine at Eucharist.

The Oxford Movement largely ignored social problems. The Christian Socialist Movement, Broad Church (1848), was led by John Ludlow, a barrister; Thomas Hughes (1822–96, *Tom Brown's Schooldays*); Charles Kingsley (1819–75, *Yeast, Alton Locke, Westward Ho!*); and F. D. Maurice (1805–72), Professor of Divinity, King's College, London. The movement died but founded the Working Men's College, North London.

Church reform

1857 Divorce obtainable in court, not by Private Act of Parliament.

  The 2 Convocations, which after 1717 had practically ceased to function, resumed general activity: Canterbury in 1852, York in 1861. Each had an upper house of bishops and a lower house of inferior clergy. Convocations were given royal licence to revise canons but Parliament, still the source of all other church legislation, was usually too busy to consider church bills. (183 bills came to nothing, 1890–1914.) Church Assembly, proposed in 1916, legalized by Enabling Act 1919. Assembly given 3 houses; house of all diocesan bishops, house of clergy, house of laity. Measures approved by all 3 houses passed to ecclesiastical committee of Parliament. On resolution of both Houses of Parliament measure received royal assent and became law. Parliament could not amend a measure, only reject or accept it. Parochial church councils 1921.

1851 First diocesan synod of clergy held by Bishop Phillpotts of Exeter.

1871 Synod of Lincoln held by Bishop Wordsworth.

1885 Disestablishment, raised by Gladstone, Joseph Chamberlain, etc., and urged by Nonconformists, dropped in election after irritating the clergy. Demand for disestablishment gradually died.

New dioceses 1847–1918:

1847 Manchester

1877 Truro

    St Albans

1880 Liverpool

1882 Newcastle

1884 Southwell

1888 Wakefield

1905 Birmingham

    Southwark

1914 Sheffield

    Chelmsford

    St Edmundsbury and Ipswich

1918 Coventry

Bishops in House of Lords: Archbishops of Canterbury and York, Bishops of London, Durham and Winchester, plus 21 most senior diocesan bishops, irrespective of particular see, are spiritual peers and sit in the House of Lords.

Nonconformists

1842 Gedney case. Privy Council confirmed that baptism by Wesleyan

Methodists was valid by ecclesiastical and civil law.

1857   Wesleyan Methodist Association joined with Wesleyan Reformers as United Methodist Free Churches.

1868   Church Rate Abolition Act.

1870   Forster's Education Act doubled state grant to Church of England and Roman Catholic schools. It also introduced board schools, paid for by rates, in which catechism or formulary distinctive of any denomination was forbidden (Cowper-Temple clause). Dissenters complained that although they had a choice of school in towns they had none in most villages. The bill angered Nonconformists, antagonized many of Gladstone's supporters and convulsed constituencies, e.g. Joseph Chamberlain, a Unitarian, became leader of Midlands Radicalism.

1871   Universities Tests Act. No declaration or oath to be made at matriculation or taking of degree.

1875   Leys School, Cambridge, founded by Wesleyan Methodists.

1878   Lay representatives at Methodist Conference.

1880   Burial Laws Amendment Act allowed Nonconformists to inter dead with services of their own sect in parish churchyard.

1881   Ecumenical conference in London of British, colonial and American Methodists.

1891   General Baptist Church and the Particular Baptist Church (Calvinist) united in Baptist Union.

1892   National Council of the Evangelical Free Churches formed.

1896   Free Church Federation.

1898   Marriage Act allowed authorized person, usually resident minister, to replace registrar in dissenting chapel registered for marriages.

1907   Methodist New Connexion (founded for reform 1797 and having 204 ministers), Bible Christians (206 ministers) and United Methodist Free Churches (438 ministers) merged as United Methodist Church.

1911   Women representatives at Methodist Conference.

1932   At London conference Wesleyan Methodists, Primitive Methodists and United Methodists merged to become Methodist Church.

General William Booth (1829–1912) local preacher with Wesleyan Methodists and minister of Methodist New Connexion, started Hallelujah Band in Walsall, which became Salvation Army 1878. It had to overcome persecution, including Sunday attacks by the Skeleton Army (founded 1883), especially outside the Eagle Tavern, City Road, London.

Charles Spurgeon (1834–92) Baptist, of the Metropolitan Tabernacle,

London, was the most popular preacher of the nineteenth century.

Roman Catholics

1829   Catholic Emancipation.

1850   Roman Catholic bishops in the United Kingdom after 300 years. One province, under Cardinal Wiseman (1802–65), Archbishop of Westminster, with suffragans at Beverley, Birmingham, Clifton, Hexham, Liverpool, Newport and Menevia, Northampton, Nottingham, Plymouth, Salford, Shrewsbury, Southwark.

The Ecclesiastical Titles Act, the result of anti-papal agitation, forbade Roman Catholic bishops to take any ecclesiastical title already appropriated to the Church of England. The act was never enforced and was repealed in 1867.

1867   Cardinal Manning, a Balliol man, persuaded Rome to ban a Roman Catholic going to Oxford or Cambridge university. For nearly 30 years Roman Catholics in England could obtain higher education only in the upper forms of Roman Catholic schools.

1878   Diocese of Beverley divided into dioceses of Leeds and Middlesbrough.

Scottish hierarchy (see Scotland).

1882   Portsmouth carved from Southwark; Menevia separated from Newport.

1883   Tothill prison site, Westminster, bought for cathedral.

1911   Three provinces: Archiepiscopal Westminster, with Northampton, Nottingham, Portsmouth, Southwark. Archiepiscopal Birmingham, with Clifton, Newport, Plymouth, Shrewsbury, Menevia. Archiepiscopal Liverpool, with Hexham and Newcastle, Leeds, Middlesbrough, Salford.

1916   Cardiff became archiepiscopal see.

1917   Brentwood separated from Westminster.

Roman Catholics estimated at:

1830	180,000
1870	1,300,000
1900	1,800,000

IRELAND

1845   Maynooth College for the education of Roman Catholic priests, which had been constituted without controversy with a parliamentary grant in 1795, now incorporated and endowed after a battle in Parliament. Similar controversy preceded the foundation of Queen's Colleges at Cork, Belfast and Galway, where no religious test was to be applied.

1846–7	Potato famine. So many Irish fled to the United States that the Roman Catholic Church there, traditionally under French influence, now resembled a rigid Irish church, with strict control exercised by priests.
1868	Gladstone's moves to disestablish Irish church, supported by House of Commons but defeated in the Lords, resulted in the fall of Disraeli ministry. Gladstone ministry disestablished Irish church (32 and 33 Vict. c. 42). Act vested all ecclesiastical property in commissioners. No bishop to sit in House of Lords. Compensation for holders of benefices, Protestant Nonconformist ministers in receipt of grant from Regium Donum, and Maynooth College. Surplus of funds to be used for the relief of suffering. Under its new constitution the Church of Ireland had a General Synod (House of Bishops, House of Representatives with 208 clergy, 416 laymen, elected triennially by dioceses).
1873	Gladstone's Irish University Bill, to create single Irish university, denounced by Irish Protestants, Roman Catholics and English Nonconformists. Defeated by 3 votes, Gladstone resigned. Disraeli refused office. After a week Gladstone resumed office.
1881	Parnell's Land League supported by most priests.
1882	£2m. of Irish Church Fund used to pay arrears of rent which tenants could not pay.
1888	Papal decree forbidding boycotting. Forty Irish Roman Catholic Members of Parliament passed resolution that the Vatican had no right to interfere with the Irish people in the management of their political affairs.
1890	Parnell divorce case. Gladstone was forced by Nonconformist supporters to make Parnell's retirement a condition of continued association of Liberals with Irish National Party. Priests refused to accept Parnell, a Protestant, as still being leader; Parnell's supporters refused to accept his resignation.
1899	Belfast Cathedral started; north transept still to be built.
1912	Ulster Protestants opposed Home Rule and threatened armed resistance to an Irish legislature.
1920	Protestant Ulster given Stormont parliament, Roman Catholic south becomes Irish Free State.

Church of Ireland - disestablished 1869
Archbishops:

Armagh	Cashel (until 1839)
Dublin	Tuam (until 1839)

SCOTLAND

Church of Scotland

Church of Scotland, established 1560, became Presbyterian 1690 after long and bloody struggle with episcopalians. Its democratic government was by: kirk session (parish minister and elders); presbyteries (ministers of district elected by General Assembly); synods (three or more presbyteries who elected ministers for General Assembly, the supreme court). The church was recognized as the established church of Scotland in the Act of Union, 1707. An act of 1712 restored to ancient patrons, unless Roman Catholic, the right of nominating ministers to benefices, thus depriving kirk sessions of right of election. Compromise of 1752, by which presbytery could satisfy itself as to 'life, learning and doctrine' of patron's nominee, did not end unrest.

1843	Third of established Church of Scotland, led by evangelical Thomas Chalmers (1780–1847), broke away because of lay patronage to form Free Church of Scotland. (2 churches reunited 1930.) Evangelical Union formed by those who left United Secession Church and by ministers from Congregational Union.
1845	New poor law transferred relief from kirk sessions to parish councils (in 1928 taken over by county councils).
1847	United Secession Church and Relief Synod merged to form United Presbyterian Church.
1875	Patronage Act reversed.
1900	United Presbyterian Church and Free Church of Scotland merged to form United Free Church of Scotland. Small group of Free Church of Scotland remained outside merger, to be known as Wee Frees. Wee Frees claimed right to retain material goods of Free Church, about £4m. Edinburgh Court of Session decided against them but House of Lords found for them. Position remedied by Act of Parliament.
1921	Church of Scotland Act gave the United Presbyterian Church complete autonomy and character of a national church.
1929	United Free Church of Scotland (538,192 communicants, 1441 congregations) and Church of Scotland (759,625 communicants and 1457 parish churches) merged to form United Church of Scotland. Small group of Free Church of Scotland left outside merger.

Episcopal Church

The Episcopal Church of Scotland is autonomous, its Primus being equivalent of archbishop.

Dioceses of Episcopal Church:

St Andrews

304

Dunkeld (held with St Andrews 1844)
Dunblane (held with St Andrews 1844)
Edinburgh
Aberdeen
Orkney (held with Aberdeen 1864)
Brechin
Moray
Ross (held with Moray 1838)
Caithness (held with Moray 1864)
Glasgow
Galloway (held with Glasgow 1837)
Argyll
The Isles (held with Argyll 1819)
Primus of Episcopal Church:

Roman Catholic Church
The Roman Catholic hierarchy was restored in 1878. It then claimed between 200,000 and 300,000 adherents in Scotland.
Archbishops:
St Andrews and Edinburgh
Glasgow
Bishops:
Aberdeen
Argyll and the Isles
Dunkeld
Galloway

WALES

1826   Calvinistic Methodist Church obtains legal existence as corporate body. Confession of Faith, attached to constitutional deed, put church in doctrinal strait-jacket.
Advocates of disestablishment claimed Nonconformist proportion of population as high as 13 to 1; the church admitted it was from 50 to 70 per cent.

1870   Gladstone appoints Welsh-speaking Welshman, Dr Joshua Hughes, to see of St Asaph, thus encouraging recovery of Church of England in Wales. But political demands for disestablishment by Nonconformists became more bitter and movement grew in power with emergence of Lloyd George, a Nonconformist. Lord Selborne led anti-disestablishment campaign. Mr (afterwards Mr Justice) Watkin Williams moved resolution in House of Commons in favour of Welsh disestablishment. Similar resolutions 1886, 1889, 1891.

1885	Disestablishment a regular election issue.
1886	Tithe riots in Wales.
1905	Liberal government of Campbell-Bannerman appointed commission to study position of church in Wales.
1910	Commission reported.
1914	Act to disestablish and disendow Welsh church. Owing to Great War act did not operate until 1920.
1922	Constitution for disestablished church: 6 dioceses instead of previous 4—Brecon and Monmouth added to Llandaff, St Asaph, St David's, Bangor. Governing Body the supreme authority, one-third of its members being clergy elected by clergy, two-thirds laymen elected by laity. Representative Body, to deal with finance, formed of elected clergy and laity. Bishops chosen by electoral college.

Notable Welsh revivals:

1818–21	at Bedd Gelert, Carnarvonshire, led by Richard Williams.
1859–61	Led by Humphrey Jones.
1904	Led by Evan Roberts in South Wales. Backed by Nonconformist resentment of the Education Act and Liberal attacks on Licensing Act ('Beer and the Bible').

Roman Catholics - see England.

13 EDUCATION AND THE PRESS

EDUCATION

PUPILS AND TEACHERS IN PRIMARY AND SECONDARY SCHOOLS

Austria

	Pupils	*Teachers*
1842	1,385,400	27,900
1850	1,450,300	29,700
1860	1,692,700	29,400
1870	1,867,300	38,200
1880	2,504,300	53,000
1890	3,229,100	68,100
1900	3,793,000	86,300
1910	4,691,000	121,700

Belgium

	Pupils	*Teachers*
1830[1]	293,000	—
1840[1]	453,000	—
1850[2]	6,989	—
1860	528,022	10,194
1870[2]	17,796	1,218
1880[2]	26,574	—
1890	644,366	—
1900	825,333	—
1910	964,526	—
1918[2]	36,063	—

[1] Primary schools only.
[2] Secondary schools only.

Bulgaria

1890 [1]	197,000	4,320
1900	352,000	9,262
1910	525,000	13,290
1918	673,000	16,011

[1] State schools only.

Croatia-Slavonia

1865 [1]	99,000	1,600
1890	172,800	–
1900	205,300	3,000
1910	272,700	3,600

[1] Primary schools only.

Denmark

1893	340,874	–
1900	–	–
1910	431,621	11,519
1918	469,489	15,091

Finland

1875 [1]	18,000	474
1880 [1]	29,000	787
1890	65,238	2,708
1900	124,449	4,595
1910	201,400	7,431
1918	239,200	9,216

[1] Primary schools only.

France

1830 [1]	42,200	–
1840 [1]	41,900	–
1850	3,369,000	–
1860 [1]	55,900	–
1870	–	–
1880	5,135,800	123,000
1890	5,684,800	146,000
1900	5,624,700	158,000
1910	5,781,000	157,000
1918 [2]	4,014,000	99,000

[1] Secondary schools only.
[2] Invaded departments excluded.

Germany

1900[1]	8,966,000	147,000
1910	11,326,000	234,400

[1] Primary schools only.

Greece[1]

1870	64,061	500
1882	91,213	1,292
1901	190,000	4,055
1910	260,000	4,641

[1] Primary schools only.

Hungary

1841[1]	26,600	800
1850[1]	18,300	1,200
1860	—	—
1870	1,189,000	20,500
1880	1,658,600	24,200
1890	2,030,000	—
1900	2,379,200	33,300
1910	2,548,600	38,200

[1] Secondary schools only.

Italy

1861	1,024,800	28,200
1870	1,628,200	41,000
1880	2,035,500	48,300
1890	2,472,500	59,000
1900	2,799,600	65,000
1910	3,473,000	72,800
1918[1]	4,325,000	121,800

[1] Teachers of primary schools only until 1918 when secondary schools included.

309

Netherlands

1839[1]	1,400	–
1850[1]	1,800	6,652
1860	402,800	8,653
1870	468,400	11,230
1880	548,400	15,331
1890	652,900	19,441
1900	753,100	26,181
1910	924,300	32,128
1918	1,049,600	37,438

[1] Secondary schools only, primary schools not available.

Norway

1840[1]	180,000	2,236
1870[1]	237,000	3,652
1880	253,500	4,934
1890	298,000	6,241
1900	349,400	8,371
1910	392,000	9,978
1918	402,200	12,397

[1] Primary schools only.

Portugal

1849[1]	42,000	1,169
1890[2]	3,500	–
1900[2]	5,200	315
1910[2]	10,600	512
1918	12,700	695

[1] Primary schools only.
[2] Secondary schools only.

Romania

1880[1]	108,000	3,010
1890[1]	191,000	4,356
1900	369,800	5,950
1910	604,200	7,862

[1] Primary schools only, secondary schools not available.

Serbia

1870	25,100	699
1880	39,100	1,005
1890	72,500	1,663
1900	106,500	2,222
1910[1]	146,000	2,500

[1] Primary schools only.

Spain

1855[1]	1,005,000
1860	1,273,500
1870	—
1880[1]	1,769,000
1890	—
1900	—
1910	—
1918[2]	51,800

[1] Primary schools only.
[2] Secondary schools only.

Sweden

1865[1]	462,000	—
1870[1]	556,000	7,800
1880	—	—
1890	704,000	13,500[1]
1900	760,000	16,600[1]
1910	815,000	23,181
1918	737,000	27,860

[1] Primary schools only.

Switzerland

1881	459,500	—
1890	504,600	11,392
1900	522,200	12,986
1910	617,200	15,727
1918	631,000	18,065

United Kingdom (England and Wales)

1850[1]	250,000	—
1860[1]	774,000	7,600
1870[1]	1,231,000	14,400
1880[1]	2,864,000	44,600
1890[1]	3,750,000	77,000
1900[1]	4,754,000	119,000
1910	5,542,000	173,800
1918[2]	270,000	14,500

[1] Primary schools only.
[2] Secondary schools only.

United Kingdom (Scotland)

1849[1]	28,000	—
1860[1]	146,000	—
1870[1]	201,000	2,400
1880[1]	410,000	6,100
1890[1]	538,000	9,600
1900	650,700	14,800
1910	752,500	21,100
1918	718,000	23,100

[1] Primary schools only.

United Kingdom (total)

1849–50[1]	278,000	—
1860[1]	920,000	7,600
1870[1]	1,432,000	16,800
1880[1]	3,274,000	50,700
1890[1]	4,288,000	86,600
1900[2]	5,404,700	188,600
1910	6,294,500	194,900
1918[3]	988,000	37,600

[1] Primary schools only.
[2] Does not include secondary schools for England and Wales.
[3] Does not include primary schools for England and Wales.

STUDENTS IN UNIVERSITIES

Austria

1842	8,590	1890	17,492
1850	11,439	1900	24,140
1860	7,993	1910	39.416
1870	11,561	1918	19,394
1880	13,264		

312

Belgium

1830	1,071	1880	4,568
1840	1,459	1890	5,663
1850	1,773	1900	5,389
1860	2,473	1910	7,910
1870	2,631	1918	10,797

Bulgaria

1895	310	1910	—
1900	483	1918	5,897

Denmark

1893	430	1910	829
1900	414	1918	1,140

Finland

1840	403	1890	1,863
1850	460	1900	2,727
1860	389	1910	3,238
1870	685	1918	2,915
1880	736		

France

1889	16,587	1910	41,190
1900	29,901	1918	29,890

Germany

1880	21,432	1910	70,183
1890	28,359	1918	95,986
1900	47,986		

Greece

1912	774
1918	1,795

Hungary

1841	1,250	1890	—
1850	838	1900	9,700
1860	1,179	1910	12,951
1870	2,629	1918	16,984
1880	4,396		

Italy

1861	6,504	1900	26,033
1870	12,069	1910	26,850
1880	11,871	1918	46,114
1890	18,145		

Netherlands

1840	1,410	1890	2,815
1850	1,082	1900	3,135
1860	1,375	1910	4,128
1870	1,240	1918	5,396
1880	1,493		

Norway

1840	600	1890	1,537
1850	550	1900	1,400
1860	550	1910	1,540
1870	1,026	1918	1,550
1880	750		

Portugal

1830	478	1880	766
1840	928	1890	1,180
1850	898	1900	1,684
1860	861	1910	—
1870	801	1918	2,472

Romania

1900	5,074
1910	3,817

Serbia

1870	224	1900	415
1880	130	1910	—
1890	466	1918	—

Spain

1857	7,528	1870	—
1860	8,611	1883	15,732

Sweden

1830	1,265	1880	–
1840	–	1890	–
1850	–	1900	–
1860	–	1910	7,659
1870	–	1918	8,928

Switzerland

1887	1,966	1910	6,831
1890	2,315	1918	7,307
1900	4,208		

THE PRESS

Date of foundation of major papers and related events:

1848	*Die Presse* (Austria) founded.
1848	Freedom of the press guaranteed in Denmark.
1855	*Daily Telegraph* (London) founded.
1860	*Aftenposten* (Norway) founded.
1864	*Diario de Noticias* (Portugal) founded.
1868	*La Stampa* (Turin) founded.
1876	*Corriere della Sera* (Milan) founded.
1887	*Le Soir* (Belgium) founded.
1889	*Arbeiter-Zeitung* (Austria) founded.
1893	*De Telegraaf* (Netherlands) founded.
1896	*Daily Mail* (London) founded.
1900	*Daily Express* (London) founded.
1912	*Pravda* (Russia) founded.

14 THE LABOUR MOVEMENT AND THE TRADE UNIONS

THE EMERGENCE OF PARLIAMENTARY LABOUR PARTIES

COMPARATIVE CHRONOLOGY OF THE FOUNDATIONS OF THE MAJOR SOCIAL DEMOCRATIC AND LABOUR PARTIES

1870	Social Democratic Party of Switzerland founded.
1871	Danish Social Democratic Party founded.
1875	German Social Democratic Party formed.
1880	Social Democratic Labour Party formed in Sweden.
1885	Foundation of Belgian Socialist Party, (*Parti Ouvrier Belge*).
1887	Workers Party founded in Norway.
1889	Social Democratic Party formed in Austria.
1892	Polish Socialist Party founded.
1893	Independent Labour Party formed by Keir Hardie at Bradford.
1894	Left-wing Hungarian Social Democratic Party formed.
1899	Social Democratic Party formed in Finland.
1900	Labour Representation Committee (LRC) formed in Britain.
1902	Luxembourg Socialist Workers Party founded.
1905	Socialist Party formed in France – an amalgamation of the Socialist Party of France (revolutionary) and the French Socialist Party (evolutionary).
1916	Labour Party formed in Iceland.

THE GROWTH OF THE SOCIAL DEMOCRATIC VOTE AND REPRESENTATION IN PARLIAMENT

		Votes	% votes	Seats
Austria				
	1907	264,431	21·0	28
	1911	310,663	25·4	33

		Votes	% votes	Seats
Belgium				
	1892	167	0·2	—
	1894	237,920	13·2	28
	1900	461,095	22·5	32
	1912	243,338	9·3	39
Denmark				
	1884	7,000	4·9	2
	1890	17,000	7·3	3
	1895	25,000	11·3	8
	1901	38,398	19·3	14
	1906	76,612	25·4	24
	1910	98,718	28·3	24
	1913	107,365	29·6	32
Finland				
	1907	329,946	37·0	80
	1910	316,951	40·0	86
	1913	312,214	43·1	90
France				
	1893	598,206	8·4	31
	1906[1]	877,221	10·0	53
	1910[2]	1,110,561	13·1	78
	1914[3]	1,413,044	16·8	103

[1] Not including the Radical Socialist Party.
[2] Not including the Radical Socialist Party and the Independent Socialists.
[3] No including the Radical Socialist Party and the Socialist Republicans.

		Votes	% votes	Seats
Germany				
	1871	124,700	3·2	2
	1877	493,300	9·1	12
	1884	550,000	9·7	24
	1898	2,107,100	27·2	56
	1907	3,259,000	29·0	43
	1912	4,250,400	34·8	110
Italy				
	1895	82,523	6·8	15
	1900	164,946	13·0	33
	1913	883,409	17·6	52

Netherlands

1888	2,020	0·9	1
1897	12,312	3·0	3
1905	65,561	11·2	7
1913	142,185	18·5	15

Norway

1894	520	0·3	–
1900	7,013	3·0	–
1906	43,134	16·0	10
1912	128,455	26·3	23

Sweden

	1902	6,321	3·5	4
	1905	20,677	9·5	13
	1908	45,155	14·6	34
	1911	172,196	28·5	64
(Mar)	1914	228,712	30·1	73
(Sep)	1914	266,133	36·4	87

Switzerland

1896	25,263	6·9	2
1902	51,338	12·7	7
1908	60,323	14·8	2
1911	80,050	20·1	17

United Kingdom

	1900	62,698	1·3	2
	1906	321,663	4·8	29
(Jan)	1910	505,657	7·0	40
(Dec)	1910	371,802	6·4	42
	1918	2,357,524	21·4	62

COMPARATIVE STRENGTHS OF EUROPEAN SOCIAL DEMOCRACY 1914

Country	Date of last election	Votes	% votes	Seats
Austria	1911	310,663	25·4	33
Belgium	1912	243,338	9·3	39
Denmark	1913	107,365	29·6	32
Finland	1913	312,214	43·1	90
France	1914	1,413,044	16·8	103

Country	Date of last election	Votes	% votes	Seats
Germany	1912	4,250,400	34·8	110
Italy	1913	883,409	17·6	52
Netherlands	1913	142,185	18·5	15
Norway	1912	128,455	26·3	23
Sweden	(Mar) 1914	228,712	30·1	73
Switzerland	1911	80,050	20·1	17
United Kingdom	(Dec) 1910	371,802	6·4	42

THE RISE OF THE EUROPEAN TRADE UNION AND LABOUR MOVEMENT

CHRONOLOGY OF KEY EVENTS 1868–1918

1868	Trades Union Congress (TUC) founded in Great Britain.
1880	Swiss Federation of Trade Unions established (*Schweiserischer Gewerkschaftesbund*).
1883	First beginnings of trade unionism in Bulgaria; a printer's union formed in Sofia.
1888	Danish Blacksmiths and Ironworkers Union formed (*Dansk Smede- og Maskinarbejderforbund*).
1889	Formation in England of National Union of General and Municipal Workers.
1890	Austrian Union of Metalworkers and Miners founded (*Gewerkschaft der Metall- und Bergarbeiter*).
1891	Formation of Norwegian Union of Iron and Metalworkers (*Norsk Jern og Metallarbeiderforbund*)
1895	In France, the *Confédération Générale du Travail* (CGT) founded.
1897	Czechoslovak Trade Union Federation formed.
1898	National Trade Union Council formed in Hungary. Foundation of Swedish Trade Union Confederation (*Landsorganisationen I Sverige*).
1899	Foundation of Belgian FGTB (*Federation Générale du Travail de Belgique*). The Norwegian Federation of Trade Unions (*Landsorganisasjonen I Norge*) formed the same year.
1902	Christian and National Socialist unions begin to emerge in Czechoslovakia. Italian Metalworkers Union (FIOM) founded.
1904	Bulgarian Free Trade Union Federation established, together with Marxist General Trade Union Federation. (These merged

in 1920 as the United General Workers Trade Union Federation.)

1905   First All-Russian Conference of Trade Unions held (for subsequent developments in Russia, see pp. 329–32).

1906   Netherlands Federation of Trade Unions founded (the NVV – *Nederlands Verbond Van Vakverenigingen*). First joint socialist – trade union conference in Romania.

1907   Confederation of Finnish Trade Unions formed (SAK – *Svomen Ammattiliittojen Keskusjäjestö r.y.*). Swiss Confederation of Christian Trade Unions established.

1909   Irish Transport and General Workers Union formed. Netherlands Catholic Trade Union Federation formed (NKV – *Nederlands Katholick Vakverbond*). The CNV (Christian National Federation) also formed in Holland to cater for Protestant workers.

1916   Trade Unions granted legal recognition in Hungary. Icelandic Federation of Labour (*Althgdusamband Islands*) established. Luxembourg Workers Union founded (*Letzburger Arbechter-Verband*).

1918   General Confederation of Labour founded.

ESTIMATES OF TRADE UNION MEMBERSHIP BY COUNTRY

Belgium
Unionization in Belgium grew extremely slowly. By 1910, it has been estimated that only 6·9 % of all workers were organized. Membership figures for the 2 principal unions, the CSC (Christian) and the FGTB (Socialist) are set out below:

CSC		FGTB	
1901	11,000	1900	31,311
1909	49,478	1910	68,844
1914	123,000	1914	129,177

Denmark

1900	77,000
1904	65,000
1908	97,000
1912	107,000
1914	121,000
1916	151,000
1918	255,000

France (total organized workers)

1894	404,440
1898	437,793
1902	614,173
1906	836,134
1910	977,350

Germany

Much the largest section of the German Trade Union movement was composed of the Socialist unions, whose membership rose by 1,838,665 from 1892 to 1914.

1892	237,094
1896	329,230
1900	680,427
1904	1,052,108
1908	1,831,731
1912	2,553,162
1914	2,075,759

In comparison, both the Christian Unions and the Hirsch Duncker unions had only relatively small memberships.

Christian		*Hirsch Duncker*	
1910	316,115	1910	122,571
1912	350,930	1912	109,225
1914	218,197	1914	77,749
1916	178,970	1916	57,666

United Kingdom: Affiliated Membership of Trades Union Congress

1893	1,100,000	1906	1,700,000
1894	1,000,000	1907	1,777,000
1895	1,076,000	1908	1,705,000
1896	1,093,191	1909	1,647,715
1897	1,184,241	1910	1,662,133
1898	1,200,000	1911	2,001,633
1899	1,250,000	1912	2,232,446
1900	1,200,000	1913	—
1901	1,400,000	1914	2,682,357
1902	1,500,000	1915	2,850,547
1903	1,422,518	1916	3,082,352
1904	1,541,000	1917	4,532,085
1905	1,555,000	1918	5,283,676

Italy (membership of CGL, Confederazione Generale del Lavoro)

1908	258,515
1910	302,400
1912	309,671
1914	320,858
1916	201,291
1918	249,039

Netherlands

As in Belgium, union development remained very slow. The NVV (Socialist) is set out below:

1906	19,000
1910	40,660
1914	80,000

The NKV (Catholic Unions) had 11,650 members in 1910 and 29,000 by 1914. The CNV (Protestant) had 6,587 members in 1910 and 11,000 by 1914.

Russia

	Economic strikes		Political strikes		Total	
	No. of strikes	No. of strikers	No. of strikes	No. of strikers	No. of strikes	No. of strikers
1895–1904	1,596	399,000	169	32,000	1,765	431,000
1905	5,780	1,439,000	8,209	1,424,000	13,955	2,863,000
1906	2,545	458,000	3,569	650,000	6,114	1,108,000
1907	973	200,000	2,600	540,000	3,573	740,000
1908	428	83,000	464	93,000	892	176,000
1909	290	56,000	50	8,000	340	64,000
1910	214	43,000	8	3,000	222	46,000
1911	442	97,000	24	8,000	466	105,000
1912	732	175,000	1,300	550,000	2,032	725,000
1913	1,370	385,000	1,034	502,000	2,404	887,000
Jan–July 1914	1,560	414,000	2,538	1,035,000	4,098	1,449,000
Aug–Dec 1914[1]	61	32,000	7	3,000	68	35,000
1915[1]	715	384,000	213	156,000	928	540,000
1916[1]	1,167	776,000	243	310,000	1,410	1,086,000
Jan–Feb 1917					1,330	676,000

[1] Excluding Warsaw region.

THE GROWTH OF TRADE UNION MEMBERSHIP, 1900—14; COMPARATIVE TABLES

	France	Germany		Italy	Britain
	CGT	Socialist	Christian	CGL	TUC
1904	150,000	1,052,000	–	–	1,541,000
1910	357,000	2,017,000	316,000	302,000	1,662,000
1914	400,000	2,075,000	218,000	320,000	2,682,000

	Belgium		Netherlands			Denmark	Total
	CSC	FGTB	NVV	NKV	CNV	LO	
1904	14,000	31,000	–	–	–	65,000	2,853,000
1910	49,000	68,000	41,000	12,000	7,000	102,000	5,055,000
1914	123,000	129,000	80,000	29,000	11,000	121,000	6,266,000

THE GROWTH OF INDUSTRIAL MILITANCY, 1896–1915

Number of Disputes (5-year average)

	France	Germany	Italy	Britain	Belgium
1896–1900	568	774	282	758	122
1901–5	691	1,363	970	427	94
1906–10	1,236	2,712	1,566	479	155
1911–15	886	2,101	953	961	201

Working Days Lost

	France	Germany	Britain	Belgium
1896–1900	1,990,600	–	6,948,000	800,700
1901–5	3,132,200	2,852,700	2,744,000	2,450,500
1906–10	4,628,600	4,954,100	5,701,000	1,605,800
1911–15	2,176,000	4,325,300	14,736,000	1,286,300

THE INTERNATIONAL CO-OPERATIVE ALLIANCE

Chronology of Main Events

1835	The 'Association of All Classes of All Nations' formed by Robert Owen. Short-lived existence.
1869	London Congress. Participation by several European countries.
1884	Further impetus at Derby Congress.
1886	Emile de Boyve, of the French Co-operative Union, proposed the idea of a permanent international organization at the Plymouth Congress.
1892	Rochdale Congress. Birth of the International Alliance of Friends of Co-operative Production.
1895	First International Congress at London. Birth of the International Co-operative Alliance.

Subsequent Major Conferences

1896	Paris Conference.
1897	Delft Conference.
1900	Paris Conference.
1902	Manchester Conference—elimination of individual membership except for countries without national organization.
1904	Budapest Conference.
1907	Cremona Conference.
1910	Hamburg Conference.
1913	Glasgow Conference.

15 THE REVOLUTIONARY MOVEMENT

The following chronology concentrates on those events most directly related to the revolutionary movement. For the other events of 1848 in Italy and Germany, see also pp. 2–5. It was to France that European revolutionaries looked for their lead, and this chronology accordingly concentrates on events in Paris.

12 Jan	Revolt in Sicily.
10 Feb	Constitution proclaimed by Ferdinand II in Naples.
22 Feb	Revolution in Paris.
24 Feb	Louis Philippe abdicates. The Republican provisional government is proclaimed under Alphonse de Lamartine.
27 Feb	National Workshops erected in France. Louis Blanc's plan for public relief inaugurated.
4 Mar	Constitution in Piedmont and Sardinia. Proclaimed by Charles Albert.
12 Mar	Revolution in Vienna starts with student demonstrations.
17 Mar	Revolution in Venice under Daniele Manin.
	Revolution in Berlin. Frederick William IV grants constitution.
18 Mar	Revolution in Milan against Austrian rule. Radetzky forced to evacuate the city.
20 Mar	Revolt in Parma.
22 Mar	Republic proclaimed in Venice.
31 Mar	German Vorparlement meets at Frankfurt.
4 May	French National Assembly meets. Elections based on universal male suffrage return a majority for moderate Republicans.
7 May	Polish rebels surrender in Warsaw.
15 May	Rising in Paris, after news of the suppression of the Polish revolt. Overturn of the government and setting up of a provisional administration which immediately collapsed.
	Second rising in Vienna.
	Revolt in Naples collapses.

18 May	German National Assembly meets at Frankfurt and suspends German Confederation.
22 May	Prussian National Assembly meets in Berlin.
2 June	Pan-Slav Congress meets at Prague.
23 June	'The June Days' in France, Louis Cavaignac suppresses workmen in effort to close workshops: thousands killed.
7 Sep	Serfdom abolished in Austria.
24 Sep	Louis Kossuth proclaimed president of committee for the national defence of Hungary.
6 Oct	Third revolution in Vienna.
31 Oct	Vienna fully in control by government troops.
4 Nov	Republican Constitution in France is promulgated.

THE PARIS COMMUNE, 1870

19 July 1870	French declaration of War on Prussia (for details of the campaign, see p. 173).
4 Sep 70	French defeat at Sedan. Republic proclaimed in Paris; formation of the Government of National Defence.
15 Sep 70	First proclamation by the Central Committee of the Twenty Arrondissements.
18 Sep 70	Siege of Paris begun by Prussia.
31 Oct 70	Surrender of French army at Metz.
4 Nov 70	Mayoral elections held in Paris.
5 Jan 71	Bombardment of Paris begun by Prussians.
6 Jan 71	L'Affiche rouge issued.
28 Jan 71	Franco-Prussian armistice declared.
8 Feb 71	Elections held for a National Assembly.
12 Feb 71	National Assembly meets at Bordeaux.
20 Feb 71	Formation of the Revolutionary Socialist Party.
23 Feb 71	Thiers Ministry formed.
26 Feb 71	Seizure of the cannon at Palace de Wagram.
1 Mar 71	Prussians enter Paris; National Assembly passes Peace Treaty.
18 Mar 71	Thiers leaves Paris for Versailles; Hotel de Ville taken over by Central Committee of National Guard.
19 Mar 71	National Guard announces elections in Paris for a Commune.
22 Mar 71	Commune proclaimed at Lyons (but virtual collapse three days later).
23 Mar 71	Commune declared at Marseilles.
28 Mar 71	Proclamation of the Paris Commune; its first decrees issued the next day.
30 Mar 71	Civil War between Paris Commune and the National Government at Versailles.
4 Apr 71	Communard forces in retreat; collapse of the Marseilles

commence.

16 Apr 71	By-elections to the Commune held.
19 Apr 71	The Commune's 'Declaration to the French People'.
28 Apr 71	Proposal mooted to form a Committee of Public Safety.
1 May 71	Creation of the first Committee of Public Safety; Versailles troops begin bombardment of the capital; Cluseret replaced at War Ministry by Rossel.
9 May 71	Resignation of Rossel; fall of the Issy Fort.
10 May 71	Treaty signed at Frankfurt between France and Germany.
21 May 71	Versailles troops enter Paris; last full session of Commune.
25 May 71	Death of Delescluze on the barricades.
28 May 71	Last barricades captured; death of Varlin.

Postscript: The first executions of condemned Communards occurred in Nov 71; in May 72 the first deportation of prisoners occurred: the International was declared illegal. On 11 July 80 a general amnesty was granted.

THE RUSSIAN REVOLUTIONARY TRADITION, 1848–1905

53	The *Free Russian Press*, founded by A. I. Herzen, begins operating in London.
55	Peasant rising in the Kiev Province.
57–67	Publication of the Bell (*Kolokol*) by A. I. Herzen.
Feb 61	The 'Peasant Reform'. Abolition of serf law.
61	Peasant risings in the villages of Bezdna in Kazan province, Kandeevka and Chernogni in the Penza province in reply to the Reform of 1861.
	Student disturbances in St Petersburg, Moscow and other towns in Russia.
May 62	P. G. Zaichnevsky's proclamation 'Young Russia'.
62–4	The secret revolutionary society Land and Freedom.
63–4	Risings in Poland, Lithuania and Belorussia.
63	The 'Kazan Conspiracy'—an attempt by Russian and Polish revolutionaries to raise a peasant revolt in Kazan province.
63–6	The *Ishutintsy* revolutionary circle St Petersburg.
Jan 64	The Zemstvo reform.
Apr 66	Attempt on the life of Alexander II by D. V. Karakozov.
70	Formation of the Russian section of the First International.
Apr	Birth of Vladimir Ilyich Lenin (Ulyanov) in Simbirsk.
May	Strike in the Neva cotton spinning mill in St Petersburg.
72	The Krengholm strike (near Narva). Publication of the first volume of *Das Capital* by K. Marx in Russian.
75	Activities of the 'South Russian Workers' Union' in Odessa.

76	Organization of the *Narodnik* society Land and Freedom (up to 1878 the Northern Revolutionary *Narodnik* Group).
Dec 76	Demonstration in Kazan Cathedral square; speech by G. V. Plekhanov.
Feb–Mar 77	'Trial of the 50'. Speech by the worker–revolutionary Peter Alekseev.
	The 'Chigirinsky conspiracy'.
78	Attempt on the life of the St Petersburg city governor F. F. Trepov and the trial of V. I. Zasulich.
78–80	Northern Union of Russian Workers in St Petersburg.
78–9	Mass strikes by workers in St Petersburg.
	Strikes at the new cotton mill.
79	Attempt on the life of Alexander II by A. K. Solov'ev.
	Land and Freedom splits up into National Freedom and Black Redistribution groups.
Feb 80	Attempt on the life of Alexander II by S. N. Khalturin (explosion in the Winter Palace in St Petersburg).
Mar 81	Assassination of Alexander II by the National Freedom group.
83	Organization by G. V. Plekhanov of the Marxist Emancipation of Labour group in Geneva.
83–4 (winter)	Rise of the D. N. Blagoev social democratic group (Party of the Russian Social Democrats).
Mar 87	Attempt on the life of Alexander III (A. I. Ul'yanov, P. Ya. Shevyrev and others).
Apr 91	Demonstration at the funeral of N. V. Shelgunov in St Petersburg.
	First May Day demonstration in St Petersburg.
91–2	Famine in 21 provinces of European Russia.
92	Disturbances in Tashkent ('Cholera Riot'). Strike in the textile enterprises in Lodz. Shooting down of workers.
93	Formation of a Marxist circle in Samara in which V. I. Lenin participated.
94	Rise of the Moscow Workers' Alliance.
95	Organization by Lenin of the St Petersburg League of Struggle for the Emancipation of the Working Class. Arrested later that year.
May-June 96	General strike of textile workers in St Petersburg.
July 96	Participation of a delegation of Russian workers in the International Socialist Congress in London.
96–7	Large-scale strikes in St Petersburg, Orekhovo-Zuevo, Ekaterinoslav and other towns in Russia.

96–9	Lenin's work on his book *The Development of Capitalism in Russia* (published 1899).
June 97	Lenin exiled to the village of Shushenskoe (Siberia).
Mar 98	First Congress of the RSDLP in Minsk.
Feb 99	First nationwide student strike.
1900	The Leninist newspaper *Iskra* founded.
Apr 01	May Day demonstrations in St Petersburg, Warsaw, Tiflis and other towns.
May	Strike in the Obukhov factory in St Petersburg.
01–2	Student disturbances in the University towns: Moscow, St Petersburg, Kazan, Kharkov.
Mar 02	Mass political demonstration by the Batumi workers. Publication of Lenin's *What is to be Done?*
Mar-Apr	Peasant disturbances in Poltava, Kharkov, Voronezh provinces, etc.
Nov	Strike of workers at Rostov-on-Don. Formation of the Socialist-Revolutionary Party (SR's).
Jul 1903	General strike in Baku. Second Congress of the RSDLP in Brussels and London. Founding of a Marxist Party.
Aug	Adoption of a programme and rules.
July-Aug	General strike in southern Russia.
Autumn	Upsurge of the peasant movement in the Caucasus and the Ukraine.

THE RUSSIAN REVOLUTION OF 1905

9 Feb 04	Japanese War; Japanese fleet attacks Russian squadron at Port Arthur.
May 04	Publication of Lenin's book *One Step Forward, Two Steps Back*.
26 Dec 04	Strike of Baku oil workers; publication in Geneva of Bolshevik newspaper *Forward (Vpered)*, edited by Lenin.
17 Jan 05	The Putilov strike; general strike in St Petersburg.
22 Jan 05	'Bloody Sunday' in St Petersburg. Waves of strikes and demonstrations throughout the country.
19 Feb–10 Mar 05	Battle of Mukden between Russian and Japanese forces.
25 Apr–10 May 05	Third Congress of the Russian Social Democratic Labour Party (RSDLP) in London.
12 May–23 July 05	Strike at Ivanovo - Vosnesensk. Formation of one of the first Soviets of Workers' Deputies.
14–15 May 05	Naval battle off Tsushima Island. Defeat of Admiral Z. P. Rozhdestvensky's squadron.

14 May (27) 05 First number of *Proletarian*–the central organ of the RSDLP edited by Lenin, appears in Geneva.

14–24 June 05 Mutiny on the battleship *Potemkin*.

22–4 June 05 Armed rising in Lodz.

31 July 05 Opening of the First (Constitutive) congress of the All-Russian Peasant Union in Moscow.

Publication of Lenin's book *Two Tactics of Social Democracy in the Democratic Revolution*.

6 Aug 05 Publication of the draft law on the establishment of the Consultative State Duma (the Bulygin Duma).

5 Sep 05 Treaty of Portsmouth between Russia and Japan.

7 Oct 05 Beginning of the nationwide political strike.

13 Oct 05 First session of the St Petersburg Soviet of Workers' Deputies.

17 Oct 05 Manifesto of Tsar Nicholas II promising political freedom and summoning the Legislative Duma.

20 Oct 05 Political demonstration in Moscow on the occasion of the funeral of the Bolshevik N. E. Bauman, who was killed on 18 Oct by the Black Hundreds.

Oct 05 Formation of the Constitutional-Democratic Party (the Cadets).

Oct-Dec 05 Formation of Soviets of Workers' Deputies in St Petersburg, Moscow, Kiev, Nizhni Novgorod, Odessa, Chita and other towns in Russia.

24–8 Oct 05 Armed rising of soldiers and sailors at Kronstadt.

Nov– Dec 05 Publication in St Petersburg of the Bolshevik daily newspaper *New Life (Novaya zhizn')* edited by Lenin.

11–15 Nov 05 Sevastopol rising headed by Lieut. P. P. Schmidt.

21 Nov 05 First Session of the Moscow Soviet of Workers' Deputies.

Nov 05 Rise of the Octobrist Party (Alliance of 17 Oct).

Dec 05 December armed rising in Moscow, Novorossiisk, Chita, Perm, Kharkov, Gorlovka, Krasnoyarsk, Sormovo and other towns.

25–30 Dec 05 First All-Russian Conference of the RSDLP in Tammerfors (Finland).

Dec 05–Jan 06 Punitive expeditions by Tsarist troops near Moscow, and in the Baltic and Siberia.

23 Apr–
8 May 06 Fourth (Unifying) Congress of the RSDLP in Stockholm.

23 Apr 08 Publication of the 'Basic Laws' of the Russian Empire.

27–8 July 06 First State Duma.

17–20 July 06 Sveaborg rising of soldiers and sailors.

19–20 July 06 Kronstadt rising of soldiers and sailors.

20 July 06	Mutiny of sailors on the cruiser *Pamyat' Azova* in Revel.
19 Aug 06	Introduction of field courts martial by the Tsarist government in order to combat the revolutionary movement.
3 Sep– 11 Dec 06	Publication of the illegal Bolshevik newspaper *Proletarian* (in Finland, Switzerland and France).
9 Nov 06	Decree of the Tsarist government on the allocation of the peasants from the commune to separate farmsteads. Beginning of the P. A. Stolypin agrarian reform.
20 Feb-2 June	Second State Duma.

THE RUSSIAN REVOLUTION OF 1917

7 Mar 1917	Large demonstrations first begin in Petrograd.
12 Mar 17	Establishment of Petrograd Soviet.
15 Mar 17	Abdication of Nicholas II; formation of a Provisional Government.
16 Mar 17	Abdication of Grand Duke Michael.
11 Apr 17	Lenin returns to Russia.
8 May 17	Resignation of Milyukov.
18 May 17	Provisional Government reorganized.
16 June 17	First Congress of Soviets held.
2 July 17	Beginning of the major summer offensive.
16 July 17	Start of the 'July Days'.
21 July 17	Kerensky becomes Prime Minister.
1 Aug 17	Kornilov appointed Commander-in-Chief (10–12 Sep, failure of the Kornilov plot).
19 Sep 17	Bolsheviks secure majority in Moscow Soviet.
6 Oct 17	Trotsky becomes chairman of the Petrograd Soviet.
25 Oct 17	Formation of the Military Revolution Committee.
7 Nov 17	Seizure of power by Bolsheviks in Petrograd.
15 Nov 17	Bolsheviks in control of Moscow.
1 Dec 17	Social Revolutionaries join the government.
3 Dec 17	Mogilev (the Russian Army Headquarters) occupied by the Bolsheviks.
20 Dec 17	The Cheka (Secret Police) established.
18 Jan 18	Constituent Assembly opens (dispersed the following day).
3 Mar 18	Treaty of Brest-Litovsk signed (for details, see p. 188).
12 Mar 18	Soviet government moves to Moscow.
13 Mar 18	Trotsky appointed Peoples' Commissar of War.
5 Apr 18	Allied expeditionary force lands at Murmansk.

The protracted Civil War in Russia continued until Nov 20, when the Red Army began its offensive against Makhno. Makhno's escape to Romania (28 Aug 21) marked the end of the last resistance to the Revolution.

THE INTERNATIONALS

The First International

Formed by Marx in London in 1864, the First International Workingmen's Association aimed to co-ordinate efforts by the working classes in different countries to establish Socialism. Disputes between the anarchists and Marxists culminated in the final break between Marx and Bakunin in 1872. The First International moved its headquarters to New York. It was finally dissolved in 1876.

The Second International

Formed in Paris in 1889. A decentralized organization, with no formal secretariat established until 1900. From an early date the Second International was preoccupied with the issue of revisionism, with Kautsky a central figure. The main congresses of the Second International were:

1905	Amsterdam
1907	Stuttgart
1910	Copenhagen

Seriously weakened by divisions over the war, the movement collapsed. In Mar 19, the Russian Bolsheviks established the Third International (the Comintern).

SUCCESSFUL ASSASSINATIONS

15 Nov 1848	Count Pellegrino Rossi (Prime Minister of the Papal States).
26 Mar 54	Ferdinand Charles III (Duke of Parma).
3 Jan 57	Msgr M. W. A. Sibour, Archbishop of Paris (by Jean Verger).
12 Aug 60	Prince Danilo of Montenegro.
10 June 68	Prince Michael of Serbia.
28 Dec 70	Marshal Prim.
24 Mar 71	Msgr Georges Darboy, Archbishop of Paris.
4 June 76	Sultan Abdul Aziz.
15 June 76	Hussein Avni (Ottoman minister).
6 Sep 78	Mahomet Ali Pasha.
13 Mar 81	Tsar Alexander II.
6 May 82	Lord Frederick Cavendish (Chief Secretary for Ireland) and T. H. Burke (Under-Secretary) in Phoenix Park, Dublin.
24 June 94	Marie Francois Sadi-Carnot, President of the French Republic (by Santo Caserio).
15 July 95	Stambulov (former Prime Minister of Bulgaria).
8 Aug 97	Antonio del Castillo (Prime Minister of Spain) (by Golli).
10 Sep 98	Empress Elizabeth of Austria (by Luccheni).

29 July 1900	King Humbert I of Italy (by Gaetano Bresci).
11 June 03	Alexander I of Serbia (together with his wife, Draga).
16 June 04	Bobrikov (Governor-General of Finland).
28 July 04	De Plehve (Tsarist minister).
17 Feb 05	Grand Duke Sergius.
13 June 05	Delyanni (Greek Prime Minister).
23 Mar 06	Redvan Pasha (Prefect of Constantinople).
11 Mar 07	Petkov (Prime Minister of Bulgaria).
29 Apr 07	Masiwoda (Montenegro Chief of Police).
1 Feb 08	King Carlos of Portugal (and the Crown Prince) shot by Buica and Da Costa.
Sep 11	Stolypin, Russian Prime Minister.
28 June 14	Archduke Franz Ferdinand (at Sarajevo).
31 July 14	Jean Jaures (French socialist leader.)

MAJOR ASSASSINATION ATTEMPTS 1848–1900

19 May 1849	Queen Victoria (by William Hamilton).
22 May 50	Frederick William IV of Prussia (by Sofelage).
2 Feb 52	Isabella of Spain (by Merino).
18 Feb 53	Francis Joseph of Austria (by Libenyi).
28 Apr 55	Napoleon III (by Pianori).
8 Sep 55	Napoleon III (by Bellemarre).
28 May 56	Isabella II of Spain (by Raymond Fuentes).
14 Jan 58	Napoleon III (the Orsini plot).
14 July 61	William I of Prussia (by Oscar Becker).
16 Apr 66	Alexander II (by Karakozow).
7 Mar 66	Bismarck (by Blind).
6 June 67	Alexander II (by Berezowski).
19 July 72	King Amadeus of Spain.
13 July 74	Bismarck (by Kullmann).
11 May 78	William I (Emperor of Germany) (by Hodel).
2 June 78	William I (Emperor of Germany) (by Nobiling).
25 Oct 78	King Alfonso XII of Spain (by J. O. Honcasi).
17 Nov 78	King Humbert I of Italy (by Passasanti).
14 Apr 79	Alexander II (by Soloviev).
30 Dec 79	King Alfonso XII of Spain (by Francisco Gonzalez).
14 Dec 80	Bratiano (Prime Minister of Romania).
17 Feb 80	Alexander II of Russia (explosion at the Winter Palace).
6 May 82	Emperor Francis Joseph (by Overdank).
23 Oct 82	Milan IV of Serbia (by Payitch).
13 Mar 87	Alexander III.
10 Dec 87	Jules Ferry (by Aubertin).

10 May 88	Alexander III.
16 June 94	Francesco Crispi (Prime Minister of Italy).
22 Apr 97	King Humbert I of Italy (by Acciarito).
26 Feb 98	George I of Greece (by Karditzis).

BIOGRAPHICAL NOTES ON MAJOR REVOLUTIONARIES

BAKUNIN, Mikhail (1814–76)
Militant revolutionary, philosopher of anarchism. Born at Tver in Russia. Originally a Guards officer. Studied philosophy at Berlin. Active in insurrection in Dresden in 1849. Arrested and condemned to death. Handed over to Russians. Exiled to Siberia. Escaped to Europe via Japan and America. Founded the International Social Democratic Alliance. Raised a revolt at Lyon in Sep 70. Discredited by his involvement in the Nechayev scandal.

BEBEL, August (1840–1913)
A founder of German Socialism. In 1871, one of the first two Socialists elected to the Reichstag. In 1875, succeeded in uniting the two wings of German Socialism into the Social Democratic Party. In 1891, at the Erfurt Assembly, the party adopted a full Marxist programme. The Social Democratic Party won 110 seats in 1912.

BLANC, Louis (1811–82)
Revolutionary theorist and politician. Born in Madrid; subsequently a law student in Paris. Influenced by writings of Saint-Simon. In 1839, published *L'Organisation du travail*. Author also of *Histoire des dix ans*, a bitter attack on the Orleanist monarchy. In 1848, Blanc was an active member of the revolutionary Provisional Government and chairman of the 'Luxembourg Commission' to conquer unemployment. Established the national workshops. Their failure forced Blanc to exile in England. Returned to become Socialist Deputy for Marseilles in Third Republic.

BLANQUI, Auguste (1805–81)
French revolutionary socialist. Born at Pujet-Théniers. Studied law and medicine. Active in 1830 revolution, but rapidly disillusioned by the Louis Philippe administration. Imprisoned in 1831 and 1836. Sentenced in 1872 for his part in Paris Commune to life imprisonment. Released, 1879.

ENGELS, Friedrich (1820–95)
The founder, with Karl Marx, of modern Communism. Born at Barmen. Lived almost continuously in England from 1842. Published (1844) his *'Condition of the Working Classes in England'*. First met Marx in Brussels in 1844. Collaborated with Marx on the *Communist Manifesto* (1848). Engels died in London in 1895.

HERZEN, Alexander (1812–70)
Russian revolutionary. Born in Moscow in 1812. First imprisoned in 1834 for his revolutionary activities. Moved to Paris (1847) and to London (1851). His most famous publication was *Kolokol* (the *Bell*). Died in Paris in 1870.

JAURÈS, Jean (1859–1914)
French Socialist leader. Born at Castres in 1859. Lectured on philosophy at Toulouse. A Deputy from 1885. Founder of major French Socialist paper *L'Humanité* in 1904. Assassinated 31 July 14.

KROPOTKIN, Prince Peter (1842–1921)
Russian geographer, explorer and revolutionary. Born in Moscow. Secretary of Russian Geographical Society; explorer of Finland and Sweden. Associated after 1872 with most revolutionary wing of the International (q.v.). Arrested in March 1874. Escaped to England, July 76. His anarchist propaganda led to his arrest at Lyons in 1883. From 1886 until 1917 lived in England again.

LASSALLE, Ferdinand (1825–64)
German Social Democrat. Born in Breslau. Active in 1848 Revolution. In 1861, published his *System der erworbenen Rechte*. Founder of the Universal German Workingmen's Association. Wrote the influential work *Bastiat-Schulze (Capital and Labour)*. Formative influence on German labour movement.

LENIN (formerly Ulyanov) Vladimir Ilyich (1870–1924)
Russian revolutionary. Born at Simbirsk. Educated at Kazan University. In 1894 organized the Union for the Liberation of the Working Class at St Petersburg.

LIEBKNECHT, Wilhelm (1826–1900). German Social Democrat. Born at Giessen. Forced to flee to Switzerland and England for taking part in Baden insurrection in 1848. Returned to Germany, 1862. Elected for the Reichstag (1874). Editor, with Bebel, of *Vorwärts*.

LUXEMBURG, Rosa (1871–1919). Extreme left German revolutionary. Born at Zamość in Poland. Wrote *Die Akkumulation des Kapitals* (1913). Leader of the Spartacist rising. With Liebknecht, was murdered in Berlin.

MARX, Karl (1818–1883). The founder of modern International Communism. Born at Trier, 5 May 18. Studied law at Bonn and Berlin. Attracted to history and philosophy. In 1842, edited the democratic *Rheinische Zeitung*. Close collaborator of Engels. Marx rewrote the *Communist Manifesto* in 1848. Settled in London, 1849. Acquired prolific knowledge of economics. His *magnum opus Das Kapital* (Vol 1) was published in 1867. Marx played a prominent role in the founding of the First International Working-men's Association (q.v.). Marx died on 14 Mar 1883 and was buried in Highgate cemetery.

PLEKHANOV, Georgi Valentinovich (1857–1918). Russian revolutionary. Born in Tambov province. In 1876 led the first popular demonstration in St. Petersburg. In 1883, helped found the League for the Emancipation of Labour. From 1883 to 1917, exile in Geneva. Russian delegate to the Second International, 1889 to 1904. With Lenin, editor of *Iskra* (Spark). Returned to Russia, 1917. Died in Finland.

PROUDHON, Pierre Joseph (1809–1865). French socialist. Born at Besançon. His publications included *Qu'est-ce que la propriété?* (1840) and his massive *Système des contradictions economiques* (1846). Imprisoned in 1848. While in prison wrote many more socialist works. Amnestied in 1860.

SOREL, Georges (1847–1922). French syndicalist socialist. His theory was set out in *Refléxions sur la violence* (1908). Argued that true socialism could only come by violent revolution. He had little impact on French trade unionists, but Mussolini was impressed with his view of the 'social myth'.

STIRNER, Max (1806–1856). Pseudonym of Kaspar Schmidt. German anarchist writer. Born at Bayreuth. Wrote *Der Einziger und das Eigentum* (1845).

BIBLIOGRAPHY

Almanach de Gotha (annual).

Anderson, M. S. *The Eastern Question 1774–1923* (London, 1966).

Berchtold, K. (ed.) *Osterreichische Parteiprogramme 1868–1966* (Vienna, 1967).

Bergasse, H. *Histoire de l'assemblée: des élections de 1789 aux elections de 1967* (Paris, 1967).

Blet, H. *Histoire de la colonisation française*, 3 vols. (Paris, 1946–50).

Bodart, G., *Losses of life in Modern Wars* (Oxford, 1916).

Brunschwig, H., *Mythes et réalités de l'impérialisme colonial* français (Paris, 1960).

Carr, E. H., *The Bolshevik Revolution*, 1917–1923 (London, 1963).

Carr, R., *Spain, 1808–1939* (Oxford, 1966).

Cruttwell, C. R. M. F., *A History of the Great War 1914–1918* (Oxford, 1934).

Duffy, J., *Portuguese Africa* (Harvard, 1959).

Edwards, S., *The Paris Commune: 1871* (London, 1971).

Falls, C., *A Hundred Years of War* (London, 1953).

Fuller, J. F. C., *The Conduct of War 1789–1961* (London, 1961).

Habakkuk, H. J. and Postan, M. (eds.), *The Cambridge Economic History of Europe*, Vol. VI (Cambridge, 1965).

Hamerow, T. S., *Restoration, Revolution, Reaction: Economics and Politics in Germany 1815–71* (Princeton, 1958).

Henderson, W. O., *The Zollverein* (London, 1965).

Horne, A., *The Fall of Paris* (London, 1965).

Howard, M., *The Franco-Prussian War* (London, 1961).

Hyams, E., *Dictionary of Revolution* (London, 1972).

Jellinek, F., *The Paris Commune of 1871* (New York, 1937).

Kendall, W., *The Labour Movement in Europe* (London, 1972).

Lewis, B., *The Emergence of Modern Turkey* (London, 1968).

Liddell Hart, B. H., *A History of the World War 1914–1918* (London, 1935).

Macartney, C. A., *The Habsburg Empire* (London, 1968).

Mackie, T. T., and Rose, R., *The International Almanac of Electoral History* (London, 1974).

Mitchell, B. R., *European Historical Statistics 1750–1970* (London, 1975).

New Cambridge Modern History, Vols. X and XI.

Puntila, L. A., *The Political History of Finland* (London, 1975).

Ramm, A., *Germany 1789–1919* (London, 1972).

Rokkan, S. and Meyriat, J. (eds.) *International Guide to Electoral Statistics* (Paris, 1967).

Seton-Watson, C., *Italy from Liberalism to Fascism* (London, 1967).

Seton-Watson, H., *The Russian Empire* (Oxford, 1967).

Smith, Denis Mack, *Cavour and Garibaldi* (Cambridge, 1954).

Spuler, B., *Regenten und Regierungen der Welt* (Wurzburg, 1962).

The Statesman's Year-Book (from 1864).

Taylor, A. J. P., *The Struggle for Mastery in Europe* (Oxford, 1966).

Williams, R. L. *The French Revolution, 1870–71* (London, 1969).

Wood, D., *Conflict in the Twentieth Century* (London, 1972).

INDEX

Most of the chapters in this book run in alphabetical sequence and for this reason we have not attempted to produce a completely detailed index. The main aim has been to allow the reader to locate the country or person by page for any major subject included in this publication.